W9-AAE-617

"Casanova and Kassum's new book provides readers with not only an in-depth analysis of the current challenges of Brazil's economy but also an insight into the desires and expectations of its people. The book shows how Brazilians dream their future."

– Alicia Bárcena, *Executive Secretary of the United Nations Economic Commission for Latin America and the Caribbean (ECLAC)*

"An objective perspective on the emergence of the Brazil dream and the challenges ahead."

– Frederico Curado, *Chairman and Chief Executive Officer of Embraer S.A.*

"This enlightening volume provides a unique perspective on Brazil's transformation into a leading global power."

– Luis Alberto Moreno, *President of the Inter-American Development Bank (IDB)*

"As Brazil, the elated and green giant, awakens and heads toward competitiveness, Casanova and Kassum provide a keen and fresh roadmap, with opportunities and pitfalls, for everyone involved in Brazil's rise."

– Humberto Ribeiro, *Secretary of Commerce and Services (SCS), Ministry of Development, Industry and Foreign Trade of Brazil*

"In a world increasingly influenced by both hard and soft powers, the authors present a knowledgeable and distinct panorama of Brazil's grand challenges and opportunities ahead."

– Antonio Ermírio de Moraes Neto, *Co-Founder of Vox Capital*

"This book provides a comprehensive analysis of Brazil's achievements and challenges as the country is on its way to attain higher levels of sustainable development and increase its relevance and influence as a global player."

– Enrique García, *President of CAF, Development Bank of Latin America*

"Drawing on extensive research, Lourdes Casanova and Julian Kassum have produced an important source of knowledge about Brazil's rise as a global power. This provocative work offers fresh insights about Brazil's emergent role in the global stage."

– Marisol Argueta, *Senior Director, Head of Latin America, World Economic Forum*

"The Brazilian dream Casanova and Kassum describe in their book is to see Brazil among the five leading economies in the world and one of the first for social justice, education and healthcare for all."

– Mario Garnero, *Chairman of Brasilinvest Group*

International Political Economy Series

Series Editor: **Timothy M. Shaw**, Visiting Professor, University of Massachusetts Boston, USA and Emeritus Professor, University of London, UK

The global political economy is in flux as a series of cumulative crises impacts its organization and governance. The IPE series has tracked its development in both analysis and structure over the last three decades. It has always had a concentration on the global South. Now the South increasingly challenges the North as the centre of development, also reflected in a growing number of submissions and publications on indebted Eurozone economies in Southern Europe.

An indispensable resource for scholars and researchers, the series examines a variety of capitalisms and connections by focusing on emerging economies, companies and sectors, debates and policies. It informs diverse policy communities as the established trans-Atlantic North declines and 'the rest', especially the BRICS, rise.

Titles include:

Lourdes Casanova and Julian Kassum
THE POLITICAL ECONOMY OF AN EMERGING GLOBAL POWER
In Search of the Brazil Dream

Toni Haastrup and Yong-Soo Eun (*editors*)
REGIONALIZING GLOBAL CRISES
The Financial Crisis and New Frontiers in Regional Governance

Kobena T. Hanson, Cristina D'Alessandro and Francis Owusu (*editors*)
MANAGING AFRICA'S NATURAL RESOURCES
Capacities for Development

Daniel Daianu, Carlo D'Adda, Giorgio Basevi and Rajeesh Kumar (*editors*)
THE EUROZONE CRISIS AND THE FUTURE OF EUROPE
The Political Economy of Further Integration and Governance

Karen E. Young
THE POLITICAL ECONOMY OF ENERGY, FINANCE AND SECURITY IN THE UNITED ARAB EMIRATES
Between the Majilis and the Market

Monique Taylor
THE CHINESE STATE, OIL AND ENERGY SECURITY

Benedicte Bull, Fulvio Castellacci and Yuri Kasahara
BUSINESS GROUPS AND TRANSNATIONAL CAPITALISM IN CENTRAL AMERICA
Economic and Political Strategies

Leila Simona Talani
THE ARAB SPRING IN THE GLOBAL POLITICAL ECONOMY

Andreas Nölke (*editor*)
MULTINATIONAL CORPORATIONS FROM EMERGING MARKETS
State Capitalism 3.0

Roshen Hendrickson
PROMOTING U.S. INVESTMENT IN SUB-SAHARAN AFRICA

Bhumitra Chakma
SOUTH ASIA IN TRANSITION
Democracy, Political Economy and Security

Greig Charnock, Thomas Purcell and Ramon Ribera-Fumaz
THE LIMITS TO CAPITAL IN SPAIN
Crisis and Revolt in the European South

Felipe Amin Filomeno
MONSANTO AND INTELLECTUAL PROPERTY IN SOUTH AMERICA

Eirikur Bergmann
ICELAND AND THE INTERNATIONAL FINANCIAL CRISIS
Boom, Bust and Recovery

Yildiz Atasoy (*editor*)
GLOBAL ECONOMIC CRISIS AND THE POLITICS OF DIVERSITY

Gabriel Siles-Brügge
CONSTRUCTING EUROPEAN UNION TRADE POLICY
A Global Idea of Europe

Jewellord Singh and France Bourgouin (*editors*)
RESOURCE GOVERNANCE AND DEVELOPMENTAL STATES IN THE GLOBAL SOUTH
Critical International Political Economy Perspectives

Tan Tai Yong and Md Mizanur Rahman (*editors*)
DIASPORA ENGAGEMENT AND DEVELOPMENT IN SOUTH ASIA

Leila Simona Talani, Alexander Clarkson and Ramon Pachedo Pardo (*editors*)
DIRTY CITIES
Towards a Political Economy of the Underground in Global Cities

Matthew Louis Bishop
THE POLITICAL ECONOMY OF CARIBBEAN DEVELOPMENT

Xiaoming Huang (*editor*)
MODERN ECONOMIC DEVELOPMENT IN JAPAN AND CHINA
Developmentalism, Capitalism and the World Economic System

Bonnie K. Campbell (*editor*)
MODES OF GOVERNANCE AND REVENUE FLOWS IN AFRICAN MINING

Gopinath Pillai (*editor*)
THE POLITICAL ECONOMY OF SOUTH ASIAN DIASPORA
Patterns of Socio-Economic Influence

Rachel K. Brickner (*editor*)
MIGRATION, GLOBALIZATION AND THE STATE

Juanita Elias and Samanthi Gunawardana (*editors*)
THE GLOBAL POLITICAL ECONOMY OF THE HOUSEHOLD IN ASIA

Tony Heron
PATHWAYS FROM PREFERENTIAL TRADE
The Politics of Trade Adjustment in Africa, the Caribbean and Pacific

David J. Hornsby
RISK REGULATION, SCIENCE AND INTERESTS IN TRANSATLANTIC TRADE CONFLICTS

Yang Jiang
CHINA'S POLICYMAKING FOR REGIONAL ECONOMIC COOPERATION

Martin Geiger, Antoine Pécoud (*editors*)
DISCIPLINING THE TRANSNATIONAL MOBILITY OF PEOPLE

Michael Breen
THE POLITICS OF IMF LENDING

Laura Carsten Mahrenbach
THE TRADE POLICY OF EMERGING POWERS
Strategic Choices of Brazil and India

Vassilis K. Fouskas and Constantine Dimoulas
GREECE, FINANCIALIZATION AND THE EU
The Political Economy of Debt and Destruction

Hany Besada and Shannon Kindornay (*editors*)
MULTILATERAL DEVELOPMENT COOPERATION IN A CHANGING GLOBAL ORDER

Caroline Kuzemko
THE ENERGY-SECURITY CLIMATE NEXUS
Institutional Change in Britain and Beyond

International Political Economy Series
Series Standing Order ISBN 978–0–333–71708–0 hardcover
Series Standing Order ISBN 978–0–333–71110–1 paperback
(*outside North America only*)

You can receive future titles in this series as they are published by placing a standing order. Please contact your bookseller or, in case of difficulty, write to us at the address below with your name and address, the title of the series and one of the ISBNs quoted above.

Customer Services Department, Macmillan Distribution Ltd, Houndmills, Basingstoke, Hampshire RG21 6XS, England

The Political Economy of an Emerging Global Power

In Search of the Brazil Dream

Lourdes Casanova
Senior Lecturer, Cornell University, United States

Julian Kassum
Independent Consultant

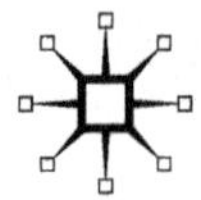

First published 2014 by
PALGRAVE MACMILLAN

Palgrave Macmillan in the UK is an imprint of Macmillan Publishers Limited, registered in England, company number 785998, of Houndmills, Basingstoke, Hampshire RG21 6XS.

Palgrave Macmillan in the US is a division of St Martin's Press LLC, 175 Fifth Avenue, New York, NY 10010.

Palgrave Macmillan is the global academic imprint of the above companies and has companies and representatives throughout the world.

Palgrave® and Macmillan® are registered trademarks in the United States, the United Kingdom, Europe and other countries.

ISBN 978–1–137–35235–4

This book is printed on paper suitable for recycling and made from fully managed and sustained forest sources. Logging, pulping and manufacturing processes are expected to conform to the environmental regulations of the country of origin.

A catalogue record for this book is available from the British Library.

A catalog record for this book is available from the Library of Congress.

Transferred to Digital Printing in 2015

To my dear husband, Soumitra Dutta, and my dear daughter, Sara Dutta. Their love and support have made my life complete.

To my beloved wife, Cecilia, who made me discover Latin America.

Contents

Figures and Tables

Figures

Tables

Foreword

Over the last few years, a part of the international media has changed its tune, moving from an ultra-optimistic view of Brazil to a more skeptical opinion. Has the country lost its way? The authors of this thought-provoking work believe it has not. For them, despite several hurdles, Brazil is on its way to becoming a player of considerable note in the new international scenario. And this is due mainly to its capacity to employ its so-called soft power, that is, its capacity to influence partners by using the attractiveness of strategic alternatives (the "Brasília Consensus").

At the foundations of such belief lies a broad-based assessment weighing up both the virtues and the drawbacks in contemporary Brazil, on a wide array of levels – ranging from economic and political institutions to corporate capacity. As part of this assessment, the authors' all-encompassing analysis covers the model for Brazilian development and for the policies employed during the Lula and Dilma administrations, seeking to shed light on the rationale behind the governmental efforts throughout this period.

This is a rather insightful work, not only for foreign readers wishing to know more about today's Brazil, but also for the Brazilian audience, because of the systematization of information and ideas taken from innumerous documents and texts on the vast issue at hand. I do not hesitate to recommend this book.

Luciano Coutinho, President of BNDES,
Brazil's National Development Bank

Acknowledgments

Writing this book has been a fantastic adventure, in which many colleagues and friends in and outside Brazil have taken an active part. Our greatest reward was being able to hear and connect with diverse viewpoints and insights about the future of Brazil, a country we respect and admire. This collection of views helped us outline what we have called in these pages the "Brazil dream".

We wish to thank all experts and practitioners who participated in the survey we conducted for this book. Their insights not only added richness to our report of survey findings, but also inspired our work and reflections. We are most grateful to Luciano Coutinho, President of BNDES, Frederico Curado, President and Chief Executive Officer of Embraer, Clóvis Rossi, journalist at Folha de São Paulo, Luiz Fernando Furlan, Member of the Board of Directors of BRF and former Minister of Development, Industry and Foreign Trade of Brazil, and Luiz Barretto Filho, President of Sebrae and former Minister of Tourism, as well as Izabela Araujo, Felipe Bastos Gurgel Silva, Welber Barral, Renato Baumann, Henrique Brusius Brust Renck, Alex Bueno de Moraes, Nestor Casado, Cláudia Costin, Demetrio Di Martino, Maria da Penha Rodrigues Raimundo, Carlos Henrique Dumortout Castro, Gabriela Falanghe Betencourt de Freitas, Nathalia Foditsch, Fernando Gómez, Maria Guadalupe, Jose Jeandson Lopes, Evodio Kaltenecker, Josilane Malvino Souza, Jorge Mariscal, Kellie Meiman, Safiya Miller, Leonardo Neves, Luiz Eduardo Pinto de Sampaio, Daniel P. Rosenfeld, Félix Peña, Eduardo Ruske Arantes Pereira, Leonardo David Sapienza, Rafael Schiozer, Leonardo F. Serrano, Guilherme Storch de Freitas, Renato Taira, Guilherme Vieira Neves, and Rasso von Reininghaus.

For their invaluable feedback and insightful comments, we owe special thanks to Paulo Afonso Ferreira, First Secretary of CNI, Diana Negroponte from the Brookings Institute, professors Henry Mintzberg from McGill University, Subramanian Rangan and Felipe Monteiro from INSEAD, Diego Sánchez-Ancochea from Oxford University and Murillo Campello, Tim Devoogd and Gustavo Flores-Macías from Cornell University, Janaina Herrera, Executive Director of NGC, Lisiane Kunst, Member of the Board of Directors of Artecola Indústrias Químicas, and

Humberto Ribeiro, Secretary of Commerce and Services at the Ministry of Development, Industry and Foreign Trade of Brazil.

This book would not have been possible without the support of the Inter-American Development Bank, INSEAD and the Samuel Curtis Johnson Graduate School of Management at Cornell University and the insights of colleagues, students and participants in the executive education programs in both institutions. Bárbara Marchiori de Assis, student at CIPA at Cornell, was also very helpful with the survey and with the social innovative initiatives. We also thank Patricio Fay from the IAE Business School in Argentina for his hospitality.

We are also grateful to Cecilia Baeza, Post-Doctorate Fellow at the University of Brasília, for her important contribution to Chapter 8, and to Richard Gallagher, for his precious help in shaping the presentation of our work. Thanks are also due to the publication team at Palgrave Macmillan for making this project possible and for their ongoing support and professionalism. Not to be forgotten is the anonymous reviewer of our manuscript whose comments greatly assisted us in the revision process. We are very pleased with the end result, but realize that some oversights and errors may still remain in the text – they are our sole responsibility.

Finally, we would like to thank our family and close ones who followed us every step of this adventure. Lourdes Casanova thanks her husband, Soumitra Dutta, and daughter, Sara Dutta, mother, parents-in-law, brothers, sisters and friends. Julian Kassum thanks his wife, Cecilia, mother, brother, parents-in-law and friends. This book would not have been possible without their inspiration, love and support and is dedicated to them.

Acronyms and Abbreviations

ABC	Brazilian Agency of Cooperation (Agência Brasileira de Cooperação)
ABDI	Brazilian Agency of Industrial Development (Agência Brasileira de Desenvolvimento Industrial)
ABRAPP	Brazilian Association of Supplemental Pension Funds (Associação Brasileira das Entidades Fechadas de Previdência Complementar)
ALBA	Alliance for the Peoples of Our America (Alianza Bolivariana para los Pueblos de Nuestra América)
APEX	Brazilian Trade and Investment Promotion Agency (Agência Brasileira de Promoção de Exportação e Investimentos)
ASA	Africa-South America Summit
ASPA	South American-Arab Countries Summit
BASIC	Brazil, South Africa, India and China
BNDES	Brazilian National Development Bank (Banco Nacional de Desenvolvimento Econômico e Social)
BNDESPar	BNDES Participações S.A.
BRIC/BRICS	Brazil, Russia, India and China/ Brazil, Russia, India, China and South Africa
BRL	Brazilian real
CADE	Administrative Council for Economic Defense (Conselho Administrativo de Defesa Econômica)
CBA	Brazilian Aluminium Company (Companhia Brasileira de Aluminio)
CBD	Pão de Açúcar Group (Companhia Brasileira de Distribuição)
CCT	conditional cash transfer
CDI	Center for Digital Inclusion
CELAC	Community of Latin American and Caribbean States
CEO	chief executive officer
CNI	National Confederation of Industry (Confederação Nacional da Indústria)
CCR	Road Concession Company (Companhia de Concessões Rodoviárias)

CPTM	São Paulo Metropolitan Train Company (Companhia Paulista de Trens Metropolitanos)
CSR	corporate social responsibility
CVRD	Companhia Vale do Rio Doce
ECLAC	United Nations Economic Commission for Latin America and the Caribbean (Comisión Económica para Latin America y el Caribe, CEPAL)
EMBRAPA	Brazilian Agricultural Research Corporation (Empresa Brasileira de Pesquisa Agropecuária)
eMNC	Emerging Multinationals
ERCo	Energy Research Company
EU	European Union
FAO	Food and Agriculture Organization of the United Nations
FPP	Favela Pacification Program
FDC	Dom Cabral Foundation (Fundação Dom Cabral)
FDI	foreign direct investment
FGV	Getulio Vargas Foundation (Fundação Getulio Vargas)
FIFA	International Federation of Association Football
FINEP	Financing Agency of Studies and Projects (Financiadora de Estudos e Projetos)
FNDCT	National Fund for Scientific and Technological Development (Fundo Nacional de Desenvolvimento Científico e Tecnológico)
FUNTEC	Technical and Scientific Development Fund (Fundo de Desenvolvimento Técnico-Científico)
GDP	gross domestic product
HIV/AIDS	Human Immunodeficiency Virus/Acquired Immunodeficiency Syndrome
IBOPE	Brazilian Institute of Public Opinion and Statistics (Instituto Brasileiro de Opinião Pública e Estatística)
IBSA	India-Brazil-South Africa Dialogue Forum
IBSAMAR	India-Brazil-South Africa Maritime
IDEB	Basic Education Development Index (Índice de Desenvolvimento da Educação Básica)
IEA	International Energy Agency
IFAD	International Fund for Agricultural Development
IMF	International Monetary Fund
INEP	National Institute of Studies and Educational Research (Instituto Nacional de Estudos e Pesquisas Educacionais)

INPE	Brazil's National Institute for Space Research (Instituto Nacional de Pesquisas Espaciais)
IPEA	Institute of Applied Economic Research (Instituto de Pesquisa Econômica Aplicada)
IPO	initial public offering
ISO	International Organization for Standardization
IT	information technology
MDG	Millennium Development Goals
MDIC	Ministry of Development, Industry and Foreign Trade
MINUSTAH	United Nations Stabilization Mission in Haiti
MBA	Master of Business Administration
MERCOSUR	Southern Common Market
MNE	multinational enterprise
MRN	Mineração Rio do Norte
NATO	North Atlantic Treaty Organization
NGO	non-governmental organization
OAS	Organization of American States
OECD	Organisation for Economic Co-operation and Development
PAC	Growth Acceleration Program (Programa de Aceleração do Crescimento)
PDVSA	Petroleum of Venezuela S.A.
PISA	Programme for International Student Assessment
Pronatec	National Programme of Access to Technical Schools (Programa Nacional de acesso ao Ensino Técnico e Emprego)
ProUni	"University for All" Programme (Programa Universidade para Todos)
PPP	public–private partnership
PT	Workers' Party (Partido dos Trabalhadores)
R2P	responsibility to protect
RwP	responsibility while protecting
SABESP	Basic Sanitation Company of the State of Sao Paulo (Companhia de Saneamento Básico do Estado de São Paulo)
SEGIB	Ibero-America's Secretariat General (Secretaría General Iberoamericana)
SOBEET	Brazilian Society of Studies and Transnational Corporations and Economic Globalization (Sociedade Brasileira de Estudos e Empresas Transnacionais e da Globalização Econômica)

UK	United Kingdom
UNASUR	Union of South American Nations
UN	United Nations
UNICA	Brazilian Sugarcane Industry Association (União da Indústria de Cana-de-Açúcar)
UNCTAD	United Nations Conference on Trade and Development
UNIFIL	United Nations Interim Force in Lebanon
UNODC	United Nations Office on Drugs and Crime
US	United States
US$	United States dollar
USGS	United States Geological Survey
VCC	Vale Columbia Center on Sustainable International Investment
WB	World Bank
WEF	World Economic Forum
WFP	World Food Programme
WHO FCTC	World Health Organization's Framework Convention for Tobacco Control
WIPO	World Intellectual Property Organization
WTO	World Trade Organization
ZPCSA	Zone of Peace and Cooperation of the South Atlantic

Introduction: Brazil at a Crossroads

Brazil has a long history of successively winning plaudits and taking flack. The country's new economic standing is increasingly being noticed, but many still doubt its ability to take the next step and fulfill its potential as a global leader on the international stage. In the 1960s and 1970s, while the country was still under military dictatorship,[1] Brazil's economic miracle caught the world's attention, before slowly vanishing with the debt crisis and finally giving way to the "lost decade" of the 1980s.

This time may be different. First, Brazil has changed. It is now a vibrant democracy, with solid macroeconomic credentials, rising human capital and an ever-growing exploitation of its abundant energy, mineral and agricultural resources. Second, the world has changed. The questioning of United States' political dominance and the deep-rooted crisis in Europe, following the Global Financial Crisis of 2007–2009, have opened new space for the rise of emerging states – and Brazil is a serious contender among them to acquire world-class political status.

Throughout the 2000s, this South American nation stood out among rising powers thanks to its pro-active diplomacy and its projection as a self-confident and engaging nation, eager to share the recipe of its political and economic success with the rest of the world. In the last few years, however, its political agenda has been marked by a resurgence of domestic issues, which have turned Brazilian leaders' attention inwards and away from the quest for greater international recognition.

Brazil's difficulties may be interpreted as the sign of an irreconcilable mismatch between its global ambitions and the pressing internal challenges that it needs to address. However, the opposite argument could be made. The emergence of Brazil as a world power and its ability to face its domestic shortcomings are deeply intertwined. By pursuing these two goals simultaneously, Brazilian decision-makers could create a virtuous circle of leadership by example, in areas ranging from its efforts to eradicate poverty to smart leveraging of natural resources. By creating both economic success and a new social order, Brazil can serve as an inspiration for the world, and especially for other emerging markets that have to also confront internal economic and social issues.

How high can Brazil go?

The aim of this book is to explore whether Brazil's rise on the global stage is beginning, or whether it has already hit a plateau. To answer this question, it offers a realistic assessment of Brazil's strengths and challenges as the country seeks to shape its own development path and play a more influential role in global affairs. What we find is that beyond the ups and downs of economic cycles and the growing pains that every rising power experiences, there are solid reasons to be optimistic about the future of Brazil. The challenges that it must face cannot be ignored. However, what observers sometimes underplay is the country's extraordinary assets and its capacity to innovate and experiment with ad-hoc solutions, many of which lie outside conventional paths.

To evaluate the potential of Brazil as an emerging global power, we looked at the country's performance across two conceptual frameworks that are commonly used to measure the power of a state in international relations: *hard power* and *soft power.*

The concept of soft power was framed by the American political scientist Joseph Nye (Nye 2004) to describe the ability of states and other entities of international relations to shape the preferences of others through attraction and persuasion. A state's soft power arises from the attractiveness of its policies, political values and culture. It contrasts with more traditional forms of hard power, which rest on a state's capacity to leverage its military and economic strength to influence the behavior of others. Hard power tends to rely on a combination of threats, coercion and incentives, sometimes dubbed a "carrot and stick" approach, where the stick may take the form of military threats or economic sanctions, and carrots include the promise of military protection or the signing of preferential trade agreements. Proponents of hard power suggest that, to win the respect of its peers, a country must keep a leading edge in the global competition for economic, technological and military power.

A remarkable feature of Brazil's ascension over the last decade has been its dominant use of soft power to raise its international profile.

Brazil is attractive and Brazilian leaders know it. Its political values, economic development model, popular culture and diplomatic confidence generate goodwill throughout the world. Its commitment to multilateralism and the peaceful resolution of conflicts makes it a cooperative player in the global governance system. At the same time, Brazil has managed to maintain an autonomous foreign policy, and has shown more than once that it is not afraid to defy Western powers. It has been able to position itself as a leading voice of the developing world and earn a seat at the high table of global governance.

While Brazil has historically emphasized soft power as a strategic means to gain influence on the global stage, the country has recently moved toward strengthening its hard power capabilities. Building on its new status as the world's seventh largest economy, the South American giant is looking to gain increased bargaining power from its position as a global supplier of key natural resources, including food, energy and minerals. It has also become a major source of investment abroad by actively promoting the internationalization of its largest domestic companies. Last but not least, Brazil is slowly establishing itself as a military power with a pro-active defense agenda.

In search of the Brazil Dream: A creative emerging power

The concepts of hard and soft power provide a useful framework to understand the kind of resources a country needs to achieve and consolidate its status as an emerging power on the global stage. In the case of Brazil, and perhaps of many other emerging nations, there is a third element that we feel should be emphasized. This third element, which can be seen as an integral part of the concept of soft power, relates to the fundamental aspiration that a nation – and its people – has for itself.

This is especially important for emerging countries who take pride in developing their own ways and not slavishly reproducing the models of traditional powers, especially if these are their formal colonial powers (such as Europe) or countries perceived as having had an imperialistic attitude toward them in the recent past (such as the United States). Models imported from or pushed by the Western world seem dated and patronizing to the next generation of emerging powers.

This third component rests on the social consensus a country is able to build for itself, across all of its stakeholders. In other words, Brazil is in the process of defining its "Brazil Dream" and gathering the resources to reach this dream.

Existing powers have historically used the aspirations and promises of their societies to project themselves on the international stage. These social constructions are often based on perception and may not always reflect reality. Here are three examples of models, which have become famous:

- The "American Dream"[2]: a vision of meritocracy where people who work hard will succeed, no matter where they come from. Through their hard work, people become homeowners, buy cars and obtain an education for their children. This dream revolves around the mythology of the self-made man.
- The "European Dream"[3], which so far applies to most continental European countries: citizens agree to pay taxes, and expect strong public services in return. Through social safety nets, a welfare state ensures that no one is left behind. This dream has a strong emphasis on humanist values, as opposed to a more materialist approach to life.
- The "China Dream"[4], which has developed more recently: all stakeholders are united to build the most powerful country in the world. While the official goal of China's leadership is to create a "socialist harmonious society", capitalism has become the favored instrument to reach this objective. There is a strong sense of working together for the common good and in support of reaching the nation's goals of growth and harmony.

What is the Brazil Dream? It is probably a mix of these three.

- Like the United States, Brazil aspires to a great deal of social mobility to fight social determinism, where the poor remain poor, and minorities are at an economic disadvantage. It is a "new world" country that values innovation and entrepreneurship. Like the United States, the population aspires to be a predominantly middle-class country. Brazil also strives to be a melting pot, where people from different ethnic backgrounds live harmoniously.
- Brazil also looks at the European model and wants good public services, such as health and education, good infrastructure and strong social safety nets such as social security, pensions and welfare programs. Like the European Union, Brazil is a proponent of multilateralism and promotes values of peace, human rights, democracy, social progress and environmental consciousness.
- Like China, Brazil wants to be respected and to build power. It wants to have a robust economy, a domestic (including state-owned)

industry base, and to create its own intellectual property and technology, so as not to be too dependent on others. Like India and many other former colonies, Brazil wants to be strong and protect its sovereignty vis-à-vis established powers.

The Brazil Dream would not be complete without a fourth element, which revolves around adding a "Brazilian twist", by leveraging what makes Brazil unique in the world: a relaxed and passionate attitude to life, which in turn fosters creative improvisation. As it has shown in the past, and as it continues to prove today, Brazil has the ability to create fresh new ideas, building from existing ones. Whether it is how to create new forms of participatory democracy, how to leverage a sudden increase in offshore oil resources, or how to continue eradicating extreme poverty in an era of slower growth, Brazil seeks to forge its own unique solutions, rather than follow others. In a sense, the Brazil Dream is to become a "creative emerging power".

A moving target

Our journey started in 1996, when Lourdes Casanova started teaching a course on Brazil and Latin America to MBAs and senior executives at INSEAD. At that time, there was a paucity of both interest in, and materials on, Latin America within business schools. Over the next decade, Lourdes Casanova led the development of dozens of case studies, chapters, books and articles about the region. A key result, which emerged from this research, was that successful Latin American firms were rapidly expanding regionally and globally and many of these firms shared special characteristics in their operational and strategic leadership. This led to Lourdes' first book on Latin America, *Global Latinas* (Palgrave MacMillan 2009).

Brazil had a special role in discussions about Latin America. The size of the Brazilian economy made it a key player in the region; however, at the same time it was often less spoken about, less discussed – in many ways it was the most powerful and yet the most often "forgotten" country in Latin America. During the two successive terms of President Lula (2003–2010), it was becoming clear that Brazil's role in the region and globally was changing rapidly. Brazil was emerging as a key regional power and an emerging global player. However, the rise of Brazil was not in isolation. Latin America needed Brazil and Brazil needed Latin America.

During this same time period, Lourdes participated in and directed several educational programs for senior Brazilian executives in collaboration with two important institutions in Brazil, Fundaçao Dom Cabral and the Instituto Euvaldo Loli of the Brazilian Confederation of Industry (CNI). Conversations before, during and after these programs with Brazilian executives, academics and government officials have proven to be very useful. On one hand, we saw the important role that both the private and public sectors were playing in the development of Brazil. On the other hand, we gathered insights into the national and political dimensions of Brazil's rise as an emerging global power – aspects that also benefited from discussions with the book's co-author, political scientist Julian Kassum. We started writing the book in 2012 and Brazil's economy was a *moving target*. The "Brazil uprising" in July 2013 motivated us to start our own survey as part of the book. We wanted to include the opinions of Brazilian stakeholders to feed the discussions on the country's opportunities and challenges as it continues to emerge as a global political and economic power. The results of this survey are presented in Chapter 8.

Overview of the book

The content of the book is divided in three parts. The first one, titled "A Champion of Soft Power", focuses on Brazil's vast array of soft power resources and includes the first two chapters.

Chapter 1 ("A Friendly Giant") offers an assessment of Brazil's soft power capabilities, evaluating its strengths and weaknesses in an area that is seen as increasingly crucial to build global leadership. We explore Brazil's ability to "seduce" the world through its warm and engaging culture, progressive values and peaceful foreign policies. The chapter also looks at areas that could undermine Brazil's accumulation of soft power.

Chapter 2 ("The Brasília Consensus: Still a Valid Model?") examines the country's hybrid development model, which combines macroeconomic orthodoxy with certain features of state capitalism, as well as pro-active social inclusion policies. We identify and analyze the five pillars of the Brasília Consensus, namely: macroeconomic stability, social programs, domestic demand, state-led industry development and political consensus.

The second part of the book, titled "A Hard Power Nation in the Making", evaluates Brazil's hard power resources, which are greater than is often believed. This part comprises chapters 3 and 4.

Chapter 3 ("Brazil's Economic Power") shows that the nation's hard power rests more on its energy, food and financial reserves than on its military capabilities – although the country is taking steps to reinforce its defense sector. We describe the key features of the Brazilian economy, including its natural resources (energy, minerals, biodiversity, agriculture), existing pockets of manufacturing and services excellence, its human capital, and its increasingly pivotal role as a global trading partner.

Chapter 4 ("Brazilian Companies Going Global") analyzes the growing presence of Brazilian multinational companies across global markets and identify the obstacles that they face on the road to become world-class players, or consolidate their status as such. Following a panorama of the current standing of Brazilian multinational companies based on the most recent global and regional corporate rankings, we discuss their motives for expanding globally and the remaining challenges they need to overcome to become world leaders in their respective markets.

The third and final part, titled "What Will Propel Brazil Forward?", explores three areas which will define Brazil's capacity to stretch its limit and fully assume the role of emerging global power. These areas are covered in chapters 5, 6 and 7.

Chapter 5 ("Strengthening Economic Competitiveness") discusses the country's economic agenda, from fostering innovation to improving physical infrastructure. We highlight examples of governmental initiatives to address the needs of agriculture, technology and business funding. The chapter also discusses Brazil's productivity challenge and its perennial infrastructure deficit. The role of public-private partnerships is explored, as well as the different forms they have taken in Brazil.

Chapter 6 ("Sustaining Social Innovation") shows that, while much has been achieved in the reduction of poverty, inequalities, crime and corruption, there is still a lot to be done. Brazil has shown that it could be a hub of social innovation in areas such as social programs and social entrepreneurship. It now needs to strengthen its education system at primary, secondary and university levels.

Chapter 7 ("In Search of a Role on the Global Stage") explores Brazil's new prominence in global affairs. We show how the country's "soft-balancing" strategy has helped it increase its influence and acquire greater autonomy on the global stage. With Brazil now a key force in multilateral institutions and a leading voice of the Global South, the chapter asks what Brazilian leaders should do with their new-found influence.

As mentioned above, Chapter 8 ("Looking for Answers") summarizes the key findings of a survey the authors conducted between July and

October 2013 in the middle of the Brazil uprising to gather the views of a number of Brazilian *movers and shakers* about some of the key themes covered in the book.

And finally, the Conclusion ("Building the Brazil Dream") summarizes the main points of the book.

Part I

A Champion of Soft Power

1
A Friendly Giant

When giving speeches around the world, Brazilian leaders tirelessly make the point that Brazil is not just the country of football and carnival. Ironically, the country has never shied away from using its popular culture to project itself onto the global stage. Promoting the image of a friendly and peaceful nation – with fun-loving and welcoming people – goes to the heart of Brazil's country-branding strategy, whether it seeks to gain influence in world affairs or to market its products in the global marketplace.

As discussed in the Introduction, what distinguishes Brazil's rise in prominence from that of other emerging powers is its quasi-exclusive use of "soft power" to pursue its foreign policy goals, at least until recent years. According to political scientist Joseph Nye, soft power rests on the ability to shape the preferences of others. This ability tends to be associated with a country's intangible assets, such as its culture, political values, institutions and policies, which are seen as legitimate or having moral authority (Nye, 2004). In the words of Paulo Sotero and Leslie Elliott Armijo (2007), "Brazil is the quintessential soft power BRIC." By contrast, China and India derive much of their international stature from being nuclear powers. Turkey possesses the second largest army of the North Atlantic Treaty Organization. For its part, Brazil has historically favored diplomacy and engagement over force or military threats, and has so far not joined the nuclear race. Since the Paraguayan war of 1864–1870, the country has lived peacefully with all of its ten neighbors. Brazil's current Defense Minister, Celso Amorim, once described Brazil's approach as "the use of culture and civilization, not threats [...] a belief in dialogue, not force".[1]

In February 2013, the *Financial Times* described Brazil as the "first big 'soft' power", whose peaceful manners and laid-back attitude make it "a kind of Canada writ large but with Carnival thrown in".[2] While Brazil's growing economic weight, its renewed interest in defense matters, and its globally active multinational companies have boosted its hard power credentials in recent years, the country has thoughtfully cultivated the image of a "peaceful giant", whose values, policies and culture generate attraction throughout the world.

This chapter offers an assessment of Brazil's soft power capabilities, evaluating its strengths and weaknesses in an area that is seen as increasingly crucial to building global leadership. What are the bits and parts of the Brazilian culture, values and policies that together depict the comforting figure of a "friendly giant" in a world torn by geopolitical tensions, cultural divisions and social stress? What are the weak spots of Brazil's soft power, and how could these affect the nation's capacity to lead and attract others?

A warm and engaging popular culture

For Joseph Nye, one of the fundamental elements of a country's soft power is its capacity to use culture as an instrument to seduce others and shape their preferences. Needless to say, the United States owes a lot of its influence to the global appeal of the "American Way of Life" fed on a daily basis by Hollywood movies and the country's dynamic entertainment industry. Rising powers, such as China, India, Turkey and Brazil, have all awoken to the importance of leveraging their national culture to win people's hearts and minds.

The good news for Brazilian leaders is that they are starting from a very strong position. The country already derives significant goodwill from its popular culture and attractive lifestyle. In a global survey of 30,000 persons across 15 countries, conducted by the social networking site Badoo.com, Brazil was voted the second "coolest nationality" in the world after the United States. Brazilian music, a key vector of its coolness, is generally associated with Samba and Bossa Nova. Somewhat surprisingly, the latest global hit was brought about by the boom of "Sertanejo Universitário", a sub-set of Brazilian country music popularized by the 30-year-old singer Michel Teló. His video-single *Ai se eu te pego* received more than 500 million views on YouTube from July 2011 to September 2013, making it the tenth most watched video of all time on the video-sharing platform. The song ranked number one in at least nine European countries and was especially popular in Spain and within the Latino community in the United States.

The international appeal of Brazilian popular culture is a particularly relevant component of Brazil's soft power resources, since the values surrounding most Brazilian cultural products are largely positive and engaging – a perfect echo of Brazil's projection as a warm and cooperative nation. A good example is the country's most famous brand, Havaianas, the colorful rubber and plastic flip-flops that are now sold in 80 countries and have become a symbol of the Brazilian lifestyle. Another powerful vector of Brazilian culture is *capoeira,* a martial art combining dance, music and spirituality, that was created by African slaves in Brazil nearly 500 years ago as a means of self-defense and emancipation. It is now a popular sport among young people from all over the world, especially in large urban centers. ABADÁ, the Brazilian Association for the Support and Development of the Art of Capoeira, is present in over 30 countries and a countless number of self-organized capoeira groups have set up shop in New York, Moscow, Jakarta, Beirut and other cultural capitals of the world.

Brazil is also famous for its *telenovelas,* which attract millions of viewers every night. Their impact goes far beyond Brazil. More than 130 *telenovelas* have been broadcast in 170 countries, including the United States, China and South Africa. Most of these serial melodramas were created and produced by Brazil's largest television network, Rede Globo, whose international channel, TV Globo Internacional is present in 118 countries. "There is no doubt that *telenovelas* are a key element of our country's soft power", said Maria Immacolata Vassallo de Lopes, from the School of Communications of the University of São Paulo.[3] Six months after being sold on the international market, the popular hit and social phenomenon, *Avenida Brasil* has become the most licensed *telenovela* in the history of Brazilian television. It has been dubbed in 14 languages and broadcast in more than 105 countries. It broke the previous record held by *Da Cor do Pecado,* which sold in 100 countries.

Paulo Coelho's best-sellers provide another example of Brazil's successful cultural exports. The novelist is one of today's most widely read authors. With over 65 million copies sold worldwide, his most famous work *The Alchemist* has been translated into 67 languages and published in more than 150 countries. Paulo Coelho, who is taken more seriously abroad than in his home country, was designated as a "United Nations Messenger of Peace" in September 2007.

A potential trap for Brazil is to let its popular culture, however appealing it may be, overshadow the richness and variety of its wider cultural scene. In the fields of architecture and plastic arts, for example, Brazilian culture enjoys a reputation for prestige and sophistication.

Oscar Niemeyer, whose work and influence has shaped the most iconic buildings of Brasília, São Paulo, Rio de Janeiro and Belo Horizonte, is widely considered as a visionary of modern architecture. The São Paulo Fashion Week, held semi-annually, is said to be the fifth largest in the world, after Paris, Milan, London and New York. Brazil's contemporary art scene has also gained a worldwide reputation, thanks to artists like Cildo Meireles, Ernesto Neto, Adriana Varejão and a generous system of corporate tax rebates for cultural sponsorships. As Matthew Slotover, co-director of London's annual Frieze Art Fair, once commented to *The Guardian* newspaper: "I've been to Russia, China and Brazil in the last few years and Brazil is the most interesting one of the BRIC[4] countries."[5]

In a recent series of articles on Brazil's soft power, *BBC Brasil* echoed the growing sentiment among Brazilian artists and policymakers that the country could adopt a more coordinated approach to promoting its culture abroad. Singer Gilberto Gil, former minister of culture, even thinks that Brazil has been neglecting culture as its economic and political profile has grown. "Since Brazil is becoming more powerful and vocal, its soft power has to grow at the same proportion as hard power," he said, adding that Brazilian cinema, plastic arts and music needed greater institutional support.[6] A better coordination of public and private initiatives in the areas of trade, technology, tourism and culture could indeed have a multiplier effect.

To promote their national culture, and to foster people-to-people exchanges, many governments have devoted growing resources to developing worldwide networks of state-funded cultural organizations. The Alliance Française, the British Council, Germany's Goethe Institut and Spain's Cervantes Institute, to name a few, have all established a solid presence across continents. Rising states are starting to follow suit, sometimes with impressive results. In just nine years, China's Confucius Institutes have opened 833 centers in 104 countries and regions. The Indian Council for Cultural Relations has established 35 cultural centers in different parts of the world, including one in São Paulo, and it is planning to open 15 more. According to a 2013 report by the British Council, the network of Brazilian cultural institutes remains under-developed, with only 29 offices, mainly in Latin America. However, as highlighted by the report, the promotion of culture will be increasingly led by non-governmental initiatives. The British Council cites Braziliality, a London-based non-profit organization that promotes "Brazilian artists abroad and international artists that have an artistic dialogue with Brazil, creating a 360 degree view of the influence of contemporary Brazilian art and culture worldwide."[7]

How hot is the "Brazil brand?"

Developing a strong country brand, sometimes called nation-branding, is especially important for emerging economies, whose local brands do not yet enjoy the powerful recognition of the Nestlés, Googles and Coca-Colas of this world. Beyond its marketing benefits, the strength of a country brand is a natural form of currency through which nations can exert influence and gain market power.

Using quantitative data and expert opinions to assess the qualities people associate with different nations, the consultancy FutureBrand created a Country Brand Index, which has become a global reference in the marketing industry. According to the 2012–2013 edition of the index, Brazil does not qualify as one of the world's top 25 country brands. Switzerland, Canada and Japan hold the first three spots. However, Brazil's rank of 28th makes it a indisputable leader in the emerging-market category, ahead of India (42nd), South Africa (43rd), Turkey (45th), China (66th) and Russia (83rd).[8]

For FutureBrand, Brazil's main assets are "steady economic growth, a burgeoning middle class and growing consumer demand, a geography rich in natural resources and beauty and a proactive government eager to play an important regional and international role". However, the report notes that "Brazilian authorities face a major and impossible-to-ignore obstacle: equality and human development."

In 2013, a special edition of the Country Brand Index took a closer look at the performance of country brands across Latin America. The results are particularly flattering for Brazil, which takes the leading spot, ahead of Argentina and Costa Rica. Based on hard data and interviews with residents, investors, tourists and government officials, Brazil receives top marks in technology, investment climate, shopping, nightlife, and culture and arts. The country gets its lowest scores in the "quality of life" sub-category, notably due to below-average rankings in education, healthcare and safety.[9]

A country with 21st-century values and policies

The soft power of a country is not only defined by the popularity and prestige of its culture. According to Joseph Nye, it also rests on two other key resources: its political values (when it lives up to them at home and abroad) and its foreign policies (when they are seen as legitimate and having moral authority). Here again, Brazil holds strong credentials, which it was able to develop by turning its main weakness – its position as a developing economy with huge societal challenges – into a major strength. As highlighted by Ana Prusa, "it is often Brazil's frankness in acknowledging that it faces serious challenges – the same challenges facing many countries in the developing world, from improving the quality of education to stimulating innovation and entrepreneurship – that gives Brazil so much credibility as a spokesperson from the developing world". The internal challenges that could potentially undermine the country's soft power have become instead a "source of legitimacy" (Prusa, 2011).

Using its own domestic experience, Brazil has managed to establish itself as a leading voice, and even a role model, in defending what Celso Amorim has called "a worldview that accords pride of place to the values of democracy, social justice, economic development, and environmental protection".[10] The country has made special efforts to project its value system and share its experience in several areas that have emerged as major global challenges for the 21st century.

Celebrating ethnic and cultural diversity

A key element of Brazil's global projection is its very nature as a multicultural nation with a strong attachment to racial diversity. About half of the Brazilian population is classified as either black or of mixed raced. Most Brazilians are descendants of indigenous peoples, Portuguese settlers, African slaves, and immigrants from Europe, the Middle East and Asia who arrived from the 19th century onwards. Home to the largest Lebanese community in the world, Brazil prides itself on being the second-largest Italian and Japanese nation. To reflect its active policy of inclusion and tolerance toward cultural diversity, the federal government of Brazil employed *um país de todos* ("a country of all") as its official slogan for many years. Brasília frequently refers to this national ideal when portraying Brazil as a potential enabler to revive the Israel-Palestine peace process. President Lula boldly summed it up in an interview to Israeli newspaper *Haaretz*: "More than 120,000 Jews live here in full harmony with 10 million Arabs. It would seem that people can learn from us."[11]

A global green leader

Brazil is far from having a clean environmental record. The country has reacted to this by positioning itself at the leading edge of global environmental governance. In 1992, it hosted the historical UN Earth Summit in Rio. In 2009, a few days after the closure of the UN Climate Change Conference in Copenhagen, then-President Lula incorporated into law an ambitious National Climate Change Policy through which Brazil voluntarily committed to reduce greenhouse gas emissions by at least 36% from "business as usual" levels by 2020.[12] In 2012, Brazil hosted the Rio + 20 Earth Summit, the biggest UN event ever organized, with over 45,000 participants. While the event was a success in terms of participation, environmental groups have criticized Brazilian diplomats for being more interested in cutting a deal at all costs (so as to improve its standing as a "global facilitator") than in actually saving the environment. Still, Brazil's recent success in reducing deforestation rates in the Amazon area, as well as its position as a world leader in renewable energies, has strengthened its standing as one of the most eco-conscious emerging powers.

Battling against hunger

In May 2010, the World Food Programme (WFP – the food assistance branch of the United Nations) honored former President Lula as a "Global Champion in the Battle Against Hunger" in recognition of his leadership in eradicating hunger and child malnutrition in Brazil and abroad. While visiting a small farm near Brasília to learn about the country's Zero Hunger (*Fome Zero*) strategy, former WFP Executive Director Josette Sheeran said that Brazil was an example to follow. The program, which inspired the launch of the "Zero Hunger Challenge" by UN Secretary-General Ban Ki-moon at the Rio + 20 Earth Summit of 2012, combines technical support for small-scale farmers, incentives to increase school attendance, food education initiatives, and the creation of subsidized restaurants for low-income populations.[13] As Sheeran noted, "Brazil has a wealth of experience that can be shared with governments eager to learn how they achieved that success and adapt it to their own countries."[14] Through the Center for Excellence Against Hunger, Brazil and the WFP have helped governments in African, Latin American and Caribbean countries run their school meal programs.

From aid recipient to donor

Traditionally an aid recipient, Brazil is slowly establishing itself as a global aid donor. According to the governmental think-tank IPEA, annual international assistance of all types totaled US$158 million in 2005 and doubled to US$362 million in 2009.[15] Part of Brazil's technical assistance activities are coordinated by the Brazilian Agency of Cooperation (*Agência Brasileira de Cooperação* – ABC), which was originally established in 1987 to channel incoming development aid. ABC now provides assistance to over 80 developing countries, mainly in Africa. While Brazil's international development funds are still small compared to those of industrialized countries, its aid efforts tend to be personalized and focus on the replication and adaptation of public strategies that it has already successfully implemented at home. Brazilian authorities emphasize that Brazil – as a developing country that has made huge progress at home in the areas of agriculture, health, education and governance – is much better placed than advanced economies to advise on the development strategies of other developing nations.

Friends with everyone

Brazil's image as a friendly nation derives not only from the warmth of its people but also from its ability to maintain positive diplomatic relationships with all kinds of states and political regimes. During his years in office, former President Lula was one of the few world leaders who maintained warm personal relations with both George W. Bush and his declared enemies Presidents Hugo Chávez, Fidel Castro and Mahmoud Ahmadinejad. Brazil sees and projects itself as a "bridge nation" between different political systems and ideologies. As pointed out by Andrew Hurrell, "the Lula government sought to play at both Davos (the World Economic Forum) and at Porto Alegre (the World Social Forum)". To a significant extent, it managed to be both the "favoured son of Wall Street" and "to claim to speak for the progressive Global South" (Hurrell, 2010a). While Brazil cannot forever be "all things to all people", it is increasingly perceived as a player that facilitates understanding between different parties and is able to generate consensus.[16]

A peacekeeper

In line with its long tradition of diplomacy and the peaceful resolution of conflicts, Brazil has taken a leading role in several UN peacekeeping operations. A prime example is Brazil's military commandment of the United Nations Stabilization Mission in Haiti (MINUSTAH). Over the years, the South American giant has provided support to UN peacekeeping efforts in 33 countries, including Angola, Mozambique, Timor-Leste and Lebanon. In 2007, Brazil was elected to lead the United Nations Peace-building Commission's talks on Guinea-Bissau. A clear motivation behind Brazil's participation in peace-building and peacekeeping operations is to affirm its standing as a global player with the political and military capacity to take a leading role in issues of war and peace. But more broadly, it serves to illustrate Brazil's altruistic behavior and its attachment to democracy. In the same vein, Brazil has vehemently opposed coups d'états perpetrated against constitutionally elected presidents in Honduras in 2009 and Paraguay in 2012.

Where does Brazil stand in the global race for soft power?

By its essence, soft power resources take the form of intangible assets that are difficult to measure and compare. To understand the key drivers behind soft power, and to explore how countries accumulate it over time, the consulting firm EY has produced a "Rapid Growth-Market Soft Power Index" in partnership with the Moscow School of Management, Skolkovo. The latest edition was published in 2012, based on data from 2010.[17]

The index is organized into three major categories:

- Global image (which measures a country's global popularity and admiration).
- Global integrity (which measure a country's propensity to protect its citizens, uphold political and social freedoms, and treat its neighbors with respect).
- Global integration (which gauges how interconnected a country is with the rest of the world).

How does Brazil fare? Not bad, but not great: it ranks fourth among rapid-growth market economies and 11th overall, behind China, India and Russia (three countries whose sheer size mechanically inflates their scoring) and above Turkey, Mexico and South Africa. Interestingly, Brazil is the rapid-growth market whose soft power increased the most since 2005, according to the report. Compared with its peers, Brazil scores above average in voter turnout, freedom, rule of law, media exports and Olympic

(Continued)

competition. Its poorest scores are found among the index's "global integration" variables. It ranks relatively poorly in the tourism and immigration categories, and importantly, its low number of world-class universities, their low level of internationalization, and the lack of command of English contribute to isolate Brazil from the rest of world and weigh down its overall ranking.

Another attempt to measure and compare nations' soft power is the annual survey published by the London-based magazine Monocle, which ranks countries according to their standard of government, diplomatic infrastructure, cultural output, capacity for education, and appeal to business.[18] In the 2012 edition of the survey, the top five spots went to Britain, the United States, Germany, France and Sweden. In an article for the *Financial Times*, Joseph Nye himself hailed Britain's performance, which he attributed to the beneficial burst of public relations produced by the successful London Olympic Games and the enduring popularity of the royal family.[19]

Brazil's position of 17th, ahead of Turkey (20th) but behind South Korea (11th) may seem disappointing. But it is one of the only three emerging powers to have made it to the top 20. Noting that much of its soft power comes from the simple fact that "we all love Brazilians", Monocle also points out the damaging impact of high-profile corruption cases on the country's global image.

Weak spots in Brazil's soft power

Soft power largely rests on the perception of the target audience. As such, it is inherently fragile and may be subject to abrupt rises and falls. A country's soft power can be undercut when its policies or actions reduce its attractiveness, or when these appear to be at odds with the ideals, values and principles it defends. The United States lost a significant amount of soft power when it decided to invade Iraq in 2003. The unilateral nature of the intervention went against commonly held international norms and reinforced the image of an arrogant United States (Prusa, 2011). In the same way, China's restrictions on political freedom can provoke enough reputational damage to cancel years of soft power-yielding initiatives by its governmental agencies.

Brazil's image as a "friendly giant" is an immense asset, but it is also one that will be hard to keep as its political influence grows and its economic and military power become more impossible to ignore. Brazil's global reputation also suffers from a number of domestic problems that continue to blight society and damage the country's global image. Education, urban crime and corruption, which we analyze in a further chapter, are among the country's most pressing challenges. What are other important weak spots in Brazil's projection as a peaceful and successful nation? Will a gradual hardening of Brazil's soft power eventually erode its charm?

The myth of racial democracy

For years, Brazilian authorities have cast their country as a "racial democracy", where successive waves of mixed-race marriages have saved the country from racial discrimination. This myth has been largely debunked in recent years, although racism remains a political taboo. This paradox was well illustrated in a survey conducted by anthropologist Lilia Moritz Schwarcz in 2000. Asked whether they were prejudiced in any way, 97% of Brazilians surveyed answered no. Asked whether they knew anyone who was prejudiced, 99% answered yes.[20] Public statistics tend to confirm the reality of a country where citizens from different races live "not separated, but not equal". According to the 2010 census data from the Brazilian Institute of Geography and Statistics, 70.8% of the extremely poor are black or brown (*pardos*).[21] The government think-tank IPEA also found that, on average, the income of whites was slightly more than double that of black or brown Brazilians.[22] Non-whites are particularly under-represented at the highest levels of government and business.

Outside observers are quick to note the disturbing gap in social status between the Brazilian white elite and the country's non-white majority. Jenny Barchfield, the Associated Press correspondent in Rio de Janeiro, paints a harsh picture of multi-racial Brazil:

> Nearly all TV news anchors in Brazil are white, as are the vast majority of doctors, dentists, fashion models and lawyers. Most maids and doormen, street cleaners and garbage collectors are black. There is only one black senator and there never has been a black president, though a woman, Dilma Rousseff, leads the country now.[23]

The government, however, is beginning to tackle the problem. Since 2001, it has encouraged federal universities to establish affirmative action programs aimed at boosting the number of black and mixed-raced university students. More than 70 public universities have introduced racial admissions quotas, a policy that was recently sanctioned by the Brazilian Supreme Court. While these programs remain very controversial (many Brazilians believe that they exacerbate racial tensions and undermine equality of opportunity), they are starting to make a difference. Black and mixed-raced students now account for 35% of college enrollments, compared to 10% in 2001. These numbers will continue to rise. In October 2012, President Dilma Rousseff enacted a new "Law of Quotas", giving Brazil's federal universities four years to ensure that half of their incoming classes were from public schools. Half of the spots must go to students from low-income families and the pool of admitted students must be representative of the state's racial makeup.[24]

Turning its back on immigration?

Brazil's image as an open and multicultural nation is increasingly put to the test in another touchy area: immigration policies. In particular, its new economic status is forcing the government and society to deal with the challenge of illegal immigration, an issue that has long been associated with first world nations. In April 2013, the western Brazilian state of Acre declared a state of emergency after a surge of illegal immigrants from Bolivia and Peru, most of whom originally came from Haiti. Some came from more distant countries, such as Bangladesh, Pakistan, Nigeria and Senegal. The authorities' response has been chaotic. "What we found was unhealthy and inhumane," reported Conectas, a Brazilian human rights organization who investigated into the conditions of a refugee camp in the city of Brasiléia.[25]

In 2012, already faced with an influx of thousands of Haitians across its Amazonian frontier, the Brazilian government reacted by awarding temporary visas to those already in the country and cracking down on new arrivals, including through deportation. Many observers in Brazil and abroad criticized these restrictions for ignoring the humanitarian plight of Haitian refugees. The government's response can be seen as a serious departure from justice minister Paulo Abrão's stated ambition to establish "an example to the world of an immigration policy that is open and democratic, that reflects our historical welcoming tradition".[26] Brazil, which traditionally lambasted the United States and Europe for their restrictive immigration rules, is beginning to adopt the same kind of selection which favors skilled professionals from rich countries, while restraining the influx of poor foreign workers.[27]

As a country that built its history through successive waves of immigration, today's Brazil finds itself surprisingly closed to foreigners. According to the economist Ricardo Paes de Barros, the number of immigrants in Brazil is half of that at the start of the 20th century, when the population was ten times smaller.[28] While Brazilian companies desperately seek engineers and other skilled professionals, the country's immigration policy makes it difficult for foreigners to work in Brazil. Beyond administrative barriers, the society's attitude toward immigration is ambivalent, and sometimes it is downright hostile. In August 2013, when a first contingent of 400 Cuban doctors arrived at the invitation of the government to support Brazil's fragile healthcare system, they were booed and insulted by their Brazilian colleagues, an attitude which the health minister, Alexandre Padilha, described as "brutal" and inciting "prejudice and xenophobia".[29]

Facing negative publicity

The world's growing interest for Brazil also means that the country has received its fair share of bad press in recent years. Twenty years after helping put a temporary halt to the construction of the world's third largest dam on the Xingu River in the heart of Amazon, British singer Sting launched a new international campaign in 2010 to dissuade the Brazilian government from restarting the project. Film director James Cameron and actress Sigourney Weaver also joined the protest. Environmentalists and indigenous groups, led by Chief Raoni of the Kayapo tribe, say the dam would damage the sensitive ecosystem and ruin the livelihoods of those who live in the area to be flooded. A photograph of Chief Raoni crying traveled the world through social media networks. It was later revealed that he was not crying in reaction to President Dilma Rousseff's approval of the project, as was initially reported. But the symbol was strong and contributed to the perception of an insensitive Brazilian government, oblivious to environmental and human rights concerns.

Football, which is a great source of Brazilian pride, also has its darker side. On June 2013, the day Brazil beat Spain 3–0 and won the Confederations Cup in Rio de Janeiro, football spectators stoned to death and decapitated a referee during an amateur game in northern Brazil, after he fatally stabbed a player who refused to leave the pitch. The incident shocked the nation and made headlines across the world, increasing the pressure for Brazil to demonstrate it is a safe place to host the 2014 World Cup. Concerns over football violence are legitimate. In 2009, a report by Mauricio Murad from the Federal University of Rio de Janeiro found that

Brazil was the number one country for football-related death. Between 1999 and 2008, 49 people died in Brazilian football stadiums as a result of violence or crowd disasters.[30]

The new "gringos"?

Finally, Brazil's soft power may be undercut by the resentment its growing economic and military power is stirring among its neighbors. In particular, the recent "hardening of Brazil's soft power" – through booming expenditures to modernize its defense equipment and new policies to prop up its own domestic defense industry (see Chapter 3) – could potentially dent its reputation as a country with strictly peaceful intent. Brazil's new interest in defense may come as a surprise given the absence of external threats and the country's historical attachment to diplomacy. As Colonel Pedro de Pessoa, commander of the Brazilian Army's Peace Keeping Operations Training Centre, puts it: "It is good if people think you are nice, but they must also think that you are capable of being bad."[31]

Concretely, Brazil needs a modern navy to patrol its territorial waters and protect its deep-water oil and gas assets. The Amazon region also needs constant patrolling due to its porous frontiers and the threat to national security they create, including illegal logging, drug trafficking and smuggling. In August 2012, in what has been described as one of the largest military operations in the history of South America, the Brazilian army launched a spectacular operation along the borders with Paraguay, Argentina and Uruguay. Some 9,000 army, navy and air force troops were deployed to reinforce security against arms smugglers and drugs traffickers. Brazil's new emphasis on controlling its border, notably through military means, is starting to generate the kind of resentment in South America that used to be associated with the United States. Some in the region have even started to call Brazilians the "new gringos".[32]

Likewise, the growing presence of Brazilian multinational companies in Latin America and elsewhere in the world has started to elicit the same type of reaction that European and United States firms have faced for years when doing business in the developing world. In 2006, Bolivia's newly elected President Evo Morales accused the Brazilian state-owned oil company Petrobras of operating in an "illegal" and "unconstitutional" way.[33] Two years later, Ecuador's President Rafael Correa expelled the construction company Odebrecht, alleging that it built a faulty hydroelectric plant on the San Francisco river. In Mozambique, hundreds of protesters blocked the entrance to a coal mine operated by mining giant Vale in a row over a compensation deal following their displacement in early 2013. The same year, activists and bloggers slammed Brazil when they learnt that Rio-based Condor Non-Lethal Technologies allegedly sold part of the tear gas that Turkish security forces used against protesters gathering in Istanbul's central Taksim Square.

Can a friendly giant lead?

A big proponent of Brazil's soft power strategy, Celso Amorim himself recognizes that "no country can rely on soft power alone to defend its interests".[34] The image of a "friendly giant" has served Brazil well. By projecting itself as a cooperative nation, Brazil was able to establish itself as a leader of the Global South and win the respect of its peers. However, as Andrew Hurrell notes, "unlike China and India, Brazil does not have the hard-power resources to claim status within a more traditionally Great Power-centric concert or club" (Hurrell, 2010b).

While the country could gain greater respect and influence through its growing economic and military might, it would be extremely hazardous for Brazil to take its soft power capabilities for granted. As we have seen, Brazil's status as a champion of soft power rests more on its quasi-exclusive use of soft power to raise its international profile, rather than on its overall position in the global race for soft power. China and India are serious contenders when it comes to leading through attraction, and Brazil is still a second-league player in the various global rankings that measure and compare nations' soft power and country-branding accomplishments.

While not yet a world leader in soft power, the country possesses a number of competitive advantages, which it could exploit even more. Its biggest strength is probably the diversity of its population. Because soft power rests on attraction, its effects largely depend on the receptiveness of those at the receiving end. As a country with people of Portuguese, Italian, Spanish, German, Lebanese, Syrian and Armenian origins – as well as a large Jewish community and a huge proportion of Afro-descendants – it is uniquely placed to address multiple audiences and bridge cultures. As illustrated by the findings of EY (formerly Ernst & Young)'s "Rapid Growth-Market Soft Power Index", a key challenge for the South American nation will be to increase its level of global integration, notably in the area of education. The soft power of Brazil is huge, and has not yet been fully tapped.

2
The Brasília Consensus: Still a Valid Model?

Speaking of a "Brasília Consensus" may seem incongruous just a few months after a wave of mass protests swept the country for the first time in decades in 2013. These uprisings took everybody by surprise. Brazil's President Dilma Rousseff certainly did not see them coming, as she enjoyed personal approval ratings of over 70% just before these demonstrations started. Still, the "Comeback Queen", as *Newsweek* magazine called her,[1] managed to survive the "Brazilian Spring" relatively unscathed. After hitting a record low of 31% in the midst of the protests, the approval rating of her government has recovered and she seems to be poised to win the presidential elections in 2014.

The protests were never about overthrowing the government or demanding a radical change of political course. To be sure, part of the Brazilian economic elite bears a serious grudge against the Workers' Party and would welcome a return to more conservative policies. However, by and large, Brazil's social compact remains strong. Despite its evident shortcomings, the country's hybrid policy model – which mixes market-oriented reforms with state-led industrial development and progressive social policies – has produced a golden decade of sustained growth and massive poverty reduction, which led to quasi-full employment and the incorporation of 35 million more Brazilians within the middle class. What the protests have shown, however, is that there remains a lot of unfinished business. The country continues to suffer from years of corruption and of underinvestment in health, education and infrastructure. For Brazilian leaders, the question is: has the model reached its limits or should it be pushed even more?

What is the Brasília Consensus?

This chapter explores the key pillars of the "Brasília Consensus",[2] an expression that has been used to describe Brazil's socio-economic development model. The Brasília Consensus is not driven by a single ideology, but rather consists of a mix of approaches and solutions that Brazilian leaders were willing to experiment with to drive the country forward. This model combines orthodox macroeconomic policies, social expenditures, the development of a strong internal market and a somewhat protectionist approach to industrial development and the management of natural resources. As Patricia Campos Mello, a reporter from the *Folha de São Paulo* newspaper framed it, "the prescription of the Brasília Consensus combines policies that could easily be on the neoliberal agenda with measures that would scare the hell out of the orthodox" (Campos Mello, 2012).

The framework is seen as an alternative to the "Washington Consensus", a term that refers to the set of pro-market reforms that were applied by the International Monetary Fund and the World Bank to Latin American countries (and other parts of the developing world) in the 1990s (Williamson, 1990, Kuczynski and Williamson 2003). It also emerged as a soft political alternative to the more radical set of socialist policies embraced by Bolivia, Ecuador and Venezuela since the 2000s. To some extent, the Brasília Consensus can also be interpreted as a democratic model of state-led economic liberalization.[3]

Brazil's socio-economic model constitutes an important element of the nation's soft power. The re-election of President Lula in 2006, with a record 58 million votes (60% of the electorate), as well as the comfortable victory of President Dilma Rousseff in 2010 have significantly lifted the moral legitimacy and political attractiveness of this model, both within Latin America and outside the region. Many Latin American leaders look to Brazil as an example, in spite of the country's recent economic turmoil. Past and current leaders of El Salvador (Mauricio Funes), Guatemala (Alvaro Colom), Peru (Ollanta Humala) and Uruguay (José Mujica) owe much of their political successes to following the Brazilian path and saying they were going to emulate the policies and governing style of Lula. Strategists from the Workers' Party played a major role in helping Humala win Peru's presidential elections in 2012.

Tying economic growth to social progress

What put Brazil on the map was its capacity to combine growth with social inclusion within macroeconomic rigor. Although the country's growth record lags behind China's, Brazil was one of the last emerging markets to take a hit during the Global Financial Crisis and was the first to see recovery begin (see Chapter 3). The country is also widely acclaimed for its success in fighting poverty. In its 2013 economic survey of Brazil, the Organisation for Economic Co-operation and Development (OECD) notes that "poverty rates have fallen visibly, in particular since 2003, regardless of the exact definition of the poverty line employed", adding that "Brazil reached the Millennium Development Goal (MDG) of reducing extreme poverty by 2015 to one quarter of its 1990 level in 2007, eight years ahead of schedule" (OECD, 2013).

Other large developing countries have made great strides in lifting many people out of poverty over the last 20 years. In fact, the reduction of poverty has been even more drastic in China. Yet Brazil's performance offers more than meet the eye. A World Bank study from 2009 revealed that when one considers the reduction of the poverty rate per unit of gross domestic product (GDP) growth per capita, Brazil did five times better than China or India (Ravallion, 2009). While China and India's economic boom was accompanied by a rise of inequality in both countries, Brazil's score on the Gini index (which measures the rate of inequality) fell from 0.61 in 1990 to a historic low of 0.53 in 2010. In other words, Brazil is the only large emerging country that has managed to secure high growth rates (until 2010), cut poverty *and* reduce income disparities.

As a mechanical effect of poverty reduction, Brazil's middle class has expanded from 38% of the total population in 2002 to 53% in 2012, according to a government study (Secretaria de Assuntos Estratégicos da Presidência da República, 2012). The study sparked a debate in Brazil because it classified as "middle class" individuals with a monthly income ranging between BRL291 and BRL1019 (between US$130 and 460 approximately[4]). By the standards of most OECD countries, those "middle class" people would be considered poor, especially when taking into account the high cost of living in urban centers, where the majority of Brazilians live. However, for the 35 million of those who climbed up to the middle class between 2002 and 2012, the change has been very tangible. It means that they no longer have to spend all their income on basic needs such as food and shelter. As the consumption boom in cars, television sets, refrigerators and mobile phones demonstrates, a deep change in the country's social stratification is at play.

This change resonates beyond material aspects as well. According to the United Nations Development Program, life expectancy rose from 66.3 years in 1990 to 73.8 years in 2012. On average, Brazilians spent 7.2 years at school in 2012, up from 3.8 years in 1990.[5] Overall, Brazil's Human Development Index climbed from 0.669 in 2000 to 0.730 in 2012. Clearly, much remains to be done for Brazil to move beyond developing-country status. Brazil ranks 85th out of 187 in the 2013 edition of the index, a position it shares with Jamaica. But it is moving in the right direction, and Brazil already performs better than the average of BRICS countries in the composite index, as well as in all of its component indicators.

The five pillars of the Brasília Consensus

The government policies of the last three Brazilian presidents have played a big role in this major accomplishment. Brazil is the only major emerging country to have put "inclusive growth" so firmly at the core of its political and economic agenda. Following the era of economic liberalization in the 1990s, the state made a forceful comeback through a series of pro-poor policies. By providing cash transfers to the poorest households, increasing the minimum wage and improving access to credit – while keeping inflation in check – the government was able to reap the benefits of a favorable international context (led by booming demand for commodities) to build a strong domestic market fueled by consumption. The winning blend of economic and social policies, which together we believe form the Brasília Consensus rests on five key pillars: (1) macroeconomic stability, (2) social programs, (3) domestic demand, (4) state-led industry development and (5) political consensus. We summarize the five pillars in Figure 2.1 before describing them one by one.

1. Macroeconomic stability

When Lula took over as President of Brazil in January 2003, one of his first moves was to reaffirm his government's commitment to the continuation of his predecessor's conservative fiscal and monetary policies. As announced in his "Letter to the Brazilian People" during the 2002 presidential campaign (which some in his party joked was in fact a letter to calm investors), President Lula promised to maintain fiscal discipline and to honor the country's debt commitments (Campello, 2013). The government of Lula even exceeded the markets' expectations by increasing its primary budget surplus target from 3.75% to 4.25% of GDP. Brazil also took advantage of its trade surpluses and large capital inflows to expand its foreign exchange reserves from US$48 billion in 2004 to over US$376 billion in mid-2013. President Dilma Rousseff has remained committed to macroeconomic orthodoxy, although lower growth makes it more difficult to uphold fiscal discipline. While Brazil's Central Bank is not formally independent, it has operated with a fair

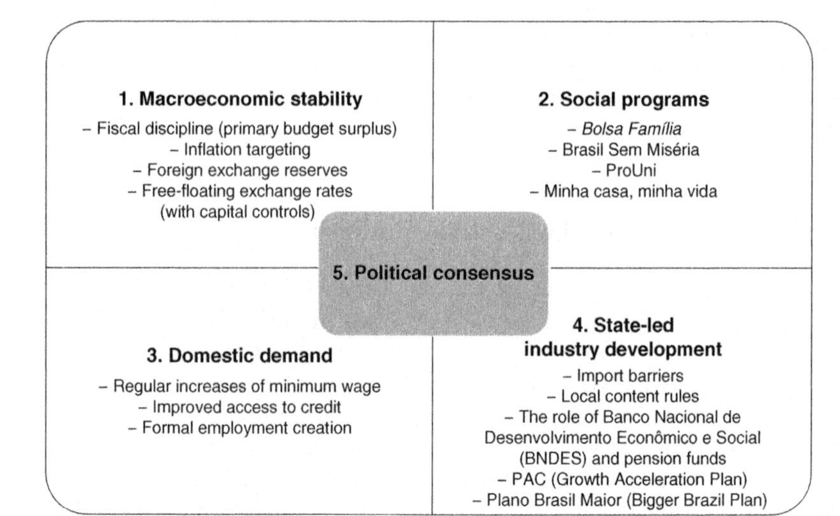

Figure 2.1 The five pillars of the Brasília Consensus.

deal of autonomy in recent years. In 1999, the government introduced an inflation-targeting regime to control inflation in the context of floating exchange rates. Since 2005, the Central Bank has had a target of 4.5%, with tolerance intervals of two percentage points above and below target. The inflation rate was at 5.59% in January 2014 (see Chapter 3 for more on Brazil's economy).

2. Social programs

Brazil is well known for its "conditional cash transfer" social programs.[6] While they are often associated with President Lula's administration, many of them were first introduced by his predecessor Fernando Henrique Cardoso. What Lula did was to make them central to the government's policies. Under the label of *Bolsa Família* (Family Grant), his government improved the coordination and increased the funding of several existing initiatives such as *Bolsa Escola*, for boosting school attendance, *Bolsa Alimentação* for maternal nutrition and *Auxílio-Gás*, a cooking gas subsidy, as well as the newly created food entitlement scheme, *Cartão-Alimentação*. These social programs, which we further explore in Chapter 6, are relatively inexpensive and remain a relatively small proportion of the total social budget (Hall, 2006). According to the government think-tank IPEA, spending on *Bolsa Família* represented 0.4% of the country's GDP in 2012 (Soares, 2012). Development

Initiatives, a non-governmental organization, found that Brazil spends nearly US$4000 per person per year on programs to fight poverty. This places Brazil ahead of China (US$1762) and India (US$864), but behind Argentina (US$5268) and Venezuela (US$4225).[7] According to the report, more than 48 million people, a quarter of Brazil's population, are now registered for government social programs. Declaring war against extreme poverty, President Dilma Rousseff launched in 2011 a new *Brasil Sem Miséria* (Brazil Without Misery) plan extending *Bolsa Família* to 800,000 families and creating targeted programs to improve access to basic services for the poorest people and help them enter the job market through professional training.

3. Domestic demand

A common perception is that Brazil's success in lifting millions out of poverty can be attributed to social programs alone. However, according to IPEA, *Bolsa Família* accounts for only 8% of total poverty reduction and for between 16% and 21% of the total decline in inequality since 2001 (Soares, 2012). Pierre Salama, a French economist, explains that economic growth was in fact the main factor, coupled with an overall improvement in employment conditions through regular salary hikes and increased job creation in the formal sector (Salama, 2010). According to the International Labor Organization, the minimum wage was BRL724 (approximately US$310) in 2014, which is almost triple what it was in February 2002, when it stood at BRL264 (measured at constant prices).[8] Overall, millions of new formal jobs were created during the two terms of Lula's presidency. Another key factor was the expansion of credit for low-income populations, a strategy that was actively fostered by the government through the public banking system. According to the OECD, the ratio of credit to GDP doubled over the last eight years and reached 54% of GDP, with 28% of outstanding credit consisting of consumer loans, including car loans (OECD, 2013:16). While this created situations of indebtedness, access to credit has been an important tool to fight poverty and strengthen domestic demand by putting more money in the hands of the poorest consumers.

4. State-led industrial development

Brazil has a long history of state intervention in the economy. The economic liberalization plan of the 1990s led to the privatization of formerly state-owned companies and opened many sectors to competition. Brazil is far from embracing open trade, however. World Bank figures show that the country's merchandise trade-to-GDP ratio was 21.1% in 2012, compared to 47% in China and 94.5% in South Korea.[9]

To promote local industry development, the government imposes stiff taxes on imports and encourages foreign manufacturers to produce from the country instead. It is not a surprise that Brazil sells the second-most expensive iPad in the world (after Argentina) and why Apple's supplier Foxconn chose Brazil to build its first iPad factory outside China. The government has also introduced local content rules to protect its automotive and energy industries. In 2012, it raised taxes on cars produced with less than 65% of locally sourced components, a move that forced several foreign car manufacturers to open plants in the country. In the oil sector, the state-controlled company Petrobras was granted exclusive rights in designated geographic blocks and a production-sharing regime was introduced for other strategic ones. Here again, local content rules require Petrobras and foreign oil companies looking to tap into the country's huge reserves to work with domestic suppliers and source equipment locally. As we will see in the following section of this chapter, state support for local industry takes many other forms as well.

5. Political consensus

The cement of the Brasília Consensus – what makes the four previous pillars stand together – is what political scientist André Singer, a former spokesperson of the Lula administration, has defined as "Lulism". To build political consensus and secure social peace, Lulism has chosen to form a pragmatic coalition of interests among various segments of Brazilian society, instead of pursuing an ideology-driven agenda. In other words, gradual reformism was favored over a direct confrontation with the interests of the elite. In particular, Brazilian manufacturers, banks and retailers were among the direct beneficiaries of the consumption-led, credit-fueled economic model championed by the government. During a lecture at the University of Oslo in 2013, André Singer noted that "the convergence of interests of the private industry sector on one side, and of the organized labor force on the other, led to the stability that allowed this political system to take the form of a sort of consensus... It was this equilibrium that allowed the government to gradually make the most significant changes in policy."[10] While Dilma Rousseff suffers from a reputation of being less amiable than Lula, she is also widely perceived as a pragmatic leader. The way she handled the massive protests of 2013 showed her attachment to constructive political dialogue. Although she remained silent at first, she quickly demonstrated goodwill and received leaders from youth organizations, including student and labor unions, pledging to open new channels of dialogue to address the movement's demands.

Similar policies, different mixes in emerging markets

Taken individually, the five pillars of the Brasília Consensus – macroeconomic stability, social programs, domestic demand, state-backed industry development and political dialogue – cannot explain Brazil's recent accomplishments on their own. It is their combination, which has helped create a virtuous circle. Other countries have used a selection of these components to build their own development model:

- **China**, for example, has pursued macroeconomic stability and championed state-led industry development. However, contrary to Brazil, it has focused until now on promoting exports rather than boosting domestic demand through the introduction social safety nets. The single-party system also renders difficult the kind of political dialogue that is taking place in Brazil.
- Since its economic meltdown in 2001, **Argentina** has adopted measures to boost domestic consumption and enhance social protection. It has also expanded the role of the state in the energy sector, by nationalizing in 2012 the oil and gas company YPF, for instance. Contrary to Brazil, the government has rejected orthodox macroeconomic policies and favored confrontational politics (notably vis-à-vis the private sector) to advance its economic and social agenda.
- **Chile** is widely seen as a paragon of macroeconomic stability in Latin America. Political decisions are mainly driven by consensus rather than polarization, but the lack of social investment explains the country's failure to reduce inequalities. The Chilean government also largely abstains from formulating industrial policies, except in the copper sector, which has been partly nationalized since 1971. Codelco, the biggest copper mining company in the world, was never privatized.

A light form of state capitalism?

The most controversial pillar of "Brasília Consensus" described above, especially outside Brazil, is the active role of the state in promoting local industry. The country is regularly accused of protectionism by its trade partners. The idea of promoting endogenous growth remains deeply engrained in the mindset of Brazilian policymakers and is a legacy of the strategy of import-substitution industrialization, which it championed between the 1950s and 1970s. State support for industry goes, in fact, much further than the imposition of trade barriers and local content requirements. Brazilian policies in this area reflect a larger trend, which has grown popular among many emerging market countries and which *The Economist* and others have labeled "state capitalism".[11]

State capitalism refers to a state-managed economic system in which the government uses capitalist tools to achieve its broader political objectives. The model differs from more socialist forms of state-controlled economy, where central planning seeks to substitute for market forces. Aldo Musacchio, an Associate Professor at Harvard Business School, defines state capitalism as "a system in which governments, whether democratic or autocratic, exercise a widespread influence on the economy, through either direct ownership or various subsidies".[12] Ian Bremmer, founder and president of the Eurasia group, offers a narrower definition: "State capitalism is an economic system in which governments manipulate market outcomes for political purposes."[13] The most common vehicle to carry this strategy is state-owned enterprises pumped up with public funds and partially listed on stock markets. Thanks to a mix of public and private capital, as well as protection from their government, they are able pursue aggressive growth plans, generally involving corporate takeovers in foreign markets. Some experts have argued that state-controlled enterprises, such as Petrobras and Banco do Brasil, have played a key role in sustaining Brazil's economic stability since the Global Financial Crisis, because their business strategies not only respond to the short-term goals of next quarter profits but also to the state's broader economic and social objectives.

In a special report on the topic, which was published in January 2012, *The Economist* explains that state-managed capitalism comes in various degrees and shapes.[14] China and Russia are the most classical examples. Most big Chinese companies – whether private or state-owned – report to the Communist Party in one form or another. In Russia, the Kremlin has established control over the country's oligarchs and placed former KGB officials at key posts of government-run corporations. Gulf monarchies apply yet another variant of state capitalism. State-sponsored modernization is largely spurred by sovereign wealth funds, whose role is to invest government revenues (often deriving from exports of oil and gas) in financial assets, real estate, infrastructure, commodities and companies – generally in foreign markets. In reality, the distinction between the two variants of state capitalism is not clear cut: China and Russia also operate sovereign wealth funds while Saudi Arabia's government is the sole owner of the oil giant Saudi Aramco and holds the majority of the shares of the country's biggest listed company, Saudi Basic Industries.

An ambiguous member of the state-capitalist camp

For *The Economist,* "Brazil is the most ambiguous member of the state-capitalist camp". Ian Bremmer contends that Brazil has begun to flirt with limited forms of state-managed capitalism, such as supporting national champions, but that it remains essentially a market economy.[15] According to Ricardo Sennes and Ricardo Camargo Mendes from Prospectiva Consulting, Brazilian multinational corporations fit somewhere between what they call the "OECD Model", where governments act predominantly indirectly to create competitive conditions for firms to develop internationally, and the "State Capitalism Model", where support by the state tends to be given directly, without which these companies would not be able to develop (Sennes and Camargo Mendes, 2009).

The Economist reports that state-controlled firms (such as Petrobras, Eletrobras, or Banco do Brasil) make up 38% of the value of the stock market in Brazil, compared with 80% in China and 62% in Russia. But the hand of the Brazilian state also reach the corporate sector through more indirect forms, first through Brazil's National Development Bank (BNDES), and through the pension funds of employees of state-owned firms, including Banco do Brasil, Petrobras and the Caixa Econômica Federal.

BNDES, the visible hand of the state

BNDES was founded in 1952 to accelerate the transition from a rural-based to an industry-led Brazilian economy (Tavares de Araujo, 2013). As a state-owned company operating under private law, BNDES continues to play a crucial role as a financing agent and investment partner for the country's corporate sector. Its stated mission is "to foster sustainable and competitive development in the Brazilian economy, generating employment while reducing social and regional inequalities". As such, it has become a key vehicle for implementing the federal government's industrial and infrastructure policies (BNDES, 2013).

By the end of 2012, BNDES held BRL715 billion (about US$350 billion) in total assets, which made it about the same size as the World Bank and more than three times larger than the Inter-American Development

Bank.[16] With BRL156.0 billion disbursed in 2012, and BRL102 billion already allocated between January and July 2013, BNDES is the main provider of long-term financing in Brazil. The bank provides loans to businesses (both directly and via accredited commercial banks), supports investment projects and finances export activities. Initially focused on infrastructure and heavy industry, it first expanded to energy and agribusiness, and is now present in virtually all sectors of the economy.

About two-thirds of BNDES loans go to large firms. The support of BNDES is crucial given that the cost of credit has been a recurring obstacle for Brazilian companies looking to expand. From 1999 to 2012, Brazil's interest rates averaged 16.27%. Long-term loans by private commercial banks remain prohibitive, and many Brazilian firms must use their own capital as their main source of funding. In such a context, subsidized loans from BNDES represent an attractive alternative for companies that the public bank considers as safe borrowers.

The Brazilian government also used BNDES as a key instrument of its counter-cyclical policies during the Global Financial Crisis. When the Brazilian real experienced an abrupt fall, several large companies, such as Aracruz Celulose, Votorantim Celulose e Papel and Sadia found themselves on the verge of bankruptcy. In Europe and the United States, governments and central banks stepped in by injecting liquidity in their financial sectors, hoping that banks would eventually lend again. In Brazil, the government asked BNDES and public banks such as Banco do Brasil and Caixa Econômica Federal to come to the rescue. Credit from the public institutions (including BNDES) rose by 50% between September 2008 and January 2010.[17]

The state as a minority shareholder

In addition to its lending activities, BNDES also directly participates in company equity through its investment arm BNDESPar. At the end of 2012, the oil and gas sector represented 30.6% of BNDESPar's portfolio, followed by mining (22.8%), electricity (12.6%) and food (7.1%). As of September 2013, BNDESPar controlled 22.99% of Brazil's largest food processor JBS,[18] 30.38% of the pulp and paper company Fibria,[19] 5.37% of Embraer[20] and 5.3% of the mining giant Vale,[21] among many others.

Through its financial support, BNDES has facilitated, and in fact encouraged, the merger of domestic firms. The underlying idea was not to create "national champions" but "international champions" who would be able to compete on a global scale. This resulted in the emergence of new Brazilian giants such as Banco Itaú Unibanco (born from the merger of Banco Itaú and Unibanco), BRF (Sadia and Perdigão) and

Fibria (Aracruz Celulosa and Votorantim Celulose e Papel). It was also thanks to financing by BNDES that JBS was able to buy a majority stake of the United States chicken producer Pilgrim's Pride and become the world's largest meat exporter. Additionally, companies with loans or equity from BNDES benefited from improved credit ratings and therefore greater access to international capital markets. By helping these companies to reach the necessary size to compete in global markets, BNDES has played a key role, albeit indirect, in turning them into genuine multinational corporations.

The future of BNDES

Critics of BNDES say that it has become too expensive (the Treasury transfers billions of reais every year to subsidize BNDES loans) and too big (it is responsible for more than 70% of long-term credit in the country). However, the governmental think tank IPEA notes that when taking into account the benefits from additional investment and income generated, the Treasury's loans to BNDES actually create a net fiscal gain.[22] The argument that BNDES has been hampering the development of the local financial industry is more difficult to counter. An OECD (2011) Economic Survey on Brazil published in 2011 explains that "while BNDES was designed to overcome the failure of private actors to enter the long-term credit segment, it is possible that the private sector has failed to enter this market in the meantime due to the strong presence of BNDES". However, the same OECD report concludes that "while this argument has some appeal in theory, the empirical evidence points to rather small effects", adding that "regardless of the role of BNDES in the past, it is clear that Brazil's future investment needs cannot be financed by a continuous expansion of BNDES' balance sheet."

The issue of financing may come back on the agenda of many global Brazilian firms. In April 2013, BNDES president Luciano Coutinho announced in an interview for *O Estado de S. Paulo* that "the promotion of competitiveness for large multinational companies is an order of business that has been concluded" and that BNDES "got as far as it could go" in providing support for the petrochemical, pulp, slaughterhouse, steel, orange juice and cement industries.[23] According to Mr Coutinho, the public bank will now focus its efforts on supporting more innovation-based sectors, such as health and pharmaceuticals, where Brazilian companies continue to suffer from a lack of competitiveness. In September 2013, Mr Coutinho also announced a big push to finance infrastructure with forecast investments of US$524 billion by 2017.

The state's indirect influence through pension funds

BNDES is not the only vehicle through which the Brazilian state finances the corporate sector. The three largest pension funds in the country, which are all directly associated with state-owned enterprises, provide another indirect way for the government to support the domestic private sector. Previ is the pension plan for employees of the government-owned Banco do Brasil. With around US$82 billion in assets, it is the largest pension fund in Latin America and was ranked 27th worldwide in 2012. Petros, the pension plan for the employees of Petrobras, is Brazil's second largest and holds around US$29 billion in assets. Funcef, the pension plan for the employees of the Caixa Econômica Federal, another public savings and loans institution, has around US$23 billion of assets and is the third biggest in the country.[24]

In 2010, these three pension funds represented 46.8% of the total investment value of Brazil's 275 pension funds, according to ABRAPP, which represents Brazil's company-sponsored pension funds. Equity investments account for a large share of their total investments. As a result, many large Brazilian companies find Previ, Petros and Funcef among their shareholders. For example, Previ owned 7.83% of the aircraft manufacturer Embraer as of June 2013.[25] At the end of 2012, Petros held 12.22% and Previ 12.19% of the food giant BRF.[26] As of January 2013, Petros and Funcef together owned 50% of the infrastructure firm Invepar.[27] In 2009, Previ facilitated Oi's acquisition of Brasil Telecom, and in 2013 its merger with Portugal Telecom, making it Brazil's largest telephone company.[28]

Previ is also a significant force behind Brazil's mining giant, Vale. It is the majority shareholder of Valepar, an investment vehicle which controls the company and holds the right to appoint nine of the board's ten directors.[29] In 2011, Brasília was said to have used Previ to force a management change at Vale, which resulted in the resignation of Roger Agnelli, who had faced repeated criticism from the government for not investing enough in Brazil. For many observers, this was a clear sign that, despite having privatized the company in 1997, the state retained significant influence over Vale's strategic direction. However, according to financial website ADFVN Brasil, Previ is now looking to gradually wind down its control over the company in order to give more freedom to management.[30]

The bigger Brazil plan

The strong hand of the state has not prevented an erosion of Brazil's industrial base in recent years. As we will see in a subsequent chapter, high levels of taxation (notably payroll taxes), inflation and tariffs on imported inputs have been a drag on the competitiveness of the Brazilian industry. Some would argue that it is precisely the strong involvement of the state that has driven up the costs of producing in Brazil. Besides the *Programa de Aceleração do Crescimento* (PAC, Growth Acceleration Program) launched in 2007 and now in its second phase (see Chapter 5), the government has reacted by launching a new industrial policy plan called *Plano Brasil Maior* (the Bigger Brazil Plan) in August 2011.

Brasil Maior is a nation-wide program aimed at boosting the competitiveness of Brazilian goods and services through taxes breaks for companies operating in labor-intensive sectors, such as clothing, footwear, furniture and software (OECD, 2011). It eliminates some charges on electricity and provides specific benefits to the automotive industry. It introduces a "Buy Brazilian" policy in public procurement rules, allowing the government to pay up to 25% more than the lowest prices to domestic suppliers. A range of measures is aimed at encouraging Brazilian exports while protecting domestic markets, for example by accelerating anti-dumping procedures and implementing stricter checks on the origins of goods. The plan also includes a big financial push to encourage research and development (R&D) spending by Brazilian firms with the support of BNDES and FINEP, the country's innovation agency.

The program drew mixed reaction from the private sector. For the US–Brazil Business Council, *Brasil Maior* falls into a long-established tradition of centrally planned, multiyear industrial policies to accelerate economic development, and offers little more than "short-term relief from foreign competition through subsidies and protection". According to the business lobby, the plan fails to address structural challenges faced by the Brazilian industry, "such as high interest rates, high energy prices, lack of adequate infrastructure, a burdensome tax system, and poor regulatory practice."[31]

Is the Brasília Consensus broken?

The rationale behind what we call Brasília Consensus has always been to develop a model of growth that would serve broader national goals of economic development and social inclusion. Has it delivered? While Brazil has a patchy record when it comes to economic growth, the drastic reduction of poverty and unemployment rates are cause for comfort. The country is often said to have withstood the Global Financial Crisis relatively well, and most political observers anticipate a new victory of the Workers' Party in the 2014 presidential elections. Nevertheless, the outbreak of massive protests in June 2013 also made evident a growing sense of frustration among many Brazilians over the lack of progress in certain critical areas.

This wave of demonstrations kicked off when São Paulo residents marched against an increase in the price of a single bus fare, from BRL3.00 (about US$1.36) to BRL3.20. The reaction of the police – who fired rubber bullets and tear gas at peaceful protesters – was met with public outrage and the movement soon expanded to other Brazilian cities. The target of the protests soon shifted from rising transport costs to a wider set of domestic issues. The general feeling among protesters was that while their purchasing power may have increased over recent years, the state was failing to deliver results in the areas for which it was responsible, such as organizing efficient and affordable transport services or improving public education and health systems. High taxes, inflation and corruption were also high among grievances. Finally, the movement crystallized over the US$14 billion dollars spent by the government to build football stadiums and prepare itself for hosting the 2014 FIFA World Cup – money, which protesters said they would have rather seen go to schools and hospitals.

Brazil saw its largest day of protests on 20 June 2013. Over one million people marched in over 100 cities across the country according to police and media reports. A poll released by IBOPE, in June 2013 showed that an overwhelming majority of Brazilians (75%) supported the demonstrations. When asked about the motives for the protests, 77% mentioned a deficient transport system; dissatisfaction with politicians and political parties (47%); corruption (32%); poor education and health care (31%), and inflation (18%).[32] A striking characteristic of the uprising was that it was largely self-organized,[33] with social media playing a key role in the mobilization. Opposition political parties and trade unions joined the crowds, but without succeeding to marshal broader support from demonstrators or public opinion.

The movement was sometimes described as "non-political". In fact, protestors came from the left, right and center. The first marches were initiated by the radical left group *Movimento Passe Livre,* which advocates free public transport. They were then joined by another wave of protesters from a totally different background, composed of mostly well-educated, upper middle-class youth who seized the opportunity to voice their dissatisfaction with the government. The movement became nation-wide when Brazil's "new" middle class joined the fray, including residents of *favelas,* who are the first to suffer from years of underinvestment in education and health.

Toward a new social agreement?

To address protestors' concerns, President Dilma Rousseff announced a "national pact" with state governors and mayors. The pact included a referendum on political reform, renewed efforts against corruption, and improvements in transportation, health and education services. The president insisted, however, on the need to maintain fiscal responsibility in order to control inflation. The quandary for Brazil's leader is that she is facing contrary demands for increased public spending and lower taxes at a time when the economy is cooling.

This situation is putting the Brasília Consensus to the test in several ways. First, addressing demands for better infrastructure and improved public services requires a shift of public support from consumption to investment. Second, reining in inflation requires boosting the competitiveness of the Brazilian industry, which many argue would be facilitated by less government interventionism, rather than more. Import barriers and high taxes contribute to raising the cost of life. The use of public funds to help BNDES finance the consolidation of domestic industries – and thereby facilitate the emergence of giant corporations – is also being increasingly criticized. A recent example is BNDES' initial support to finance the merger of the Brazil's retailer Pão de Açúcar and the Brazilian operations of Carrefour. This deal, for which BNDES later decided to withdraw its support, would have given the combined company 27% of the national and 69% of São Paulo state's retail market.

Which way ahead

Going forward, it is unlikely that the next leader of Brazil elected in 2014 will make any radical change to the hybrid framework of policies that constitute the so-called Brasília Consensus. The strategy of tying economic growth to social inclusion will remain at the core of the political agenda and will continue to call for innovative policy approaches. Brazilian leaders have shown that their approach is fundamentally pragmatic and that they are willing to try "whatever works". Full economic liberalization and a complete retreat of the state are highly unlikely, so is a shift to a bigger state and greater government control of the private sector. And, while social programs are important, they are only "palliative" in nature, while long-term solutions involve broader economic factors, such as continuous growth productivity gains and price stability. Securing full employment and a "living" minimum wage will also be crucial.

The Brasília Consensus is, by its essence, a combination of models. Like Chile, it places great emphasis on macroeconomic stability and fiscal responsibility. Like Venezuela, it takes a pro-active approach to reducing poverty and inequalities through ambitious social programs. Like China, the state takes an active role in promoting industrial development and the rise of the corporate sector. The originality of the Brazilian way is that it does not envisage these individual goals as exclusive, but as mutually reinforcing each other. As such, the Brasília Consensus serves as a possible inspiration for other emerging markets, which all try to have a stable macroeconomic framework and generate social inclusion. Upgrading the Brasília Consensus has now become a necessity. It will not only help advance the country's economic and social development, but also keep feeding the country's soft power on the global stage by reinforcing its standing as a policy innovator and achiever.

Part II

A Hard Power Nation in the Making

3
Brazil's Economic Power

What defines a world economic power among nations? And is Brazil ready to take its place as one of these world powers? Until 2011, the answer appeared to be "yes", on the heels of a decade of robust GDP growth, which reached an average of 4.2% per year between 2003 and 2012, and peaked at 7.5% in 2010 (see Figure 3.1), and a historically low unemployment rate at around 5.4% – combined with a bright future in oil and natural resources, a growing manufacturing base, and the rating of Brazil's debt as "investment grade" since 2008 by rating agencies Standard & Poor's and Moody's the following year.[1] Since then the economy has cooled, with GDP growth slowing down to 2.7% in 2011, 0.9% in 2012 and pushing back to 2.3% in 2013, while social and infrastructure issues continue to loom. However, there is still a consensus among numerous stakeholders that Brazil's time has come as a respected world economic power. Brazil is the fifth biggest country in the world by landmass and population, the second biggest emerging market after China and the seventh largest economy in the world (OECD, 2013, IMF, 2013).[2] Its sheer size makes Brazil a key country in the world.

Many countries become world leaders through the "hard power" of military or economic strength. However, Brazil's modern history has rarely emphasized military might: while Brazil's armed forces of over 300,000 people represent the largest standing force in Latin America, and its history has involved armed conflicts ranging from its 1822 war of independence to the Paraguayan war in the late 19th century, modern Brazil neither seeks nor exerts military power on either a regional or a global level. For more than 100 years, Brazil has been a country at peace with its neighbors.

While the political scientist Joseph Nye recently described a shift in focus from a country's military to economic power as being behind the notion of "hard power", this concept still revolves around the idea of pressuring others using threats, force and incentives.[3] The United States,

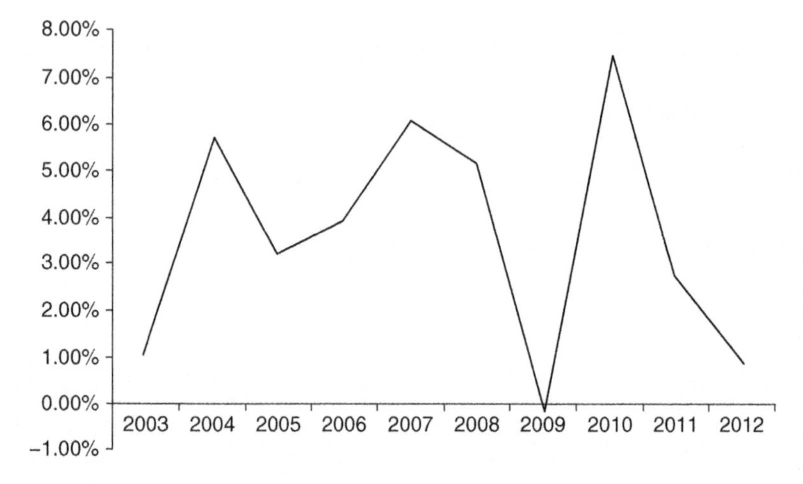

Figure 3.1 Brazil's GDP growth between 2003 and 2012.
Source: Authors based on World Bank data http://databank.worldbank.org/ (Accessed on 20 August 2013).

for example, has done this by negotiating trade deals, investing in other countries, providing financial aid and then threatening to withdraw this aid or create economic sanctions if a country does not support Washington's foreign policy goals. Through its investments in Africa, China is also building a new sphere of influence for itself.

Brazil certainly has greater bargaining power now, thanks to its export diversification, both in terms of trade partners and types of exports. But it does not yet have substantial hard power, as emphasized by Andrew Hurrell (Hurrell, 2010b). At least, it is not a country that is regularly using its hard power resources to influence other states' behavior. However, Brazil is rapidly building economic and market power based on its sheer size, as well as its abundance of three of the world's critical needs: energy, food and minerals. Brazilian multinationals are also growing in importance, as we discuss in the following chapter. These factors allow Brazil to negotiate in more equal terms to other nations, and give the country important resources that may increase its own hard power for the future. Therefore, its ability to use its influence on the world stage to achieve its desired outcomes is here to stay, and is projected to increase rapidly over the decade to come.

A large and growing economy

This economic activity is reflected in Brazil's nominal GDP's growth over the past decade; a growth rate, however, that has been dwarfed by that of China (whose nominal GDP has reached US$8.3 trillion in 2012) over this time period; a country that has commanded much press and market mindshare. Compared with Russia (US$2 trillion), India (US$1.8 trillion) and South Africa (US$384 million) – the other BRICS nations besides China – however, Brazil's GDP growth has been impressive, with nominal GDP expanding by nearly a factor of five across the ten years from 2002 through 2012, reaching US$2.25 trillion.

When we turn our attention to the growth of GDP per capita, the results are similarly impressive. In current United States dollars, Brazil's nominal GDP per capita reached US$12,789 in 2012, increasing by more than a factor of six since 1980, and by over an order of magnitude since the mid-1970s. This GDP per capita compares favorably with other BRICS nations, in fact far exceeding that of South Africa (whose GDP per capita reached US$7,500), China (US$6,076) and India (US$1,492), and a bit lower than the one of the Russian Federation (US$14,300).

With foreign reserves at US$377.5 billion as of mid-2013, an external debt of US$397.5 billion, and a gross public debt representing about 55% of its GDP (a bargain compared to developed countries like the United States, Japan and some European countries), Brazil's public finances seem to be under control.[4]

Clouds on the horizon? Avoiding a currency war

Like all major world economies, Brazil's fortunes are intertwined with those of its investors and trading partners. One of the risks of this interdependency is the specter of a *currency war*, where competing countries devalue their currency against those of their partners, making exports more attractive at a cost of rising import costs and domestic prices. Such a currency war between the United States and its partners in Europe was widely viewed as contributing to the Great Depression of the 1930s.

During the 1990s, and due to the changes implemented by Brazil and other Latin American countries such as trade liberalization, privatization, market deregulation and fiscal reforms, Foreign Direct Investments (FDI) in Brazil rose from US$18 billion in the beginning of the 1990s to US$108 billion in 1999. This later fell to US$45 billion in 2002, following the wave of financial crises, which had successively hit Asia in 1997, Russia in 1998 and Argentina in 2001–2002. But a new and massive surge of FDI once again took place following the Global Financial

(Continued)

Crisis of 2007–2009, with the flight of capital to Brazil's stable and growing economy.

As Brazil's economy continued to grow, late in the first decade of the 21st century, fueled by this surge of foreign investment, as well as increasing commodity prices and other factors, its currency the Brazilian real (BRL) soared by 60% against benchmark currencies such as the United States dollar between 2009 and 2012. This had the effect of significantly eroding Brazil's competitiveness. This in turn led Brazilian Finance Minister Guido Mantega to declare in September 2010 that the world was in the midst of a global currency war, leading Brazil to impose new capital controls. Today, this picture has reversed dramatically: as of August 2013, the real dropped 18% against the United States dollar since the beginning of the year, the largest decrease of any of the BRICS countries.

The resulting impact on consumer prices was one of the deep causes of the massive social protests of 2013 throughout Brazil, instigated by public transit fare hikes and extending a host of economic and social issues. Analysts have pointed to underlying economic issues as the Brazilian economy has softened, including an inflation rate that inched above the government's target rate of 4.5% to 6.5% in July 2013, as well as endemic issues with productivity, infrastructure and capital investment. This triggered the Brazilian Central Bank to increase the benchmark Selic rate to 9% in August 2013.

By then the Brazilian government had invested close to US$60 billion to shore up its currency, and expressed faith in the underlying strength of its economy – at one point, leading President Dilma Rousseff[5] to decry comments from media sources as "information terrorism". While the mood in Brasília could currently be described as one of cautious optimism, the events of early to mid-2013 underscore the importance of a strong, stable currency to Brazil's economic future. Sudden currency swings make the economic environment very volatile and not easy for companies to handle. For instance, when the value of the Brazilian currency goes down, Brazilian companies with debt in United States dollars and revenues mainly in Brazilian reais, see their debt increase in reais.

A self-sufficient country: Brazil's wealth of natural resources

At a time in history when access to resources is becoming critical for many nations, Brazil is (with Russia) one of the two self-sufficient countries in the world, thanks to its abundance of natural riches, including iron ore, manganese, bauxite, nickel, granite, limestone, clay, sand, tin, gold, platinum, uranium, gems, petroleum, phosphates, timber and water. With much of its agricultural and energy potential yet to be tapped, Brazil's future economic power will lie in its ability to supply an increasingly larger part of the world with many of its basic needs.

Energy: Becoming a key player

Leveraging a wide mix of sources, ranging from oil to renewable energy sources, Brazil has reached a level of self-sufficiency in energy. It is one of the world's leaders in biofuel, through its program to promote the development of sugar-based ethanol, an energy source that now meets over 15% of Brazil's domestic energy needs. But a major and disruptive development in Brazil's energy future has now become one of the key factors in pushing the country forward onto the world stage.

Starting in 2007, the state-owned oil company Petrobras announced the discovery of massive oil and natural gas deposits off the southeast coast of the country. These recently discovered deposits of fossil resources, which are estimated as amounting to a full two-thirds of Brazil's existing reserves, come at a time of great tension in world energy markets. As it continues to develop the necessary infrastructure for tapping these resources, Brazil is poised to take its place among the major oil exporting countries. According to the International Energy Agency, today Brazil is the world's 12th largest oil producer. Some experts forecast that it may become, in two years, the biggest producer in Latin America, bypassing Venezuela. It should be among the top five oil producers in the world by 2020.

In the meantime, Brazil enjoys an unusually diverse mix of energy sources, as shown in Figure 3.2, including a wide range of alternative and renewable forms of energy. A quarter of its energy comes from plant sources such as sugarcane or other biomass, and close to another 20% comes from hydroelectric power and other renewable sources. According to the Energy Research Company (ERCo[6]), 85% of Brazilian-produced electricity comes from renewable energy, mainly hydroelectric power. The country openly champions "green" energy sources: for example, the environmentally conscious major city of Curitiba uses

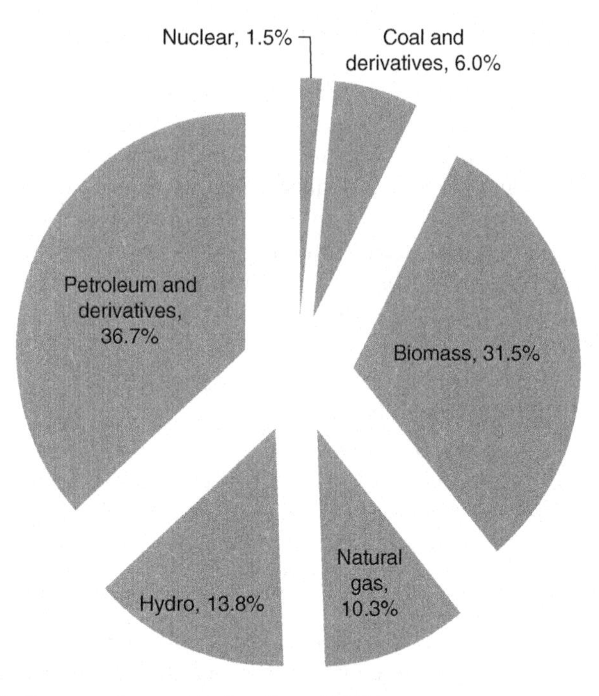

Figure 3.2 Sources of energy in Brazil as of 2012.
Source: Authors based on Urban Times, "Brazil: Courting Risk and Reward", 29 March 2012, http://urbantimes.co/magazine/2012/03/brazil-energy-policy-ethanol-or-fossil-fuel/ (Accessed on 12 October 2013).

alternative biofuels for a key portion of its transit fleet, and even employs a flock of sheep to trim the grass at its parks.[7]

However, it is in petroleum that much of Brazil's future economic prospects lie. Petrobras, Brazil's biggest oil company and former state monopoly until 1997, recently parlayed its expertise in deep-water off-shore drilling into the 2007 discovery of the Tupi oil fields below 6,500 feet, in what is known as the "pre-salt layer", a geological formation off the southeastern coast of Brazil. Later re-named the Lula oil fields (formerly Tupi, in the Santos basin), in honor of Brazil's then president, this remains the largest oil finding in the Western hemisphere since the 1980s. Later, the discovery in 2008 of the almost equally large Jupiter oil fields off the coast of Rio de Janeiro further consolidated its position as a key world source of oil for the future.

As a result, Petrobras became in 2010 the fourth largest company in the world by market capitalization following its public stock offering.[8] The impact of these pre-salt oil discoveries in Brazil as a whole cannot be underestimated. As shown in Figure 3.3, these discoveries boosted

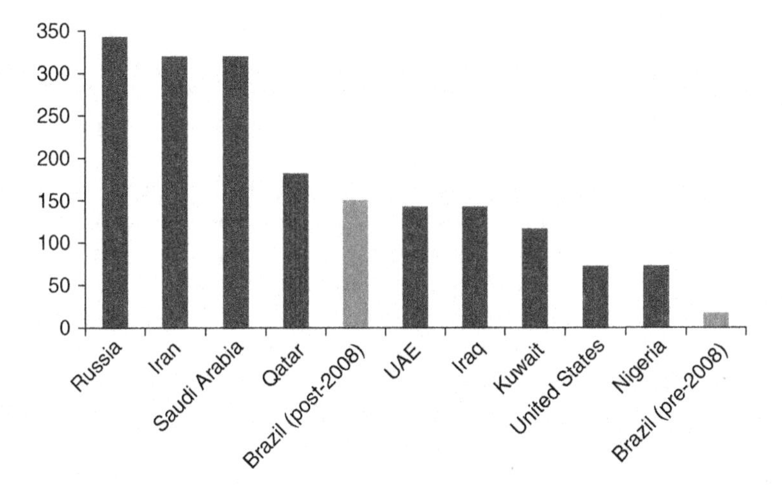

Figure 3.3 Brazil's oil and gas reserves before and after the 2007–2008 discovery of pre-salt layer oil fields among top ten countries, 2010 (billion barrels of oil equivalent).
Source: Authors based on Citibank report, "The Brazilian Energy Sector", September 2012.

Brazil's oil reserves by nearly a factor of ten, making it one of the top five reserves in the world. By 2020, Brazil will have a projected output of 6.1 million barrels of oil per day, of which 4.2 million barrels of oil per day will come from Petrobras, from the current production of 1.9 millions of barrels per day.[9] Leveraging this potential oil output will require expensive investments in drilling and refining infrastructure in the future, and investments in exploration have taken resources from existing oil fields and their production levels. Petrobras's revenues reached US$145 billion in 2012. The company took its place among what are now known as the "New Seven Sisters"[10] of the industry. As of 2012, it has become the most valuable brand in Brazil: the "Petrobras" brand has been valued at nearly US$10 billion by WPP, a marketing group.[11] By comparison, with natural gas reserves of over 350 billion cubic meters, which currently supply over 10% of the country's energy, Brazil only ranks 37th among world gas producers.[12]

A home grown innovation: Sugarcane-based ethanol

The other major energy trend that looms large as part of Brazil's growing bargaining power is the growing global demand for bioenergy.[13] Its vast resources for the production of sugarcane have made it the second biggest producer of ethanol in the world, after the United States, currently supplying 30% of a world market that reached nearly 25 billion liters in 2013. As the world's largest sugarcane producer,[14] it has a privileged position in the production of ethanol because of its mastery of the technology, its favorable climate and its availability of land suitable for growing cane, without causing widespread deforestation or competition with food production.

In Brazil, sugarcane is used to produce both sugar and alcohol (hydrated and anhydrous ethanol). The sugarcane agro-industry involves various steps, from growing the cane, to management of inputs, wastes and by-products, to storage, transport and sale of the final product. The industry is noted for its versatility, since most mills can make both sugar and ethanol in varying ratios, with the mix depending on the profitability of each product, as well as co-generated electricity from cane stalks and leaf litter.

Ethanol production first became significant with the 1975 launch of the government's ProÁlcool Program, instituted in response to the 1973 oil crisis. The aim of the program was to reduce Brazil's dependence on imported oil for fuel cars. Production of fuel ethanol under this program peaked in 1986–1987 at 12.3 billion liters, and later declined in the 1990s as the market sector turned its attention to sugar, a global commodity with many more marketing and financing options, as the price of a barrel of oil tumbled to US$12 in 1998. But at the turn of the millennium, heightened environmental awareness and rising oil prices prompted a renewed focus on producing ethanol. Two important reasons for the renewed demand were the commitments by countries under the Kyoto Protocol and the development of flex-fuel cars, which are able to run on any mixture of gasoline and ethanol, or either fuel alone.

COSAN, Brazil's largest bioenergy supplier, projects that the world is currently on the cusp of a massive increase in demand for biofuels over the next decade. First, renewable energy standards are growing – in the United States, for example, the Renewable Fuel Standard will require 21 billion gallons of biofuel to be used by 2022, and Brazil itself currently mandates a mix of 25% ethanol and 75% petroleum for its vehicles. Second, after a lot of lobbying from Brazil, tariff barriers are dropping in the United States, which is eliminating a 54 cents-per-gallon tariff that has excluded much of Brazilian ethanol, while the European Union is negotiating a new free trade agreement with Latin American Mercosur countries.[15] Finally, massive untapped markets such as China are beginning to open up to biofuels.

Another key issue turns out to be Brazil's home court advantage. Global concerns over biofuels, particularly those made from corn, like those made in the United States, have centered around how they have raised the price of food and upset the food chain. There are currently few, if any, such concerns about the use of Brazilian sugarcane. The Brazilian Sugarcane Industry Association (UNICA) estimates that less than half of 1% of land in Brazil is used for growing sugarcane, meaning that it has not affected food prices to date. Further, Brazilian cane ethanol is less expensive[16] to produce versus other biofuel sources, such as corn, wheat or beets. It uses significantly less fossil fuel to produce, and generates fewer greenhouse gases than corn. About 91% of cars being manufactured today for the Brazilian market have "flex-fuel" engines, i.e., engines which can run with ethanol, gasoline or any combination of both. Consumers are free to choose between the two alternatives.

So where does this changing world market leave Brazil? The answer is, with a great opportunity that is also a challenge. Brazil currently struggles to meet its own needs for ethanol, and is hampered by both its current production capacity and poor infrastructure. According to UNICA, the sugarcane industry will need to both double production and invest US$80–100 billion in infrastructure improvements between now and 2020 to meet projected demand. A fragmented market is a further issue: the industry leader COSAN only represents 9% of the market, and has moved toward a joint venture with Shell to compete more effectively with other giant global energy companies.

A key resource for the world: A wealth of minerals

Iron ore and other minerals are vital to feed the rapid industrialization of emerging markets, as well as growing market demand elsewhere. Brazil is home to a wealth of mineral deposits, which in turn gives it a key role as a supplier and exporter of materials such as iron ore, bauxite, copper, phosphates and other raw materials. Some of the specific raw materials where Brazil plays a strategic export role include the following.[17]

Iron ore. Brazil is the world's third largest producer of iron ore, a critical mineral used in the production of steel and other metals. Although its 2011 production of 467 metric tons is dwarfed by China's production volume of 1,200 metric tons, Brazil's output still roughly equals that of the other BRICS countries combined, and it is a leading exporter. Its position in the global marketplace is illustrated in Figure 3.4.

Bauxite. This core component of aluminum has enjoyed steadily increasing demand. With 13% of world production, Brazil is currently the third largest producer of bauxite, behind Australia and China. Mining firm MRN accounts for 70% of Brazilian production as of 2010, with Vale and CBA representing most of the rest. According to figures

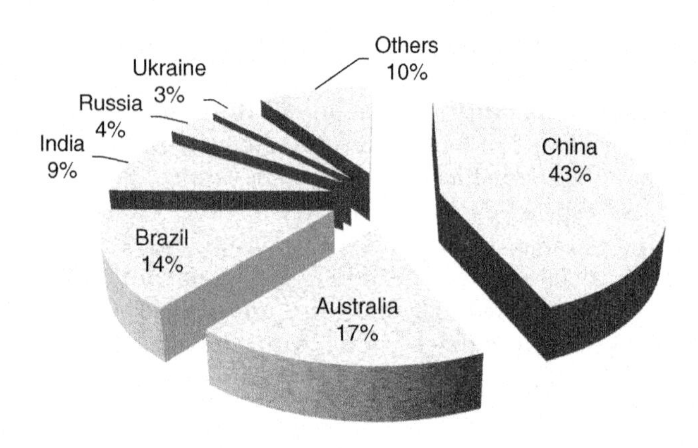

Figure 3.4 Iron ore production per country as of 2011.
Source: Authors based on USGS (Mineral Commodity Summaries) http://www.usgs.gov/ (Accessed on 25 August 2013).

from the US Interior Department agency USGS, Brazil also sits on the fifth largest reserves of bauxite in the world, at 2.5 trillion metric tons.

Copper. This mineral is central to the production of electrical wiring, as well as building materials and other applications. Brazil's 2011 output of 400,000 tons makes it the world's 5th largest producer of copper, with Vale accounting for 60% of Brazilian production and Canadian firm Yamana Gold representing another 25%. Vale's Salobo mine project, which received government approval for operations in late 2012, promises to add up to another 100,000 tons annually to Brazil's capacity after it begins operation in 2014.[18]

Nickel. Nickel is a key material used in metal alloys, notably stainless steel, which by itself accounts for over 60% of world demand. Brazil's 2011 production of 70,000 metric tons places it among the world's top 10 producers of nickel, largely on the strength of global market leader Vale, within an overall market of 1.8 million metric tons, according to USGS figures.

Brazil's key position in raw materials has been a double-edged sword for its economy: this sector commands much of the country's export trade and FDI, which means that these financial inflows do not translate to jobs and infrastructure at the same level as in more manufacturing-focused economies. Nonetheless, this vast natural resource represents an important part of Brazil's economy, and its position relative to growing world resource demands forms a substantive portion of its potential for hard power on the world stage.

The lungs of the world: The Amazon

Brazil's tropical forests, including the Amazon basin, have been referred to as its "green treasure". It is a key part of the global environment. However, this treasure has been under attack: as of 2012, roughly 12% of the original Amazon has been lost to deforestation in the last 40 years.[19] This development has led to widespread global concerns over its potential effects on greenhouse gases and biodiversity.

Figure 3.5 shows the trajectory of Amazon forest cover over time, using statistics from Brazil's National Institute for Space Research (Instituto Espacial de Pesquisas Espaciais, INPE) and the UN Food and Agriculture Organization (FAO). From the mid-20th century through to the 1990s, the conversion of forests to farming and ranching land grew with the Brazilian government's blessings, both in offering land ownership incentives to those clearing the land, and in the development of infrastructure, such as the 1970s Trans-Amazon Highway. Exploiting these resources was seen as an important factor to achieve both economic growth and the repayment of Brazil's massive foreign debt at the time.

During this period, Amazonian land became increasingly lost to farming, ranching and logging – particularly the latter two, due to the unsustainable poor soils often left behind after clearing hardwood rain forest. Ranching became particularly well suited to this region, which

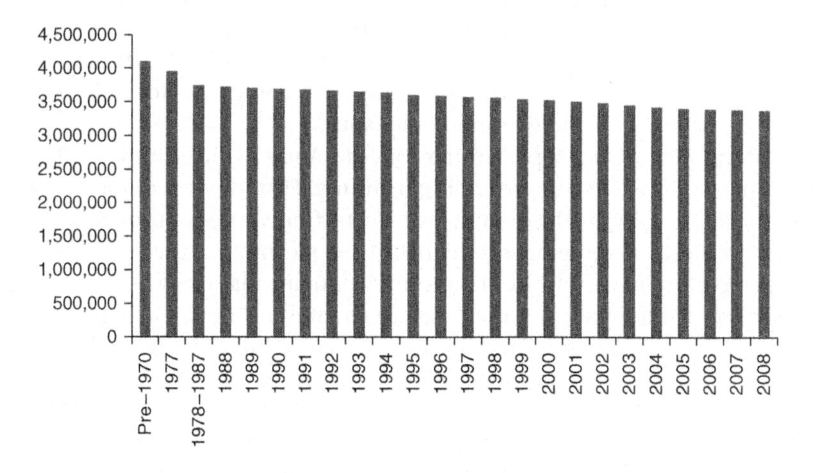

Figure 3.5 Amazon rain forest surface (km^2) 1970–2008.

Source: Authors based on Butler, Rhett A., "Calculating Deforestation Figures for the Amazon", Mongabay.com, 2010. http://rainforests.mongabay.com/amazon/deforestation_calculations.html (Accessed on 5 October 2013).

offered grasslands for grazing. Ranchers in the Amazon were frequently displaced economically from other parts of the country, as a result of competing interests from the sugarcane industry, as demand for sugar and ethanol-based biofuels have continued to increase.

Today, diplomatic negotiation and environmental action have begun to reverse the rate of deforestation in the Amazon. Brazil was party to the 1992 United Nations Framework Convention on Climate Change – a non-binding treaty proposing compensation in exchange for limits on deforestation – and later ratified the 1997 Kyoto Protocol as a developing nation exempt from greenhouse gas emissions limits. The activism of non-governmental organizations (NGOs) such as the World Wildlife Fund and Greenpeace, both of whom are very active in the Amazon, has also been a factor. The results of both of these efforts have been government action, ranging from the cessation of logging permits to the establishment of hundreds of thousands of square kilometers of protected areas.

The future of the Amazon rainforest also has some political and cultural overtones. Some Brazilians point to Western economies such as those in Europe, which underwent substantial deforestation for development or agricultural purposes earlier in their histories, and openly question why a different standard is applied to their country. For example, in 2008, President Lula noted that it is "Brazil that is in charge of looking after the Amazon".[20] Others express concerns over the perception that some NGOs have an environmental agenda that does not always consider Brazil's best interests. At the same time, Brazil has progressively moved toward increasing protection of the rainforest in both its environmental and development stance.

Regardless of one's perspective on the Amazon, it is important to understand two realities regarding its future. First, the loss of forestland has continually evolved in recent years from state-sponsored activity to illegal development, which in turn means that the focus of its preservation must shift from diplomacy and negotiation to legal action. Second, while protecting the Amazon remains a concern, its long-term rate of destruction continues to decrease as a result of increased awareness and stricter environmental laws, as well as improving economic opportunities elsewhere.

A new frontier: A global agricultural powerhouse

Between now and 2050, the United Nations estimates that the global population will rise from 7 billion to 9 billion people. With the conjunction of population growth and rising incomes – leading to increasing consumption of animal food sources who themselves require being fed – global demand for food is expected to double over this time period. Increasingly, crops will also become used for bioenergy and other industrial purposes. The looming specter of population growth and its concomitant demand for agricultural resources has led *The Economist* magazine to coin the term "agro-pessimism" to describe the mood of the coming age.[21]

According to the Brazilian weekly magazine *Exame*, Brazil has become the fourth largest agricultural producer in the world, after China, the United States and India. It is already the world's largest exporter of orange juice, coffee, sugar, soybean and maize. As such, it is uniquely positioned to become a strategic supplier of agricultural products for this new, resource-competitive world. As the world's fifth largest landmass, it is the largest country in the southern hemisphere, and has the most arable land in the world, of which only 12% is under cultivation. Its agricultural exports now represent one of its most promising future growth areas.

The growth of Brazil's agricultural sector has evolved steadily over time. According to the FAO, Brazil has long been a substantial net exporter of food, and the two decades between 1990 and 2010 have seen overall agricultural exports increase more than sevenfold to peak export levels of US$60 billion in 2010, as shown in Figure 3.6. By 2020, the FAO predicts that Brazil will become the leading exporter of 14 key consumables, including chicken, pork, beef, orange juice, soybeans, coffee, corn,

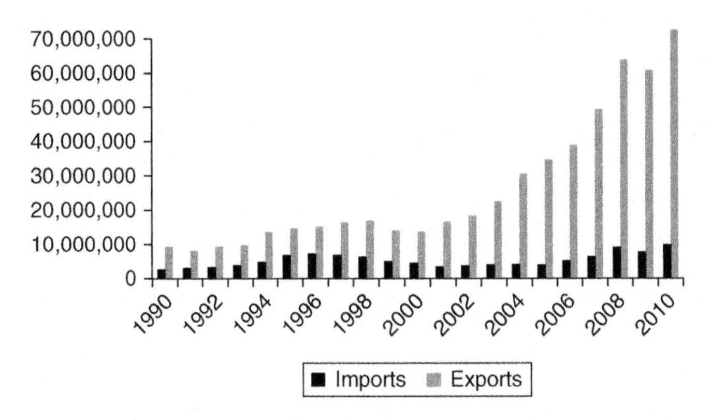

Figure 3.6 Brazil's agricultural imports and exports, 1990–2010 in US$.
Source: Authors based on FAOSTAT database, 2013. http://faostat.fao.org/ (Accessed on 1 August 2013).

bananas, chocolate and tobacco, and projects a further 40% growth rate for Brazilian agriculture over the next decade.[22]

Specific high-value exports in Brazil include soybeans, sugar and chicken, representing close to a quarter of its total agricultural exports. It also is the largest exporter by volume of tobacco leaf, a politically contentious area that nonetheless remains a major agricultural crop with high demand and relatively low demand elasticity (see box).

Brazil and tobacco: Mixed objectives

Brazil is currently the world's largest exporter of tobacco, and the second largest tobacco producer after China. Tax revenues from the sale of tobacco totaled over US$3 billion in 2011.[23] At the same time, the country has taken a creditable lead role in addressing the problem of tobacco use as a public health issue among its own population.

Brazil is a party to the World Health Organization's Framework Convention for Tobacco Control (WHO FCTC), a global public health treaty enforcing numerous evidence-based tobacco control measures, such as high cigarette taxation and bans on most tobacco marketing and advertising. It was the first country to ban package descriptors such as "light" and "low-tar", which have not been shown to be safer for smokers. Brazil also has aggressive requirements for graphic warning labels covering 100% of the back and 30% of the front of cigarette packs. Following the lead of São Paulo in 2009, smoking is now banned in enclosed public places countrywide.

At the same time, tobacco remains a very successful export for Brazil, particularly given export declines among competitors such as the United States and Africa. While Brazil has implemented programs to encourage its tobacco farmers to shift to other sustainable crops in the long term, the sheer number of existing smokers worldwide consuming an addictive good will likely ensure the economic future of tobacco in Brazil for some time to come.[24]

While building a dominant position as a food exporter is a clear sign of growing market power, Brazil's approach to agriculture belies its soft-power roots as well, because it is now exporting its agricultural know-how to Angola, Mozambique and other African countries. In a world where large-scale private agribusiness and government subsidies have gone hand-in-hand in other key food exporting countries, Brazil focuses on technology for sustainable agriculture as well as a free-market system that encourages trade, a model that could translate well to other developing countries. Brazil's increasing agricultural productivity has grown on the backs of scientific research that has optimized the use of its arable land, in areas such as plant breeding and reduction of soil acidity, as well as a growing economy of scale from its vast resources. While the developed world, the United States, the European Union and Japan rely heavily on subsidies, Brazil has become a major agricultural powerhouse by introducing technology and, as of 2011, it has increased the productivity of grain growing in the agricultural sector by 150%, with only a 25% increase in cultivated land.

While the popular image of Brazil is sometimes associated with the destruction of Amazon River rainforest land for the sake of agriculture, in fact the majority of its growth in farming has taken place in its vast plains, such as the *cerrado* tropical savannah regions in the states of Goiás and Minas Gerais. This growth can be easily sustained in the future, given Brazil's abundance of resources. This competitive advantage, combined with projected world demographics over the next several decades, promises to make food and agriculture exports an increasingly key component of Brazil's future market power.

Defending Brazil's natural resources

Throughout history, most wars ultimately have had their roots in conflicts over resources. A peaceful nation known for cooperating with its neighbors, Brazil is nonetheless aware of the need for a strong defense to protect its interests in the future.

Brazil's Minister of Defense Celso Amorim, lays out this case very simply in an article for Project Syndicate: "Brazil's abundance of energy, food, water, and biodiversity increases its stake in a security environment characterized by rising competition for access to, or control of, natural resources. In order to meet the challenges of this complex reality, Brazil's peaceful foreign policy must be supported by a robust defense policy."[25]

So, while Brazil has historically lived in peace with its neighbors and has long since (so far) opted out of the nuclear arms race, refining and modernizing its military strength has become a priority for the future. This new direction takes several forms, including:

- Bilateral defense cooperation with partners in Africa, as well as the Zone of Peace and Cooperation of the South Atlantic (ZPCSA), a treaty organization spanning both sides of the South Atlantic.
- Military cooperation exercises with fellow BRICS (Brazil, Russia, India, China and South Africa) countries such as Ibsamar a regular trilateral naval exercise with South Africa and India.
- Increasing moves toward joint development of defense technologies with other nations.

In 2012, Brazil's military expenditure represented US$33 billion, which is much less than that of world leaders such as the United States at US$682 billion (4.4% of GDP) and China at US$166 billion (2% of GDP). Still, this represents a 30% increase since 2001, and Brazil is now the world's 11th biggest military spender. Brazil was the eighth largest defense exporter in the 1980s (thanks to Embraer) but has gradually lost ground over time. The country has recently engaged in an unprecedented shopping spree aimed at replacing aging equipment and strengthening its military capabilities. In particular, Brazil seeks to build or acquire nuclear-powered submarines, helicopters, as well as jet fighters, for which it has evaluated offers from French, Swedish, Russian and United States constructors. The country is also taking steps to reinforce its own defense industry. Its goal is to increase exports of defense and security materials, as well as the number of Brazilian companies providing military goods and services. None of this changes Brazil's basic "soft power" focus on international cooperation and dialogue, nor its support of world diplomatic bodies such as the United Nations. However, in a world where global conflicts have erupted at alarming speed, its stance reflects a new realism designed to preserve the future of its development.

Pockets of manufacturing and service excellence

While agriculture represents 5.5% of GDP in Brazil and employs about 20% of the labor force, industry accounts for 27.5% of GDP and around 14% of the jobs, while services account for 67% of GDP and 66% of the employed population. Manufacturing and services act as creators of jobs for the domestic economy, are key in the development of infrastructure, and are a source of exports and innovation. They also serve as an important part of the visible public "brand" of a nation. For example, Japan's 1980s growth in manufacturing quality in areas such as automobiles were key in shedding the country's post-World War II low-cost "made in Japan" image, and building the global reputation of "Japan, Inc".

Brazil's main industries are textiles, shoes, chemicals, cement, lumber, iron ore, tin, steel, aircraft, motor vehicles and parts, and other machinery and equipment. It has shown the potential to compete effectively in the global market in several areas. Its potential has yet to be fully realized, because of the need for better infrastructure and the lack of skilled, educated professionals among the local population. It also qualifies as a challenging place to start a business in terms of bureaucracy and costs. That said, there are specific pockets of manufacturing and service excellence that demonstrate Brazil's ability to continue growing in this area. We highlight below aerospace in manufacturing, and banking and information technology in services.

Aerospace: Embraer is an aircraft manufacturer that currently controls much of the market for small, fuel-efficient regional jets. While far from being Brazil's largest company, with revenues close to US$6 billion in 2012, it has grown rapidly from a revenue base of less than US$1.5 billion in 2009, and is a very visible symbol of both a quality global product and as an example of Brazil's prowess in aerospace engineering. It competes with Bombardier as the third biggest airplane manufacturer of the world.

Banking: Banco do Brasil S.A. is the largest bank in Latin America, with assets of over half a trillion in United States dollars, as of 2013. Publicly owned by the state but traded on the São Paulo Stock Exchange, it now has nearly 50 service locations outside of Brazil, and its profitability is a key factor in the funding of public social programs. Other successful Brazilian banks include Itaú Unibanco, Bradesco, and Santander Brasil. Brazilian banks have traditionally been early adopters of technology and online access and have been fostering the IT sector.

Information technology (IT): IT represents the largest single source of jobs for college-educated Brazilians, with over 15% of professional positions in 2013.[26] Stefanini, an IT services firm that has expanded all over the world, and was ranked as one of Forbes Magazine's top ten innovative companies in Brazil, is a prime example of the growth and global reputation of this sector.[27]

The rise of the Brazilian corporate sector is discussed at greater length in Chapter 4. It must be noted, however, that many of Brazil's largest and most successful firms – such as mining giant Vale and energy leader

Petrobras – trade in areas such as natural resources or agricultural products. The development of a successful manufacturing and service sector on the global stage remains a work in progress, and is set to play an increasingly important part of the world's perception of Brazil as a global economic power.

A global player in the making: Looking back 40 years[28]

The Brazilian magazine *Exame* commemorated the 40th anniversary of its corporate ranking of the *Melhores & Maiores* ("The Best and the Biggest") in 2013 by looking back at the changes Brazil has experienced since 1973. Back then, half of Brazilians lived in urban areas, compared with the 80% who do today. Average life expectancy has also increased from 53 to 74, child mortality has decreased from 115 to 16 per 1,000, and illiteracy has dropped from 33% to 10%.

In the 1970s, Brazil was under a military dictatorship that had started in 1964, and the media was censored. Many left-wing activists, including the current President Dilma Rousseff, fought against the authoritarian regime. Meanwhile, Brazil was experiencing an "economic miracle" with a growth rate of 14% in 1973. Since then, however, the country has endured several crises, including the oil shocks of 1973 and 1979, and inflation reaching a peak of 6,821.3% in April 1990. From 1985 to 1999, eight economic plans were implemented, six different currencies circulated, and nine different presidents governed the country during this tough period. In March 1985, the country returned to being a democracy, while the market started opening to foreign competition in the late 1980s and 1990s and a number of state-owned enterprises were privatized, notably the telecommunications giant Telebras in July 1998.

The economic improvements that followed impacted the lives of most Brazilians. Today, statistically, there is a cell phone for every person and one car for every Brazilian family. Global and local companies have benefited as well, and the revenues of the 500 largest Brazilian companies in 1974 have increased ten times from US$173 million in 1973 to US$1.3 trillion at the end of 2012. But the composition of these 500 companies has changed dramatically: only 230 out of the 500 companies listed as the largest in the country in 1974 are still in business, many with different names or corporate structures. Among the 230 surviving companies, only 87 were ranked among the top 500 companies in 2013.

Many Brazilian companies have gone out of business over the past 40 years due to globalization, a trend which was accentuated in the late 1980s and early 1990s by the economic turmoil. Former President Fernando Collor de Mello (1990–1992) initiated the process of economic liberalization, removing import barriers to around 500 products such as computers and automobiles. Many firms did not survive competition from multinationals, which offered products at lower prices, and with more advanced technology. Investments in innovation became the solution to keep many companies in business – and in many cases, sowed the seeds for Brazil's current economic maturity.

Source: Exame Melhores i Maiores: As 1,000 Maiores Empresas do Brasil. Edição Especial 40 Anos. Julho 2013.

Brazil's human capital

Currently the fifth most populous nation in the world, Brazil is home to 200 million inhabitants, and it has quadrupled in size since 1950. While its current growth rate has slowed to 1.26%, similar to the world population as a whole, it is projected to continue growing to 206 million people by 2030.[29]

While the population is aging in Europe and Japan, Brazil is a relatively young country, with nearly 62% of its population being under the age of 30. On the world stage, its demographics put its 2010 average age at 30.5, making it one of the youngest major economies, with an average age nearly 15 years younger than other established countries such as Japan.[30] The country is highly urbanized, with 85% of the population living in cities and nearly 10% living in the principal cities of São Paulo and Rio de Janeiro. It is overwhelmingly Catholic, with its Catholic population of 74% being the world's largest community of this faith. The vast majority of Brazilians consider themselves religious.

Brazil has long been one of the world's more racially diverse nations, as stated and further discussed in Chapter 1. The 2010 census showed that the country was home to 91 million white residents (47.7% of the population), 82 million people who define themselves as "multi-racial" (43%); 15 million people of African descent (7.6%); with the remainder being of Asian descent (1.1%) and indigenous (0.4%), according to the census' own racial classifications.

So what does this human capital represent from an economic standpoint? First, a huge and young potential labor force that is largely on the job. Unemployment levels in Brazil were at record low at 4.2% in January 2014 after having been below 6% for the last two years.[31] This number is similar to those during Brazil's superheated economy of 2011, during which unemployment rates reached a low of 4.7% amidst widespread labor shortages. And, it is less than half of the double-digit unemployment rates of the early 2000s, which exceeded 13% as recently as 2003.[32] Brazil has maintained a relatively stable employment profile in recent years, however, shortages exist in many skilled labor areas, such as science and technology, a problem which is partly due to deficits in Brazil's educational system.

Second, Brazil has evolved to become one of the world's great consumer societies, with higher per capita spending on personal items than other cultures, relative to income level. In addition to the future of Brazilians as workers, there is a bright future for them on the world stage as consumers. The perspective of gaining greater access to Brazil's booming consumer market serves as a great bargaining chip for bilateral and multilateral trade negotiations. A renewed focus on leveraging human capital at all levels of society has clearly contributed to Brazil's growing world standing.

Trading with the world

One of the more critical aspects of economic power is a country's leverage as a trading partner, both as a customer for the world's products, and as a provider of goods and services to other nations.

According to Development Economics, Brazil's imports and exports have both increased nearly fivefold since the dawn of the 21st century, to US$238 billion and US$256 billion, respectively, in 2012.[33] Behind this increase is particularly strong growth in agriculture and industry, as well as modest but steady growth in the services sector.

Who are Brazil's key trading partners? The answer depends upon *when* you ask the question. Historically, North America, particularly the United States, have represented Brazil's most important economic relationship. This relationship is still important, although China is now Brazil's most important trade partner. It is the destination of 17% of Brazil's exports and the origin of 15% of its imports, followed by the

United States (the destination of 11% of Brazil's exports and the origin of 14.7% imports) and its neighbor Argentina (7.4% of imports and exports) and followed closely by Germany (origin of 6.4% of imports) and the Netherlands, where 6.2% of its exports go. A relatively new trading partner is South Korea (origin of 4.1% of imports). Brazil still maintains a trade surplus with China and a deficit with the United States, while Argentina is a more equal partner. Iron ore represents 15% of its exports, followed by oil (8.3%), soybeans soya oil cake (7.8%), raw sugar (6.3%), poultry (2.9%) and coffee (2.6%), resulting in a majority of its trade revolving around raw natural resources and agriculture.

During the Global Financial Crisis of 2007–2009, trade between Brazil and the United States dropped precipitously, at a time that saw China suddenly and rapidly emerge as Brazil's largest trading partner, as shown in Figure 3.7. China's economic and manufacturing juggernaut over the past decade has been a clear factor, as has a growing trade environment between China and Latin America in general. Brazil's trade is quite equally distributed between China, United States, the European Union and its Latin American neighbors.

The inflow of FDI into Brazil ranked it among the top six recipient countries in 2012, as shown in Figure 3.8. It had reached US$76 billion in 2012, compared with an average of US$2 billion in the 1980s. As mentioned earlier, much of this FDI surrounds Brazil's massive agricultural and natural resources, which do not have the same effects on the domestic economy as manufacturing trade in terms of job creation. However, Brazil has clearly grown in stature as a country that attracts foreign capital.

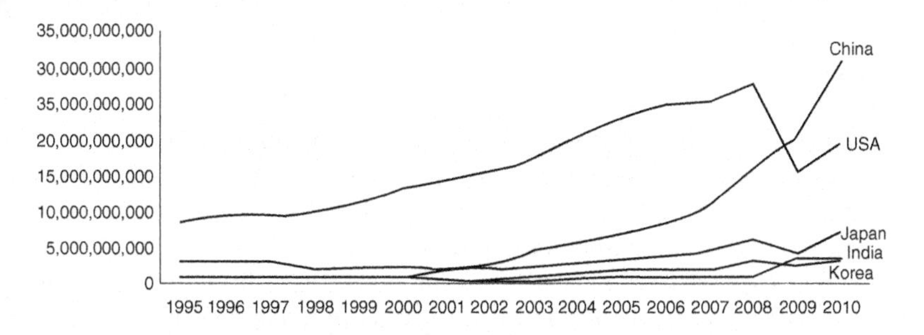

Figure 3.7 Total volume of exports with key trading partners, 1995–2010.
Source: Authors based on data from Development indicators from World Bank and United Nations Conference on Trade and Development (UNCTAD).

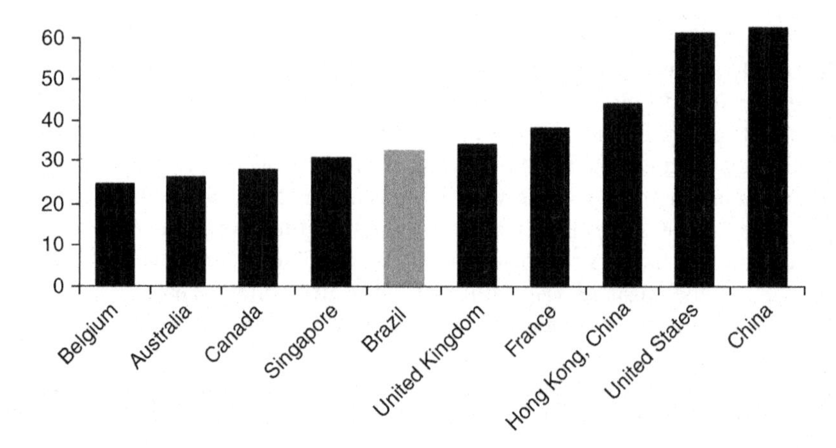

Figure 3.8 Global inflows of foreign direct investment Q1/Q2 2012 in US$ billions.
Source: Authors based on Development Indicators from the World Bank http://data.worldbank.org/ and UNCTAD (Accessed on 25 September 2013).

An investment-grade economy

As a closing point, perhaps the most important recognition of Brazil as an economic powerhouse – and a country with economic influence on the world stage – has been the recognition of its national debt as being investment grade, a rating conferred upon Brazil in 2008 by global rating agency Standard and Poor's,[34] and later by Moody's. Brazil's growth of its foreign exchange reserves has also shown its power by buying United States Treasury bonds. Currently, Brasil is the fifth biggest holder of United States debt after China, Japan and the Caribbean banks, and it is becoming a lender of the International Monetary Fund (IMF), while at some point in the recent past it was one of the biggest recipients of IMF loans.

One cannot underestimate the impact of this rating on Brazil's economy and future prospects. Historically, countries without investment-grade ratings from a globally recognized rating agency have been required to pay much higher interest rates when they issue bonds, which in turn raises the costs of borrowing and hurts their competitive posture. In the process, its economic infrastructure and status as a second-tier financial power often becomes self-perpetuating over time.

Against this backdrop, this rating recognizes how far Brazil's economy has come. Known in decades past for hyperinflation and currency issues, as well as the infrastructure of a developing nation, it is a recognition that things have changed. Today, Brazil can boast of single-digit inflation over much of the past decade, substantial economic growth and, above all, a strong position as a broker for the world's resource needs in the decades to come.

Brazil has so far survived with its current debt rating intact, through the economic events beyond the Global Financial Crisis. This looms as an important factor in its future economic power, as many of the key challenges it faces in the future – including building infrastructure, creating a more highly skilled workforce, and continuing to reduce poverty and economic inequity – will require capital investment, and ultimately public financing.

While much remains to happen in these areas, as will be discussed in more detail in subsequent chapters, Brazil appears to have turned a fundamental corner in its position on the world stage. In a very real sense, its current investment-grade ratings serve as an important and symbolic cornerstone for its future growth and development, as well as recognition of how far it has come.

4
Brazilian Companies Going Global

Recent years have seen a fundamental shift in Brazil's attitude toward global markets, and the world has taken notice. As one very visible example, aircraft manufacturer Embraer is regularly cited as a prominent emerging-market multinational, and a leader in a highly competitive and technology-intensive sector. In another key area, food products, meatpackers JBS and Marfrig have propelled Brazil to become a dominant force in the global beef industry in just a few years. Brazilian brands have started to spread internationally, for example, Havaianas, whose flip-flops are a fashion statement worldwide.

Previously, Brazilian industry was seen as mainly playing to local and regional markets. This perception often had as much to do with convenience as it did with competitiveness: between a large domestic market and the immediate availability of natural resources at home, Brazilian firms were often seen as having little incentive to expand their activities globally. The boom in outward investment from 2002 to 2009 marked an important shift in these attitudes, and today Brazilian business is a growing force in the world market.

This chapter explores the universe of Brazilian multinational companies. Who are the most active Brazilian players in the global market and how "multinational" are they? What are their motives for expanding globally, and what are the remaining challenges they need to overcome to become world leaders? We first present a panorama of the current standing of Brazil's multinational companies based on the most recent corporate rankings. We then look at the main driving forces behind their globalization, as well as the various obstacles they face on the road to becoming world-class players.

Why is it important for a country to have multinational companies? While small and medium-sized enterprises create many jobs and constitute the backbone of any economy, the presence of large companies that operate globally provides an invaluable source of research and development, growth, knowledge and innovation for their home countries.

Not only do multinational companies bring significant tax revenues, they also help local suppliers connect with global production chains and contribute to improving the overall "country brand", which ultimately benefits all sectors of the economy. Furthermore, a country's multinationals often represent one of the most visible aspects of its economic hard power. As Brazil seeks to play a more influential role in global political affairs, the active operations of Brazilian companies on a worldwide scale provide a source of economic leverage and prestige through which the country can acquire and wield power in international relations.

Brazilian multinationals: Reaching a critical mass?

"It is time for Brazilian businessmen to abandon their fear of becoming multinational businessmen," urged former Brazilian President Lula while addressing the Portuguese Industrial Association in 2003.[1] Ten years later, looking at the current standing of Brazilian firms in the annual Fortune Global 500 ranking, it is hard to tell whether President Lula's vision has been fulfilled or not. On one hand, Brazil has made an important breakthrough, with a total number of eight firms among the world's top 500 companies (by revenue) in 2013, compared to only three in 2005 (see Figure 4.1). It is well ahead of Mexico (three firms), stands on equal terms with India and is slowly catching up with South Korea. Closer to home, Brazil outshines its Latin American neighbors: 13 Latin American companies have made it into the top 500, eight from Brazil, three from Mexico, one from Venezuela and one from Colombia[2] (see Table 4.1).

On the other hand, Brazil's performance pales by comparison with the spectacular incursion of Chinese firms, whose total number in the Global Fortune 500 ranking increased more than six fold since 2005 to reach 89 in 2013 (Figure 4.2). Asian firms from other countries factor highly on this list as well, including 14 from South Korea, eight from India, and six from Taiwan. Overall, almost one in three of the companies (143) listed come from emerging countries, while eight years ago in 2005 only 9% (47) were represented (Figure 4.3).

When compared with other countries of similar economic weight, Brazil also lags behind. While Brazil was the world's seventh largest

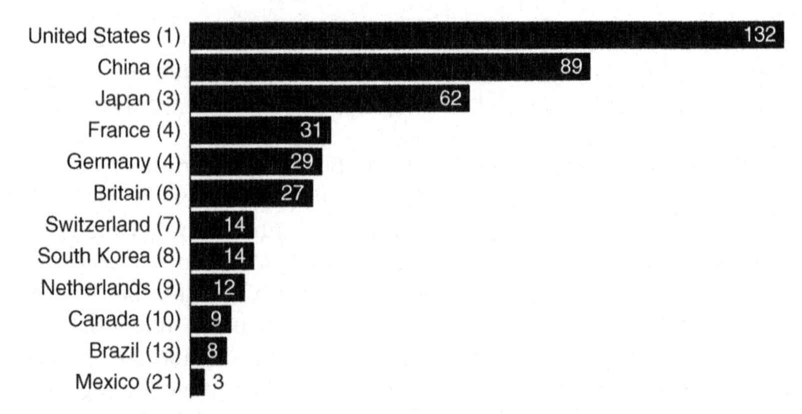

Figure 4.1 Number of companies listed in the Fortune Global 500 ranking, 2013, on the right and the position in the ranking by total number of companies on the left.
Source: Authors based on data from Fortune Global 500 (2013 edition).

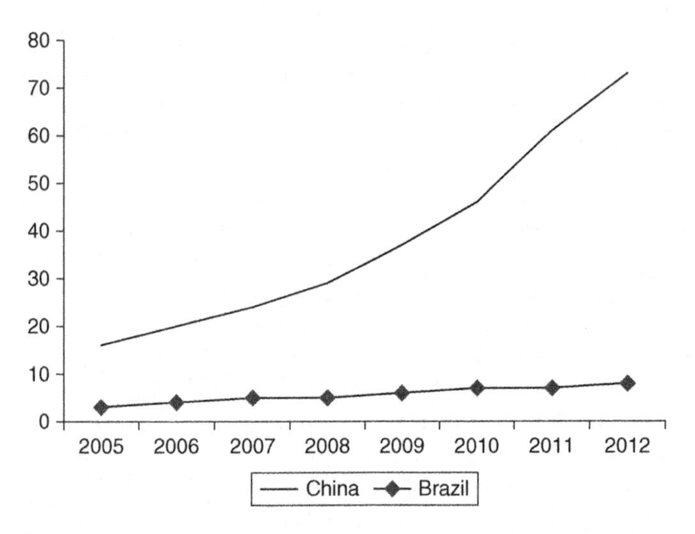

Figure 4.2 China and Brazil: Year-on-year evolution of the number of companies listed in the annual Global 500 ranking of Fortune (2005–2012).
Source: Authors based on data from Fortune Global 500.

Table 4.1 Largest Latin American firms, according to the Global 500 ranking of Fortune (2013 edition)

Rank 2013	Company	2012 revenues ($ billions)	Country	2012 profits ($ billions)
25	Petrobras	144.1	Brazil	11.0
36	Pemex	125.2	Mexico	0.2
368	PDVSA	124.5	Venezuela	2.7
116	Banco do Brasil	72.1	Brazil	5.8
168	Banco Bradesco	56.0	Brazil	5.8
158	América Móvil	58.9	Mexico	7.0
210	Vale	47.7	Brazil	5.5
275	JBS/Fibroi	38.7	Brazil	0.4
280	Ecopetrol	38.3	Colombia	8.2
366	Itaúsa-Investimentos	31.1	Brazil	2.3
420	Ultrapar Holdings	27.6	Brazil	0.5
449	CBD	26.1	Brazil	0.5
491	CFE	23.6	Mexico	−1.5

Source: Authors based on data from Fortune Global 500 (2013 edition).

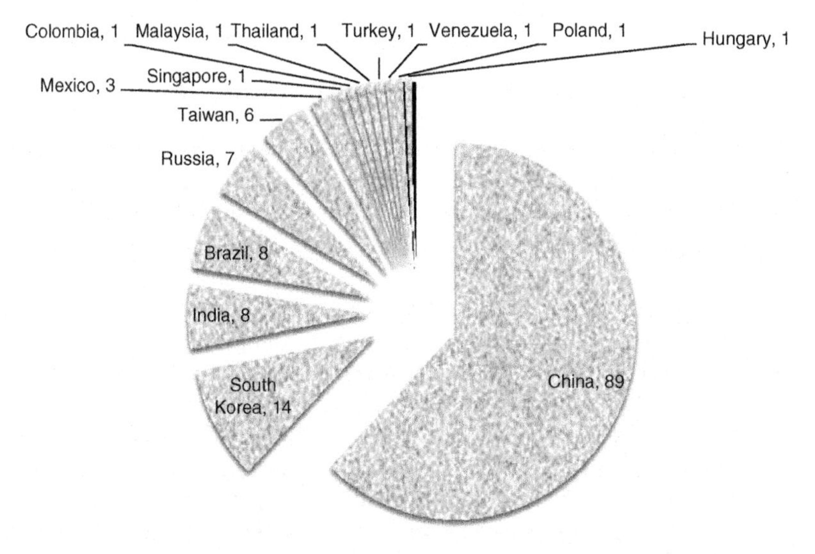

Figure 4.3 Distribution per country of 143 emerging multinationals in Fortune Global 500, 2013 edition.
Source: Authors based on data from Fortune Global 500 (2013 edition).

economy in 2012, it ranks only 13th in terms of total number of companies ranked per country. By contrast, United Kingdom with a nominal GDP roughly equal to that of Brazil, is home to no less than 26 Global 500 companies. With a GDP 25% smaller than that of Brazil, India is already on a par with the South American giant (Figure 4.4).

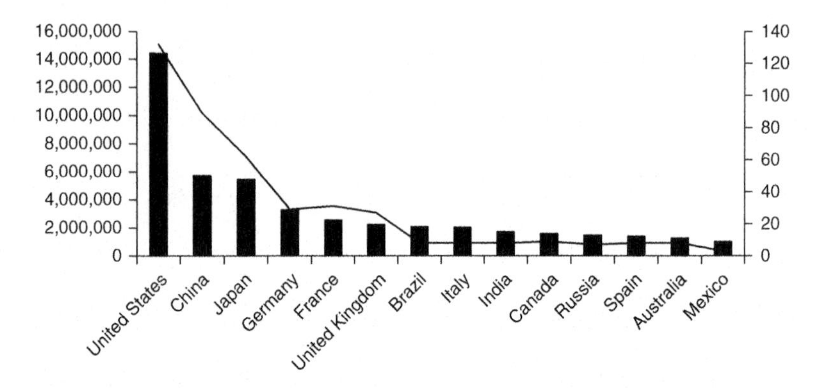

Figure 4.4 Nominal GDP (bars, left axis) and number of Fortune Global 500 per country (right axis, line), 2013 edition.
Source: Authors with data from World Bank and Fortune Global 500 (2013 edition).

According to the *América Economía* ranking of 2012, Latin America's 500 largest companies together sold US$2.67 trillion of products, which is equivalent to the combined sales of the 14 largest companies in the world.[3] The three largest companies on the continent, Brazil's Petrobras, Mexico's Pemex and Venezuela's PDVSA, share membership in the hydrocarbon sector in a region that concentrates one-fifth of the world's oil reserves and mining. The rise of other champions is related to the emergence of the new middle class in the region and the subsequent increasing demand for consumer products. Examples are the Mexican telecommunications multinational América Móvil, Brazilian food processor JBS-Friboi and Brazilian retailer CBD (also known as Grupo Pão de Açúcar). The Brazilian banks Banco do Brasil, Bradesco and Itaú-Unibanco have also seen their retail and consumer finance businesses increase with the growing ranks of middle-income families.

One way to reflect on the relative scarcity of large Brazilian companies is to look at the concentration of wealth within the country's corporate sector. In 2012, the ten largest Brazilian companies accounted for 40% of the accumulated revenues of the country's top 100 firms, signaling the fact that the biggest Brazilian companies concentrate a lot of power with

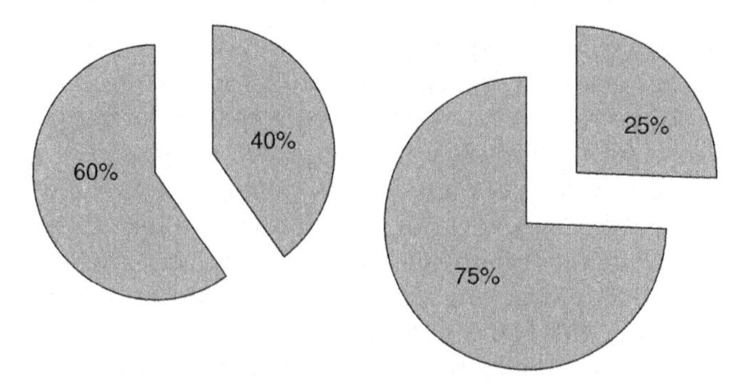

Figure 4.5 Concentration of corporate revenues in Brazil, and the world.
Source: Authors based on data from Revista Exame, América Economía, Fortune Global 500 (2013 edition).

respect to the rest of their counterparts. At the world level, the ten largest companies accounted for only 25% of the top 100 corporate revenues (see Figure 4.5). In other words, the performance in global corporate rankings of a handful of very large firms such as Petrobras and Vale should not hide the relatively smaller presence of average-sized Brazilian multinational companies.

Leading Brazilian multinationals: A sample

Will the next supercomputer come from Brazil? Probably not in the near future. But more so than almost any country in Latin America, Brazil's global influence is likely to show up in the food we eat, the energy we use, and increasingly the consumer products and services we buy, among many other areas. The global footprint of Brazil's industry has steadily been expanding beyond its traditional base of natural resources and manufacturing.

The brands of the marquee firms that represent Brazil's industry to the world, such as Petrobras, Vale or Embraer are well known. Beyond these firms, however, Brazil has made steady and fundamental inroads into areas ranging from food processing to information technology (IT) services. This section profiles some of the current leading multinational firms that continue to grow beyond Brazil's borders.

JBS-Friboi

JBS, headquartered in São Paulo and founded in 1953, is Brazil's largest multinational food processing company and has close to 125,000 employees. JBS produces fresh, chilled and processed beef, chicken and pork, and also sells by-products from the processing of these meats. The company has inaugurated itself as the world's most far-reaching multinational in the beef sector, with the purchasing of several stores and food companies in Brazil as well as the 2007 acquisition of the US's third-ranked beef and pork firm Swift & Company (now known as JBS USA), giving the company global rights to the Swift brand. The following year, JBS acquired Smithfield Foods' beef business, renaming it JBS Packerland. JBS's production structure is embedded in consumer markets worldwide, with plants in the world's four leading beef-producing nations (Brazil, Argentina, the United States and Australia), and serving 110 countries through exports.

Banco Itaú Unibanco

Banco Itaú was a former Brazilian bank founded in 1945 that joined forces with Unibanco in 2008 to form Itaú Unibanco. After the merger, the bank became the 10th biggest in the world by market capitalization and it has now fallen to 16th position. It is traded in the São Paulo Stock Exchange, as well as the New York Stock Exchange, with headquarters in São Paulo. The company's operational areas include commercial banking; life insurance, pension plans and saving bonds; foreign business; consumer credit and the corporate investment bank subsidiary Itaú BBA. Banco Itaú provides an assortment of financial services including credit, insurance policies, investing tools, credit cards, saving accounts, pension plans, cash management, international trade financing, business transactions, processing, mortgage loans, project financing and asset management, among others. The bank is present in Brazil, as well as 18 other countries including Argentina, Switzerland and the United States.

Stefanini

Stefanini was established in 1987 as an IT training company and has become a major IT company, with over 17,000 employees. Stefanini operates across 73 offices in 30 countries expanding the Americas, Europe, Africa, Australia and Asia. Stefanini provides offshore, onshore and near-shore IT services, including application development and outsourcing services, IT infrastructure outsourcing including help desk support and desktop services, systems integration, consulting and strategic staffing to Fortune 1,000 enterprises around the world. With a base of over 500 active clients, including more than 300 multinationals, Stefanini has a presence in industries such as financial services, manufacturing, telecommunications, chemical, services, technology, the public sector and utilities. Its corporate global headquarters are located in São Paulo, Brazil, with European headquarters in Brussels and North American headquarters in metropolitan Detroit.

TOTVS

TOTVS is another leading Brazilian IT company and the second-largest in Latin America, with 53.1% and 35.6% of the market share, respectively. TOTVS develops and markets licenses to use computer-based systems as well as providing implementation, related consulting, advisory and maintenance services, primarily in Brazil, but also globally. TOTVS has revenue of US$690.0 million and net income of US$101.0 million, and it is traded in the São Paulo Stock Exchange. It is the largest application software company in the emerging markets and the sixth largest in the world, with 1,890 employees. The company was founded in 1983 in São Paulo and today has more than 26,000 customers in 23 countries. The company serves various industries such as agribusiness, infrastructure, construction and projects, health, logistics, transportation, educational, legal and others.

Natura

Natura is a cosmetics company with a compelling brand and vigorous growth in international and domestic markets. Natura is the premier Brazilian manufacturer of beauty products, household and personal care, skin care, solar filters, cosmetics, perfume and hair care products. It also sells products through agents in many countries across the world. Luiz Seabra founded Natura in 1969, and it became a public company listed on the São Paolo Stock Exchange in 2004. It has revenues of US$3.2 billion and net income of US$420.3 million, with 6,620 employees. Natura uses a direct sales model, using consultants who are incentivized to build quality relationships and fulfill the needs of customers. In 2012, it had more than 1.2 million consultant resellers and operates throughout Argentina, Brazil, Chile, Colombia, France, Mexico, Peru, the United States, Australia and the United Kingdom, among others. Natura emphasizes its image as an environmentally friendly, sustainable company using organic products and working toward a sustainable planet. The company also takes satisfaction from its passionate research and development activity, and advertises ordinary women rather than supermodels in its promotions.

Fibria Celulose

Fibria Celulose SA is a Brazilian company with 15,000 employees, engaging in the production, sale and export of short fiber paper pulp, including the bleached eucalyptus kraft pulp used in the manufacture of toilet paper, uncoated and coated paper for printing and wiring, and coated cardboard for packaging. The company was created from the merger of Aracruz and VCP, positioning itself as a global leader in pulp, with production exceeding six million tons of pulp and paper across seven factories in five Brazilian states. Much of its production is exported to Europe, North America, Asia, and elsewhere. It has revenues of US$3.0 billion, and is traded in the São Paulo Stock Exchange, as well as the New York Stock Exchange.

BRF

Headquartered in Itajai, BRF (formerly Brasil Foods) is one of the chief food processing companies in the world, formed from the merger of Perdigão and Sadia. BRF takes part in the raising, production and slaughtering of poultry, pork and beef, as well as in the processing and sale of fresh meat, milk and dairy products, pasta, frozen vegetables and soybean derivatives. It operates 61 plants in Brazil, five in Argentina, two in Europe, and an upcoming one in the Middle East. BRF has revenues of US$13.9 billion and has 129,510 employees. BRF is traded on the São Paulo Stock Exchange, as well as the New York Stock Exchange. The company's competitors are JBS, Marfrig, Tyson Foods and Bunge.

AmBev – The best company in 40 years[4]

When Brazilian business magazine *Exame* asked the CEOs from 1,000 of the largest Brazilian companies which company was the best in Brazil over the last four decades, 23% chose AmBev, the brewing company Companhia de Bebidas das Américas ("Americas' Beverage Company"). This company was officially established in 1999, when the Brahma brewery from Rio de Janeiro joined its rival Antarctica from São Paulo, creating the third largest brewing company in the world. However, the story actually starts in 1989, when Jorge Paulo Lemann, Marcel Telles and Beto Sicupira purchased Brahma, a traditional brewery founded in 1888.

Despite the fact that none of them were experts in the brewing business, they helped the company succeed by implementing an efficiency culture with the support of the consultant Vicente Falconi, who was hired shortly after the acquisition of Brahma and is still today the company's advisor. At the time of

Brahma's acquisition, a team of 34 employees produced 17,000 bottles of beer per hour; nowadays, nine employees can produce 63,000 bottles per hour. Indeed, for every BRL1.00 of revenue (about US$0.45), AmBev makes BRL0.50 profit (about US$0.23). To reduce its production costs, AmBev also promotes an annual review of all expenditures, known as "zero-based budgeting", and ties employees' remuneration to the company's performance.

In order to maintain this performance, AmBev invests in innovation, creation of new products, and diversification of its portfolio. The company also produces the soda Guaraná Antarctica, and sells and distributes PepsiCo products in Brazil and in other Latin American countries, such as Pepsi, Lipton Ice Tea and Gatorade. More recently, AmBev has been evaluating the possibility of entering the juice market and competing with the Coca-Cola Company, the producer of Del Valle juices.

Since the merger of Brahma and Antarctica in 1999, AmBev's revenues have increased six times, reaching US$15.7 billion, with profits of US$5.1 billion. During this same period, its market capitalization has increased 2,670%, compared to an average of 176% of other stocks negotiated at Bovespa. In March 2012, AmBev became the largest company in the country, beating out mining giant Vale. On 26 June 2013, AmBev was valued BRL246 billion at Bovespa (about US$112 billion) – BRL46 billion (about US$21 billion) above Petrobras, which is traditionally the highest valued company. This resulted from an ambitious round of growth by acquisition: over the last decade, AmBev has acquired six companies in Latin America, including the Argentine brewery Quilmes in 2002, the Republic Dominican brewery Presidente and Grupo Modelo (Corona) in Mexico in 2012. In addition, AmBev AB has now become part of InBev, the largest brewer in the world, following a merger with Belgian company Interbrew in 2004 and the acquisition of the American beer giant Anheuser-Busch in 2008.

Source: Exame Melhores i Maiores: As 1,000 Maiores Empresas do Brasil. Edição Especial 40 Anos. Julho 2013.

Growth choices: Size versus global reach

Corporate rankings come in many forms. Some evaluate companies on the basis of their revenues, others on their market capitalization.

Whatever criteria are chosen, the semi-public energy giant Petrobras is Brazil's largest company (see Chapter 3). The state-controlled Banco do Brasil is the country's largest bank.

The examination of corporate rankings nonetheless comes with an important caveat. Not all big companies qualify as *multinational* companies to the same extent. Some of the firms listed in the Global Fortune 500 ranking may be very large in terms of revenues and number of employees, but have a limited presence in overseas markets. In 2010, the Brazilian think-tank, Sociedade Brasileira de Estudos e Empresas Transnacionais e da Globalização Econômica (SOBEET) and the Vale Columbia Center on Sustainable International Investment (VCC) published a study on 30 listed Brazilian multinationals. According to the study, in 2009 Vale was the Brazilian company with the largest foreign assets abroad, at nearly US$35 billion. It alone accounted for about 40% of total foreign assets held by the top 30 Brazilian companies (see Figure 4.3). With almost US$14 billion of foreign assets, the steel company Gerdau, which never qualified for the Global Fortune 500 ranking, was closely behind the energy giant Petrobras (US$16 billion) (Table 4.2).

Another authoritative source is the Transnationality Ranking of Brazilian Companies published every year by the Fundação Dom Cabral (FDC), based in Belo Horizonte in the state of Minas Gerais.[5] According to the 2013 edition of the ranking, Brazil's most internationalized company is the food processing company JBS-Friboi, followed by Gerdau, the largest steel producer in Latin America, and the software company Stefanini IT Solutions. With 140 production units worldwide, JBS-Friboi

Table 4.2 Ranking of non-financial Brazilian companies by foreign assets, 2009

Rank	Company	Sector	Foreign assets (in millions of US$)
1	Vale	Mining	34,934
2	Petrobras	Oil and gas	15,937
3	Gerdau	Steel	13,916
4	Votorantim	Conglomerate	7,809
5	JBS-Friboi	Food	5,296
6	Camargo Corrêa	Conglomerate	2,161
7	Marfrig	Food	1,529
8	Ultrapar	Oil and gas	1,514
9	Embraer	Manufacturing	1,378
10	Weg	Manufacturing	509

Source: Authors based on data from SOBEET and Vale Columbia Center.[6]

is the firm with the highest percentage of employees abroad, and the highest ratio of foreign revenues to total revenues. Stefanini IT Solutions has the highest ratio of foreign assets to total assets. Vale, for its part, has the strongest international foothold, with subsidiaries in 38 countries outside Brazil.

The Transnationality Ranking offers some intriguing revelations. Metalfrio, one of the world's largest manufacturers of commercial refrigeration equipment, has now become the sixth most internationalized Brazilian company. This performance is the result of a series of acquisitions in Turkey, Russia and the United States over the years. With total sales of less than US$500 million in 2012, Metalfrio is, however, largely absent from corporate rankings based on company size. Conversely, Petrobras, Brazil's largest company, ranks only 26th in the 2012 Transnationality Ranking. In other words, the biggest Brazilian companies are not necessarily very internationalized, while the most internationalized Brazilian companies are not necessarily very big.

Investing beyond their natural markets

The year 2006 was a turning point for the Brazilian economy. For the first time, total outflows of FDI outweighed total inflows into Brazil, which themselves reached record levels in the mid-2000s. From 2000 to 2003, outward FDI from Brazil averaged less than US$1 billion a year. From 2004 to 2008, the average jumped to nearly US$14 billion. Such prowess was largely seen as evidence of the take-off of Brazilian multinational companies and their increasingly active presence in the global markets. Until 2009, Brazil had the largest stock of outward FDI from all emerging countries. Its FDI outflows started going down in 2009, in response to the aftermath of the Global Financial Crisis. Total outflows were negative in 2009 and 2011, due to the repatriation of capital, mainly through intra-firm lending by foreign affiliates of Brazilian multinational enterprises (MNEs) to their parent firms.[7]

What have been the main destinations of Brazil's outward FDI? Numerous studies have highlighted the strong Latin American focus of Brazilian firms' international activities. Before expanding to industrialized markets or other emerging markets, Brazilian companies have traditionally begun by establishing operations in their natural markets: countries from their immediate geographical neighborhood. But only a handful of Brazilian multinationals (e.g., Gerdau, Odebrecht, Samot) have established a major presence in Mexico, the second biggest economy on the continent. In the meantime, several Mexican companies (e.g., Grupo Carso, Telmex, América Móvil, Bimbo, Homex, Cinepolis) have made significant investments in Brazil. It is interesting to note that between 2005 and 2010, Mexico's FDI in Brazil represented US$4.7 billion, while over the same period Brazil invested only US$684 million in Mexico (ECLAC, 2012).

It is worth noting also that the top destinations of Brazilian FDI in the period 2001–2010 were jurisdictions in the Caribbean that are generally known as tax havens, such as the Cayman Islands, the British Virgin Islands and the Bahamas. Some European countries, such as Austria, the Netherlands and Luxembourg have also been used by Brazilian companies to settle subsidiaries or special purpose entities through which they channel their outward investments. This practice has been widely construed as a way for Brazilian firms to reduce their tax burden and bypass domestic regulations. As a consequence, the exact geographic distribution of Brazilian outward investments is difficult to assess, since Brazilian companies often use intermediary vehicles located in deregulated jurisdictions to make their investments in third countries.[8]

Leaving aside tax havens and the specific case of European countries used to settle special purpose vehicles, the United States was the first destination of outward investment stock from Brazil in 2010, followed by Denmark and Spain (see Figure 4.6). In Latin America, Argentina and Uruguay were the two main recipients of Brazilian FDI. Asia and Africa accounted for a very low share of total outward Brazilian FDI. However, their share may increase as Brazilian companies from the extractive industries, agribusiness and the construction sector increasingly look to invest in countries from these two regions.

This overall picture is corroborated by FDC's 2012 Transnationality Ranking of Brazilian Companies, which highlights the strong regional focus of most multinational Brazilian firms, while also revealing the proportion of the Brazilian companies in the ranking with subsidiaries (often of less importance) in North America (57%), European Union (46%), Asia (44.4%) and Africa (27%).

Increasing market power: The drivers of internationalization

Why have Brazilian companies expanded their operations outside their home country, and what are the strengths and weaknesses they have exhibited in doing so? In the following part of this chapter, we look at the trajectories of former Brazilian "national champions" and family-owned companies, and examine the main drivers and specificities of their internationalization.

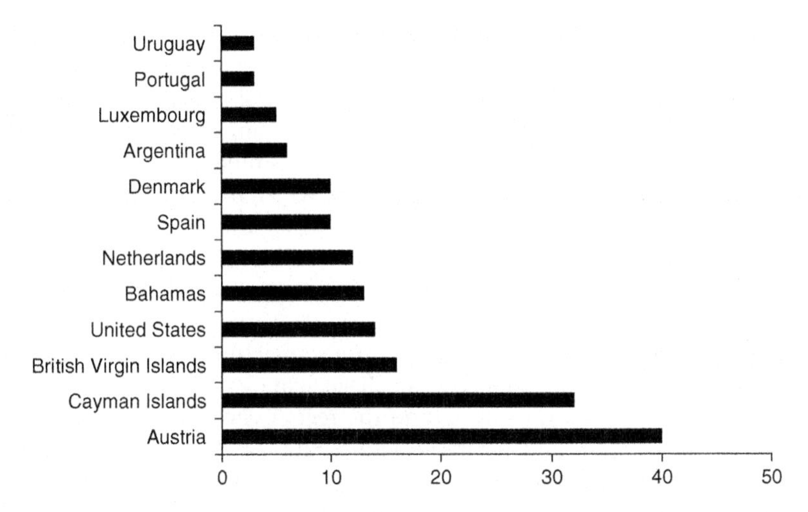

Figure 4.6 Geographic destination of outward Brazilian Foreign Direct Investment in 2010 (in US$ billions).
Source: Authors based on SOBEET and Columbia Vale Center (2012), *Outward Foreign Direct Investment from Brazil and its Policy Context, 2012,* http://www.vcc.columbia.edu/files/vale/documents/Profile-_Brazil_OForeign Direct Investment_10_May_2012_-_FINAL.pdf (Accessed on 25 April 2013).

From "national champions" to global players

To capture the specificities of large Brazilian multinational companies, it is fundamental to understand the continent-wide context from which these companies have emerged. As pointed out by Sinha (2005), Ramamurti (2012) and Santiso (2013), high tariffs, underdeveloped capital markets, inadequate levels of research and development, market domination by family-owned conglomerates with risk-averse cultures, and a turbulent political and economic climate have historically frustrated the emergence of globally oriented Latin American firms. These factors, combined with state protection, have fostered the growth of large-scale family-owned companies, which favored expansion in their domestic markets, often through sector diversification. When not family-controlled, companies from the continent have often been state-owned and based on primary resources like oil, gas and metals.

This state of affairs has largely applied to Brazil, together with a policy tendency to promote "national champions" that prevailed until the economic liberalization era in the 1990s. National champions can be defined as directly or indirectly state-backed firms protected from competition, which benefit from government export subsidies and are designated vehicles for national industrial policy objectives such as employment, economic growth and international prestige (Casanova, 2009b). Brazil's policy of nurturing national champions was and to a certain extent still is deeply interwoven with its broader economic policy of import substitution industrialization, which reached a peak in the 1960s and 1970s.

Forty years later, many of yesterday's national champions feature among Brazil's most prominent global companies. During its long years as a state-owned enterprise (1969–1994), the aircraft manufacturer Embraer was largely shielded from competition and developed a market niche in the supply of small jet planes for the civilian and military markets, both in Brazil and the region. Due to a conjunction of adverse internal and external factors, Embraer faced heavy losses and was privatized in 1994, with foreign ownership limited to 40%. The company's operations were rationalized and sales abroad boosted its growth. Embraer is today the world's third largest manufacturer of commercial aircraft and has established operational units in the United States, Portugal, France, Singapore and China. The company is now looking to extend its presence in Africa's rising aviation sector.

Vale is another example of a former state-owned giant, which grew in isolation from 1942 to 1995, before taking off as publicly traded company. The Companhia Vale do Rio Doce (CVRD), as it was known prior to 2007, first developed as an industrial conglomerate with wide interests in shipping, railroads and forestry, as well as mining. Its privatization took place in several phases during the period 1995–2002. Vale is now publicly listed in the São Paulo, New York, Hong Kong and Madrid stock markets. Following a series of joint ventures and acquisitions, the company strengthened its hold on the domestic market and built capacity at the global level to meet the booming demand for commodities from rapidly growing emerging countries. The boldest move of all took place in 2006, when Vale made a US$17.8 billion all-cash acquisition of the Canadian nickel producer, Inco. With operations in 28 countries, the Brazilian mining giant is now present on all continents and is the largest producer of iron ore and iron ore pellets, and the second largest producer of nickel.[9] With revenues of almost US$48 billion in 2012, Vale is one of the three largest metals and mining companies in the world, alongside the Australian BHP Billiton and the Anglo-Australian Rio Tinto. Although the company is now publicly traded, the Brazilian government still has a golden share and an indirect stake of 5.3% through BNDES, the national development bank.

Another classic Brazilian national champion is Petrobras, which was founded in 1953 and benefited from a state monopoly on oil until 1997. Unlike Embraer and Vale, Petrobras is only partially privatized and remains under government control. In September 2010, it became the Brazilian company with the largest market capitalization, and fourth largest in the world in 2010, after a world-record initial public offering (IPO) of US$72.8 billion in São Paulo to fund its offshore development plans.[10] The company still retains significant advantages from state support, which has proved particularly helpful when negotiating with foreign governments for exploration rights. As of November 2013, it had operations in 24 countries outside Brazil, including Angola, Argentina, Benin, Bolivia, Gabon, Namibia, Nigeria and the United States. With over 80,000 employees, revenues of US$144.1 billion and profits of US$11.0 billion in 2012, Petrobras trades on the stock exchanges of São Paulo, New York, Madrid and Buenos Aires.

Driving forces behind internationalization

While it is only in the last years that Brazilian companies have started to attract the attention of international markets, their global expansion is not a new phenomenon. Similarly to companies from other Latin American countries, the internationalization process of Brazilian firms occurred in four successive phases (Casanova, 2009a). The first phase – in the 1970s and 1980s – witnessed modest signs of internationalization, with some companies starting to export to and establish operations in their so-called "natural markets" in countries with a cultural affinity. Target markets included Latin American countries, but also Spain and Portugal, as well as Portuguese-speaking African countries.

It was during this period that many family-owned companies, such as engineering and construction services firm Odebrecht, the family-owned conglomerates Votorantim, Camargo Corrêa and Andrade Gutierrez, the construction company Tigre, and electrical devices producer WEG started their first business operations abroad. Following its short-lived "economic miracle" in the 1960s and early 1970s, Brazil suffered a long period of economic stagnation triggered by the debt crisis in the 1980s. Hard pressed by falling sales at home, internationalization became the only viable option for these companies to keep growing. Large construction firms faced with falling public investment increasingly looked to foreign markets to stay afloat. For example, Odebrecht began its international operations in 1979 with infrastructure projects in Chile and Peru. In 1984, the company first set foot in Africa with the construction of a hydroelectric power plant in Angola.

The second phase broadly corresponds to the "Washington Consensus" years (1990–2002), during which Latin American governments, encouraged (and to a certain extent obliged) by the IMF and the World Bank, abandoned their import-substitution policies and adopted pro-market strategies, including the privatization of state-owned enterprises in telecommunications, mining, energy, transportation and infrastructure. In Brazil, the impact of this "competitive shock" was twofold (Cyrino and Tanure, 2009). First, it forced the best-positioned Brazilian companies to restructure their operations in order to survive in the face of heightened competition from local subsidiaries of foreign multinationals. Firms sought to consolidate their positions domestically by pursuing efficiencies, comparative advantages and foreign financing and, inevitably, accelerating their international expansion. Second, it exposed the most fragile companies to acquisitions by foreign firms, and ultimately meant weaker companies faced extinction.

A third phase can be identified, beginning around 2002, with soaring commodity prices and high growth rates facilitating a more aggressive global expansion of Brazilian firms, notably through the acquisition of foreign firms and assets (Casanova, 2009b). This phase particularly benefitted resource-based companies, whose strong cash position permitted large-scale acquisitions in both advanced and emerging markets. It was during the 2000s that Vale, Petrobras and several other companies experienced their most intensive internationalization phases.

The fall of Lehman Brothers in September 2008 and the Global Financial Crisis that ensued marked the start of a fourth phase with global investments moving from the "North" (i.e., Europe and the US) to the "South" (i.e., emerging markets). The investment risk had switched to the developed world, while thanks to the growth drivers to be found in emerging markets, they had become "El Dorado". In 2011, FDI inflows into Latin America and the Caribbean reached US$154 billion, 28% more than in 2010. Latin America was the region that recorded the highest percentage increase in FDI inflows, which brought its share of global inward FDI to 10% (ECLAC, 2012). For Brazilian companies this meant that new sources of growth are located in other emerging markets or simply at home and, as a result they divested international assets.

Besides these broad macroeconomic factors, a number of firm-specific objectives have stimulated the international expansion of Brazilian firms. In the case of Petrobras and Vale, investments abroad have been chiefly motivated by the desire to secure access to other natural resources in foreign markets. Other companies, such as Embraer and bus manufacturer Marcopolo have "followed the client" by focusing on opening commercial offices and subsidiaries abroad in order to better serve local markets and become more responsive to customers' needs. Circumventing tariff and non-tariff barriers has been another major motive for investing abroad. By opening production units in key markets instead of limiting themselves to exports, Gerdau in the steel industry and orange juice producer Cutrale were able to overcome trade barriers and break into the protected markets of developed countries. Finally, several firms have used the internationalization process as a way to learn and acquire new skills by competing in sophisticated markets with demanding consumers (Casanova, 2009b, Cyrino and Tanure 2009). In 2005, beauty products company Natura opened a retail store in Paris, through which it was able to connect with the latest consumer trends, while disseminating its brand name in the world's most iconic perfume and cosmetics marketplace.

The best and the biggest in 2012: A year to be forgotten

The 500 biggest Brazilian companies together had profits of US$34.4 billion in 2012, approximately half of the previous year's profits. Such bad results were unexpected, especially considering that Brazilian companies were urged by the Minister of Finance, Guido Mantega, to invest and prepare themselves for a GDP growth of 4%. However and in spite of the fact that growth only reached 0.9% in 2012, the 500 biggest companies still broke revenue records, growing to 1.8% to US$1.047 trillion in 2012 after breaking the US$1 trillion barrier the year before. While this was a small increase, particularly in comparison with 7.3% growth the previous year, such growth shows that Brazilian businesspeople have learned how to tackle the persistent *voo de galinha* (e.g., "chicken flights" or short-lived economic spurts) in the economy, while managing to maintain growth.

A good example of this ability to adapt is BRF, the Brazilian food company presented earlier in this chapter. BRF was taken by surprise when the drought in the American Midwest substantially increased the prices of corn and soybean crops, which are responsible for 70% of the production costs of poultry. As a consequence, the company's profit suddenly fell from US$199 million in 2011 to US$10 million in 2012, representing a drop of 95%. Despite the challenges, BRF's revenues increased in 2013, reaching US$13 billion.

(Continued)

Other Brazilian companies were also impacted by the economic slowdown. For instance, the revenues of the Brazilian mining and metal company Vale dropped 18% in 2012, mainly because of falling prices for minerals and steel. The company's profits fell even more, from US$15 billion to less than US$2 billion, a reduction of 87%. For companies that have their costs indexed in dollars, 2012 was also not a very good year. Revenues for the airline Gol went down 6%, and its deficit was US$624 million, while Gol's competitor TAM had a deficit of US$600 million, influenced by the volatility of the Brazilian real and higher fuel prices and before being acquired by the Chilean LAN.

Factors behind these results include (1) the persistence of the European crisis, as well as the slowdown of the Chinese economy; and (2) the fact that many companies depend mostly on the external market. Domestic factors had an impact on the 2012 results as well: for example, Brazilian utilities Eletrobras and Chesf lost US$8.8 billion between them, representing 41% of the total deficit of the 500 biggest companies that ended 2012 in the red.

The investment rate ended the year at 18.1%, more than one percentage point below the 2011 rate, and the default rate increased from 6.8% to 8.1%. Industrial production fell 2.6% in 2012, indicating that government's programs to encourage consumer purchases were no longer having the same positive effect.

Source: Exame Melhores i Maiores: As 1000 Maiores Empresas do Brasil. Edição Especial 40 Anos. Julho 2013.

The ability to navigate in turbulent waters

Another distinctive feature of emerging Brazilian multinational companies is the resilience forged from years of doing business in a volatile market. For decades these firms have thrived in a domestic environment marked by unstable economic conditions, as well as complex regulatory frameworks, infrastructure challenges and a very diverse business environment. While these factors may have impeded their long-term growth and development, their ability to deal with limited infrastructure and financial instability has become one of the major competitive advantages of these Brazilian firms, especially when doing business in other geographies with similar constraints. It is important to recognize that Brazilian managers, as with managers from other emerging countries, have learned to manage in turbulent waters (Cuervo-Cazurra, 2012), which serves as another competitive advantage in driving the internationalization process.

For example, BRF was able to develop unique logistics expertise by building a world-class distribution network for its frozen and refrigerated products. Through its Sadia brand, BRF enjoys a strong foothold in the Middle East. Its shipments to the region accounted for 32% of its total exports in 2011, with products sold in the United Arab Emirates, Saudi Arabia, Egypt, Kuwait, Qatar, Bahrain, Iran, Iraq, Jordan and Lebanon. Another example is Vale, which had to create vast transport networks integrating mines, railroads, ports and ships to transport and export its mineral resources. Today the company operates approximately 10,000 kilometers of railroad network and claims to have the largest mineral vessels in the world.

A long road to becoming world-class players

Brazilian firms continue to face daunting challenges in their globalization. Many of these are not specific to international activities, but relate to the general business environment that prevails in their domestic market. It is common for Brazilian entrepreneurs to complain about the "*custo Brasil*" or the "Brazil cost", an expression used to describe the operational complications and added costs associated with doing business in Brazil. These include excessive bureaucracy, a byzantine tax system, high labor costs, the underdevelopment of infrastructure and corruption. According to the survey of outward investors conducted by SORBEET and the Columbia Vale Center in 2010, the top-ranking *internal* barrier to the internationalization of Brazilian firms was the tax burden (19% of respondents), followed by currency fluctuations (17%), competition with projects in Brazil (14%), high credit costs (11%), and the lack of skilled human resources (8%).

Beyond these homegrown factors, Brazilian companies also face a number of challenges that derive from the prevailing global economic competition. Among the principal *external* barriers to internationalization, respondents to the SORBEET and Columbia Vale Center survey cited tough competition in mature markets (31%), the regulatory environment (14%), difficulties in managing international operations (10%), barriers imposed by local industry (9%) and difficulties in raising funds in overseas markets on competitive terms (9%). The lack of double taxation treaties was also mentioned.

Until recently, the promotion of outward investment has never been a high priority for Brazilian policymakers. The internationalization process of Brazilian multinationals (Fleury and Fleury, 2011) has been largely driven by companies themselves, unlike in Spain, where the banking sector has played a key role, or in China, where the government is a key driving force for the global expansion of Chinese companies. Apart from the financial support of BNDES and some stand-alone programs to support the internationalization of Brazilian companies, there is no holistic approach to strengthen their position in global markets. This contrasts with the more aggressive stance adopted by several Asian countries (notably South Korea and China) to increase the global competitiveness of "strategic" industries (Cyrino and Tanure, 2009).

In addition, Brazil has only signed 14 bilateral investment treaties with other countries, a very low number compared with the 90 signed by China and 61 signed by India.[11] Similarly, Brazil is at risk of remaining a bystander to the dramatic reconfiguration of the global trading system that may unfold as a result of the new generation of mega-trade agreements currently being discussed, such as the Trans-Pacific Partnership, which groups economies from the Pacific Rim and the Trans-Atlantic Trade and Investment Partnership between the European Union and the United States. As a member of the Mercosur trading bloc, Brazil cannot sign trade agreements with other countries on its own. The long-term risk of this looming economic isolation of Brazil is that Brazilian companies get increasingly sidelined from global value chains and transnational production networks.

Looking ahead

For many years, Brazilian firms have been shy about going global. Brazil's corporate sector still lags behind those of equivalent economies, particularly when compared with the dynamism of Chinese and Indian companies. Although the last few years have witnessed an important process of "catching up" and several Brazilian corporations are now recognized as global leaders in their respective sectors, many more qualify as global companies "in the making". Indeed, some of the most internationalized Brazilian firms are still relatively small companies and their expansion may take the world by surprise, as occurred with the stellar rise of the meatpacking companies JBS, Marfrig and BRF, which all took leading positions in only a few years.

The expansion of Brazilian multinational companies first started in neighboring Latin American countries and then extended to the rest of the world. Brazil's size and richness in natural resources has nourished some of the domestic conglomerates that later went global. Furthermore, the role of government has been instrumental through policies to protect and promote the development of "national champions", along with the use of development loans by the public development bank BNDES to foster the competitive development of Brazilian companies in strategic sectors and support their international expansion.

The literature on emerging multinational companies (Casanova 2009b, Khanna and Palepu, 2010, Guillén and García-Canal, 2013, Santiso, 2013) provides extensive insights into their internationalization strategies, entry modes, success factors and remaining obstacles to their further global expansion. International and national corporate rankings established by the financial press and research institutes also give a clear view of the hierarchy of Brazilian firms, whether in terms of size, revenues or presence abroad. What is less clear is how the globalization of Brazilian companies will continue going forward. Is there room for continuous expansion? How many of them are consistently winning global market shares and have entered the top ten in their respective industries? How does their performance compare to those of their Chinese, Indian, Mexican or South African counterparts?

Finally, a question remains over the commitment of Brazilian companies – and of the Brazilian government – to internationalization. In 2011, the replacement of Roger Agnelli by Murilo Ferreira as Vale's chief executive was widely interpreted as a sign of the government's intention to favor domestic investments over the expansion of the company's global activities. With the country's immense infrastructure needs to prepare for the World Cup in 2014 and the Rio Olympic Games in 2016, it is not surprising that many Brazilian companies are starting to look inward again. For instance, Petrobras is divesting from the United States and Argentina as part of a worldwide asset-selling plan to fund the development of its deep-water oil discoveries off the coast of Brazil.

While it is too early to tell whether the "re-nationalization" of globally active companies will become a generalized trend, it is clear that the promotion of homegrown multinational enterprises is still not among the government's highest priorities. The announcement by BNDES of the end of its policy to support the international expansion of domestic companies in sectors deemed strategic, such as food processing or petrochemicals, also signals the beginning of a new era for Brazilian multinationals. Looking ahead, the Brazilian champions of tomorrow will increasingly need to rely on their own strengths to fulfill their global potential, and invest more in innovation in the long-term.

Part III

What Will Propel Brazil Forward?

5
Strengthening Brazil's Competitiveness

Brazil is a country whose recent GDP growth and political stability were achieved against the backdrop of numerous endemic social and economic issues. A subsequent chapter explores many of the social issues of crucial importance for the country's development, ranging from poverty to crime and corruption, as well as the potential of its human capital. Here, we examine the economic challenges that hold back the rise of Brazil in relation to other economies, with a focus on deficits in competitiveness, innovation capabilities and infrastructure.

History has shown that massive social, cultural and economic change can take place within the space of a generation. Sometimes, these changes spring from external forces, such as the Marshall Plan for the reconstruction of Europe at the end of World War II. At other times, they spring from conscious leadership decisions, such as how public-private partnerships fueled Japan's emergence as an export power in the 1980s, or how a renewed focus on economic incentive has fueled China's continuing growth since the 1990s.

We believe that such change is possible in Brazil, as evidenced by recent gains in both the social and economic realms, as well as a renewed willingness on the part of its government to invest more in areas ranging from healthcare to infrastructure. The very public profile it will enjoy as host of the 2014 World Cup, as well as the 2016 Summer Olympic Games may turn out to be symbolic of the rise of a new Brazil, as long as tough choices and priorities are made in the years to come.

Moving ahead in competitiveness and innovation

Brazil's recent economic growth is, in some ways, an anomaly compared with that of many other emerging economies, in the sense that it has been driven by factors linked to its natural resources (e.g., the development of agriculture and mining), versus industrial or technological competitiveness. One study framed this in terms of the so-called "natural resources curse", where inelastic demand for primary resources can disincentive investment in other economic sectors, including industry, manufacturing and knowledge-based services. Brazilian business leaders have expressed a concern about the risk of "de-industrialization" in the face of global competition, which is also driven by human capital factors, such as deficits in Brazil's educational system and a concomitant lack of skilled professionals.

However one frames this issue, Brazil's world rankings on competitiveness and innovation are disproportionately low relative to its size and overall growth. For example, Brazil ranked 116th in the World Bank's 2014 Doing Business Report, 56th in the World Economic Forum's 2013 Global Competitiveness Report and 64th in the Global Innovation Index published by the World Intellectual Property Organization (WIPO), Cornell University and INSEAD (www.globalinnovationindex.org).

China, in 35th position, is better ranked than Brazil (64th) in the Innovation Index. In particular, the Asian giant is better positioned in many indicators such as assessment in reading, mathematics and science (30 points for Brazil versus 100 for China), Research and Development (R&D) (27.2 for Brazil and 41.5 for China), ease of paying taxes (39.1 for Brazil versus 60.5 for China), university rankings (46.5 points for Brazil versus 74.9 for China), ISO 14001 environmental certificates (11.6 points for Brazil versus 55.3 points for China), and firms offering formal training (60.2 points for Brazil and 100 for China). Relative to Brazil, China's score is twice as high in patent families filed in at least three offices, and three times as high in total computer software. China also multiplied by eight its high tech exports including creative exports where China doubles Brazil.

In global terms, investments made by innovation policies in Brazil since 2004 have not been as productive as expected. Experts agree that the areas where Brazil must improve much further include government procurement of advanced technology products and university-industry collaboration in R&D. Both areas are included in current governmental programs and improvements depend exclusively on their actions and willingness to change. The availability of scientists and engineers and patents per capita are two factors where Brazil is positioned far behind China and other BRICS countries. In addition to educational and skills deficits (which are further discussed in the next chapter), the lack of an effective patent culture in academia, where most scientists are concentrated, discourages innovation.

Brazil's culture is not hostile to individual effort or innovation, and the country is well known for certain pockets of know-how and technology. For example, aircraft manufacturer Embraer, which is presented at greater length in Chapter 3, redefined the global market for regional jet transportation and is gaining ground in the broader market for airliners. Brazil is one of the world's manufacturing and design centers for

Brazil's technology gap: More than a competitive issue

In Brazil, the need to improve technology infrastructure includes other aspects beyond the sale of technology products. By the late 20th century, large multinationals that had set up and remained in the country from the automotive, banking and telecommunications sectors, were major consumers of information technology, software, communications and internet services, as well as consumers of technological innovations. As such, they contributed significantly to the growth of the internal market in these areas.

However, the demands from these sectors could not be totally supported by the local technology industry, as Brazil did not have an organized science, technology and innovation structure, and this sector had undergone a serious economic and management crisis during the 1980s and 1990s. This crisis would only start to be solved by the end of the 1990s, with the creation of the Sectorial Funds for Science and Technology (Fundos Setoriais para Ciência e Tecnologia), funded by Brazil's Ministry of Science and Technology (FNDCT). This move ultimately helped Brazil create tens of thousands of new university researchers and allowed the development of a growing Brazilian industry of software and services mature enough to warrant the subsequent implementation of a Research, Development and Innovation Policy. The local banking sector, Banco do Brasil, Banco Itaú-Unibanco or Bradesco was also an early adopter of technology to survive during the hyper inflationary years (1980–1994). One could argue that, unlike other countries in Latin America, the Brazilian banking sector survived the volatile economic environment by using technology. The software was developed initially in-house but, later on, companies such as Politec were the suppliers of choice.

automobiles from multinationals such as Volkswagen, General Motors and Fiat, the latter of which sells more cars in Brazil than in Italy. The country is also known for technological achievements in areas including bioengineering, e-government, banking and technology. The term "Made in Brazil" carries no negative connotations on the global stage.

So what stands between Brazil and a stronger global competitive and innovative position? First and foremost, moving past economic growth that revolves around agriculture and natural resources requires development of its human capital, as we discuss in the next chapter. This includes improving the country's educational system, successfully encouraging families to comply with mandatory school attendance through programs such as *Bolsa Família*, improving global connections for its colleges and universities, and supporting the growth of skilled professionals.

At an economic level, a key part of the competitive equation lies in stronger partnerships between government, academia and the private sector, along lines that have been shown to be successful in other countries such as China and Singapore. In particular, several government initiatives have grown to address the needs of agriculture (EMBRAPA), technology (FINEP), and business funding (BNDES). We look at them in more detail in the sections below.

EMBRAPA – Brazilian Agricultural Research Corporation (Empresa Brasileira de Pesquisa Agropecuári)

The Brazilian Agricultural Research Corporation (EMBRAPA) was founded in 1973 as a state-owned organization affiliated with Brazil's Ministry of Agriculture. Its mission statement is to provide "feasible solutions for the sustainable development of Brazilian agribusiness through knowledge and technology generation and transfer". As a research center, it examines areas that are critical to the future of agribusiness in Brazil, ranging from animal production to information technology. Some of its key successes include improved crop yields and planting techniques, integrated crop-livestock systems, and the successful introduction of new crops such as soybeans, leading United States agriculture writer Mike Wilson to describe EMBRAPA as "the engine behind Brazil's economic miracle".[1] Thanks to its efforts, Brazil has been able to increase productivity by 150% over the last 30 years – while only increasing 20% of the landmass dedicated to agriculture and the sector promoting economic growth.

BNDES – National Bank of Economic and Social Development (Banco Nacional de Desenvolvimento Econômico e Social)

The BNDES, a federal government company, is now the main long-term financing instrument for investments in all segments of the economy, including at regional level and for social and environmental projects. Since being founded in 1952, BNDES has supported agriculture, infrastructure, commerce and the services sector, offering special lending terms for micro-, small and medium-sized companies, as well as multinationals. The bank has also provided social investment credit for education and health, family agriculture, basic sanitization and urban public transportation. BNDES supports infrastructure projects, acquisition of equipment and exports of goods and services. It also helps to strengthen private company capital structures and provides non-refundable financing to projects that contribute to social, cultural and technological advancement. In its 2009–2014 Corporate Planning, BNDES placed a special emphasis on innovation, local and regional development, as well as social and environmental development.

As one example in the technology sector, BNDES launched Prosoft – or the Integrated Sectorial Program for Software Exports and Correlated Services – a program designed to help grow R&D investment and exports in the software industry, as well as to strengthen the Brazilian operations of multinational software and IT firms. Various initiatives were set up under this program, including *Prosoft Empresa* (Prosoft Company), which provides direct or indirect support in the form of financing or shareholding participation to eligible Brazilian companies; Prosoft Comercialização (Prosoft Commercialization), which finances the acquisition, in the domestic market, of software and related services; and Prosoft Exportação (Prosoft Exports), which finances exports of software and services developed in Brazil, along with the Cartão BNDES (BNDES Card), a credit card-like instrument for financing the acquisition of new assets and inputs by micro-, small and medium-sized companies.

FINEP – Financing Agency of Studies and Projects (Financiadora de Estudos e Projetos)

FINEP is a government organization linked to the Ministry of Sciences and Technology (MCT) that finances scientific, technological and innovation projects, with the mission of "promoting the economic and social development of Brazil, through government support to science, technology and innovation in companies, universities, technological institutes and other government or private institutions".

FINEP was created in 1967 to institutionalize the Financing Fund of Studies of Projects and Programs, created in 1965. Subsequently, FINEP amplified the work of BNDES, and its Fundo de Desenvolvimento Técnico-Científico – FUNTEC (Technical and Scientific Development Fund), which was created in 1964 to finance the implementation of post-graduate programs at Brazilian universities. In the 1970s, FINEP financed the implementation of new research groups, the creation of thematic programs, the expansion of the science and technology infrastructure and the institutional consolidation of research and post-graduate study. It has stimulated collaboration among universities, research centers, consultancy businesses and contractors.

Some of the economic successes attributed to FINEP financing include the development in the early 1980s of the EMB-312 Tucano airplane by the Brazilian airplane manufacturer Embraer, which opened the way for their airplanes to become an important part of Brazil's exports; Petrobras' research and human capital projects, in partnership with universities, which contributed to their expertise in deep-water exploration technology that is now leading the country to energy self-sufficiency, and numerous projects led by EMBRAPA (see above) that in turn drove the technological development of the Brazilian agribusiness system to become one of the most competitive in the world.

APEX – Brazilian Trade and Investment Promotion Agency (Agência Brasileira de Promoção de Exportação e Investimentos)

This agency acts strategically to lead more companies into the international marketplace, diversify and aggregate value to export transactions, increase trade volumes, consolidate the presence of the country in traditional markets and open new market frontiers for Brazilian products and services. To fulfill its goals, it offers solutions in the areas of information, export qualification, commercial promotion, marketing and internationalization. The agency wants to promote and facilitate the internationalization of Brazilian companies. With its headquarters in Brasília, APEX has offices all across Brazil and well as in Angola, Belgium, China, Cuba, Russia, the United Arab Emirates and the United States.

ABDI – Brazilian Agency of Industrial Development (Agência Brasileira de Desenvolvimento Industrial)

This is a more recent government agency created in 2004 and linked to the Ministry of Development, Industry and Foreign Trade (MDIC),

Brazil's productivity challenge

Despite Brazil's recent economic growth, experts often point to Brazil's dismal track record on productivity: according to the Boston Consulting Group, barely a quarter of its growth in GDP over the past decade was due to improvements in productivity, with the remainder coming from growth in employment – numbers that are severely out of step with other growing economies.[2]

A 2013 *Economist* article lays much of the blame at the lack of fundamental government reform, comparing its onerous business tax codes and bloated pension obligations with the country's historically poor infrastructure. Brazilian pensions average 70% of pay at age 54 and payroll taxes are close to 60% of salaries, while infrastructure spending is described as "skimpier than a string", at roughly 1.5% of GDP.[3]

In its 2013 Economic Survey of Brazil, the OECD insists on the country's need to boost productivity growth, which the Paris-based intergovernmental organization says "requires addressing infrastructure deficiencies, high labour costs and low skill levels, a high tax burden and an onerous tax system, excessive administrative burdens, shallow credit markets and barriers to international trade" (OECD, 2013).

While infrastructure and technology remain critical factors for improving Brazil's productivity, opinions such as these underscore the importance of fiscal and trade policy as well: according to *The Economist,* businesses face one of the largest shares of taxes among the developing world (36%), onerous import and customs regulations, and entrenched levels of government bureaucracy. Many of these are entrenched issues whose solutions will require political will, as well as economic growth in the future. With general elections looming in 2014 for both Brazil's President and National Congress, the future trajectory of Brazil's productivity concerns will at least in part be a question for the country's electorate to decide.

which has the mission of promoting the execution of the Industrial Policy jointly with Foreign Trade and Science and Technology Policies. Its most important goal is to help the government to implement Brazil's new industrial policy, in particular, the *Plano Brasil Maior* (Bigger Brazil Plan, see Chapter 2).

Each of these agencies, some of which date back decades, are part of a renewed focus on government efforts to work with the private sector in improving Brazil's competitiveness and innovation, particularly in the industrial and technology sectors. In a very real sense, it is following a blueprint that has worked for other countries that have successfully transformed their economies.

Government support and involvement is clearly far from the only factor in its competitiveness – people still speak of the "Brazil cost" (*Custo Brasil,* mentioned in the previous chapter)[4] of corruption and bureaucracy in doing business.

The flow of goods and people: The persistent infrastructure deficit

Brazilian truck drivers and ship's captains often wait for days to load or unload their cargo in the crowded port of Santos, the largest in Latin America. Mass transit systems in major cities such as Rio de Janeiro or São Paulo are ill equipped to handle rush hour crowds or growth. More than half of Brazil's major airports are running at or beyond their capacity. And roads are so bad that the head of Brazil's national logistics organization stated in 2013 that they increase the cost of truck transportation, the lifeblood of its agricultural system, by over 60%.[5]

Brazil has a longstanding infrastructure deficit problem, the result of years of underinvestment on the part of government that dates back to the economic crises of the 1980s and 1990s. With some exceptions, roads, ports, airports as well as the overall state of transport, and services in general are not up to the standards that should be expected from the world's seventh largest economy. According to a McKinsey study cited by the *Financial Times,*[6] Brazil's stock of infrastructure totals only 16% of the GDP, versus a norm of 70% for most countries.

Even today, during a period of relative economic stability since 2003, levels of investment in infrastructure have been very low: Brazil currently spends roughly 1.5% of its gross domestic product on infrastructure, compared with a world average of 3.8%, versus 13% in China, and less than half of what multilateral institutions recommend to sustain a

4% economic growth rate. Combined with decades of neglect, this creates a serious functional infrastructure deficit that is holding back the country from further growth, particularly as more people at all levels enter its workforce.

Since 2007, Brazil's Accelerated Growth Program (PAC) has invested hundreds of millions of Brazilian reais toward infrastructure improvements. In the first phase, up to 2010, the program allocated US$349 billion, of which 63% had been invested. The second PAC was launched in 2010 announcing additional investments of US$526 billion up to 2014 for new projects, and the conclusion of those initiated during the first phase of the program. The program invests in logistics, energy and social development under six major initiatives: Better Cities (US$31.3 billion, quality of life in cities), Bringing Citizenship to the Community (US$12.6 billion, social inclusion), My House, My Life (US$152.5 billion, housing, see Chapter 6), Water and Light for All (US$16.6 billion, sanitation and electricity, see Chapter 6), Energy (US$255.3 billion and post-2014, an estimated US$343.9 billion, renewable energy, oil and gas) and Transportation (US$57.3 billion, highways, railways and airports). In the different programs and as of 2013, Brazil plans to substantially increase its level of investment in infrastructure, spending nearly a trillion Brazilian reais (US$407 billion) over the next few years. It has also begun to embark on an ambitious program of public-private partnerships (PPPs), described in more detail below, where public infrastructure assets ranging from toll roads to airports are being put into the hands of private operators as subsidized or for-profit enterprises with attractive rates of return. Some specific plans including ports, roads, mass transit, airports and waterways are described below.

Ports: Brazilian public ports are currently critically overcrowded, causing cargo bottlenecks on both land and the sea. As of 2013, the Federal government is committing over US$20 billion to reforms on three fronts: the development of new public ports, improved access to ports through improvements such as dredging, and the opening of numerous public ports to private investment – including Latin America's largest port at Santos in São Paulo state. This influx of private investment is expected to improve both capacity and efficiency for the affected ports.[7]

Roads: Only 13.5% of roads were paved in Brazil in 2012, according to World Bank data, versus 100% of roads in Western countries. Brazil is responding to these concerns with increased moves toward privatization; in addition to a longstanding policy of having private firms operate major toll roads and collect tolls, a series of ten-year contracts have been issued to private operators. In 2013, President Dilma Rousseff announced the Logistic Investment Program (PIL) to provide US$22 billion in long-term funding for infrastructure improvements.

Mass transit: In major metropolitan areas such as Rio de Janeiro and São Paulo, commuters are faced with the twin nightmares of insufficient public transit capacity and clogged roads, in a country where there is still tremendous over-dependence on the automobile.[8] Dissatisfaction with the state of public transit led directly to the 2013 civil protests throughout Brazil, triggered by increases in transit fares that were subsequently reversed.

Looking to the future, one of the most visible short-term upgrades to Brazil's mass transit will be the construction of new subway lines, bus lines and a light rail system in Rio, in advance of the 2016 Olympics, accounting for nearly US$1 billion of the US$4 billion budgeted for mass transit upgrades in Brazil as of 2013. Public-private partnerships have recently been forged to upgrade São Paulo's subway system, as discussed in more detail below, and other cities nation-wide are slated for mass transit investments. Monorails, an inexpensive alternative to subways, are also sprouting up in São Paulo as an alternative to other forms of commuting.

Airports: Most of Brazil's major airports currently operate at or beyond their full capacity, the result of steady growth in air travel over the past decade, without a concomitant increase in airport infrastructure improvements. Privatization has been a key strategy for coping with this increase: in 2011, for the first time, public-private partnerships were created to remodel and expand Guarulhos and Viracopos-Campinas international airports in São Paulo, as well as the capital, Brasília's, airport. In the former case, flight capacity is scheduled to increase by nearly 25%, along with expanded parking and a new international terminal. In late 2012, Rio de Janeiro's Antônio Carlos Jobim (Galeão) airport and Confins airport in Belo Horizonte were also opened to private partnerships, which in turn are expected to raise nearly US$5 billion in investment.[9]

Waterways: Waterways are a vital transportation link, particularly in remote regions such as the Amazon. Elsewhere in the country, they are often underutilized compared with other transportation channels, such as trucking. Numerous challenges remain in utilizing Brazil's waterways better, ranging from integration with roads and railroad regulations that

Can monorails ease Brazil's traffic congestion?

What carries thousands of passengers at the height of rush hour – and needs no driver?

In North America, monorails are extremely rare forms of transportation except for short-distance travel like in airports and amusement parks such as Walt Disney World (whose monorail system transports over 150,000 people per day). Elsewhere in the world, however – particularly in Asia, where monorails have long been a staple in countries such as Japan – they have gained traction as a means of moving large numbers of people in urban areas.

In São Paulo, where commuting volumes are at a crisis point, monorails have emerged as a viable solution for rapidly expanding the city's transportation infrastructure. The new Expresso Tiradentes line, which is currently under construction, will extend Line two of the current São Paulo Metro. When completed in 2015, it will be able to carry nearly 50,000 people per hour in each direction. Canadian firm Bombardier, the lead contractor on this project, is also creating Brazilian jobs in the process by planning construction of most monorail cars at its plant in Hortolândia.[10]

Why monorails? According to *Financial Times'* columnist Robert Wright, monorail projects like these require only half the cost and half the construction time of traditional metro systems. He describes trucks carrying concrete pillars and rails at night to be rapidly constructed over existing roadways. And once constructed, these automatically controlled, driverless systems can carry a similar volume of people as existing metro systems. They also have a strong safety record, with the world's most heavily used monorail – in Walt Disney World – logging only one fatality in over four decades of operation.[11]

In São Paulo, the new Expresso Tiradentes line will be the first of two major monorail routes planned for the city, the other of which is the forthcoming Gold Line or Line 17 between the planned São Paulo-Morumbi station and São Judas. According to Luis Ramos, Bombardier's director of communications for South America, "Monorails could be Brazil's contribution to world transport technology."

require the use of Brazilian ships for cabotage. By 2025, the government hopes to nearly double the use of its waterways to 29% of transportation, investing over US$6 billion in the process.[12]

In many of these cases, a mix of government investment and private partnerships, described in more detail below, are seen as the keys to long-term improvement in infrastructure. In the former case, Brazil is leveraging its economic success to make permanent improvements in its economic capacity; in the latter case, it is attempting to change a culture and reduce the cost of doing business by harnessing the energy and efficiency of the private sector. If successful, these efforts can potentially become a model for government efforts in many other areas.

Could public–private partnerships be the solution?

One of Brazil's key tools for improving its infrastructure and making capital investments is PPPs.[13] Under these partnerships, private firms are contracted to provide public services by Federal, state or municipal governments. This allows these government entities to decentralize their investments in infrastructure to these private companies, while in turn harnessing the economies and profit incentive of the private sector to run these more efficiently.

The partnerships take one of three forms: so-called *regular concessions,* where the private partner is compensated for its services through users fees; *sponsored concessions,* where the government complements the private partner award through public budget funds in a risk-sharing arrangement, for cases where user fees are not sufficient to offset the investments made by the private partner; and *administrative concessions,* where it is not possible or convenient to charge user fees, and the private partner is compensated exclusively through public funds. Note that even in a regular concession, the government may provide funds to the private partner in order to maintain the economic balance of the contract, as well as possible negotiated revenue guarantees or rates of return. Legislation supporting regular PPPs dates back to 1995, while sponsored and administrative concessions were incorporated into follow-on legislation in 2004. Some examples of these include the following.

Federal PPP: The Pontal Irrigation Project. This project is located in the city of Petrolina, in a semi-arid region of the state of Pernambuco in the northeast of Brazil (São Francisco river valley).[14] The Brazilian government transferred the operation of 33,526 hectares of land to the private sector for 25 years. The PPP contract was signed as a sponsored concession under which, in addition to the fees charged from users, the private partner's revenues are also complemented with government contributions paid by the public authority. The private partner's responsibilities are to construct, operate and allocate the lands to agribusiness users, who will have freedom in selecting their crops. The PPP fund guarantees 100% compensation to the private partner in case the Ministry of National Integration breaks the agreement.

State PPP: Minas Gerais.[15] Following the federal legislation, the states also enacted or amended a PPP law aimed at attracting private investments by increasing the guarantees that were provided in the past. Minas Gerais was the first state that passed a PPP law in 2003, even before the Federal PPP Statute was passed. The state of Minas Gerais has four contracts of PPPs under execution, including (1) a highway MG-050 PPP signed in 2007, (2) a PPP signed in 2009 to build a prison complex with a capacity of 3,000 people, (3) a PPP signed in 2010 to build integrated service centers in six municipalities and (4) the PPP for the renovation of the Mineirão Stadium for the World Cup, signed in 2010.

State/Municipal PPP: São Paulo.[16] The state of São Paulo has three contracts of PPPs under execution benefiting its principal municipality. The fourth line of the Metro of São Paulo is the first example of PPP implementation. The contract was signed in November 2006 with a consortium led by CCR (Companhia de Concessões Rodoviárias), a toll road company in Brazil and one of the major private toll road concession groups in Latin America. The project involves a 30-year concession to operate a 12.8 km stretch of subway in São Paulo, the biggest city in Brazil. Also, the São Paulo Metropolitan Train Company (CPTM) signed an administrative concession PPP in 2010 for Line eight – Diamond, involving an investment of BRL993 million (about US$447 million). The private partner is responsible for delivering 36 new trains and providing fleet maintenance for 20 years.

In 2009 the "Alto Tietê" PPP was signed between SABESP, the state-owned water treatment company of São Paulo, and Galvão Engenharia S/A. The project aims to expand the Taiaçupeba water treatment plant, constructing 17.7 km of new pipelines and four reservoirs with a capacity to store 70 million liters of water. This PPP involves an investment of BRL300 million (US$132 million).

Will hosting the 2016 Olympics help or hurt Brazil's economy?

When observing the competitive jockeying that takes place every four years to be the host city for the Summer or Winter Olympics, one can imagine that it is a prize that must come with major economic benefits for the eventual winner. But is this accurate?[17]

There is no clear answer to this question, because there is no obvious metric for this. Does it involve the Olympic Games themselves breaking even? Or a clear financial benefit to the massive amount of public infrastructure spending that accompanies each Games? Or a more intangible public relations dividend that springs from having your country host up to a million new visitors and be seen by billions of global television viewers?

In recent years, some analysts have pointed to the economic aftermath of spending heavily on specialty sports facilities for a one-time event – for example, the city of Athens now faces a annual maintenance bill of more than US$750 million on its venues from the 2004 Olympics, with many of its facilities now boarded up, and its post-Olympic glow did not prevent the country from falling into economic ruin three years later. Others have cited the displacement of regular tourism and commerce that the organization of these major events may cause. Still others caution that Rio de Janeiro's persistent reputation for crime will be on display in 2016 alongside its 34 gleaming Olympic facilities, nearly a third of which will be new.

Nonetheless, the mood of many observers could be characterized as positive, or at least cautiously optimistic. The city of London,[18] whose 26 million annual visitors dwarf Rio's rapidly growing rate of two million per year, experienced a 7% net increase in tourism during its 2012 Summer Olympics. Barcelona also became a major touristic destination after its 1992 Olympics, indicating a possible major tourism boost for Rio and Brazil. One study from the National Bureau of Economic Research, a United States organization, showed that countries who hosted the Olympics, or even bid for them, experienced a sustained 30% growth in exports that may correlate the organization of major events like this with a greater openness to global trade. And a recent expert panel hosted by the *New York Times* was largely positive about the possible impact of the 2016 Rio Olympics, pointing to gains ranging from infrastructure improvements to an improved self-image for past Olympic cities.[19]

A prescription for competitiveness and innovation

Brazil's problems with the basic components of competitiveness and innovation – including basic infrastructure, transportation capacity and technology – are endemic issues whose roots date back to an economy that was often in crisis over the past several decades. They represent a longstanding mindset of tending to what is urgent for survival, as opposed to building the foundations for long-term growth. And ironically, these problems have become severely exacerbated with Brazil's recent economic success. The country now enjoys higher employment levels in cities where people face long and crowded commutes, increasing levels of exports through ports that are backed up for days, and economic opportunities that often lack the technology to support them.

The seeds of changing this reality have begun to be sown, not only by a change in Brazil's economic fortunes, but by changes in philosophy. Following the lead of other successful growth economies in recent history, Brazil's current political leadership has been following a path that understands both the role of government investment in economic growth, and the value of creative public-private partnerships. By trading investment capital for future opportunities for the private sector, fueled in turn by growth, it is applying leverage as well as resources toward the future.

There is a very symbolic aspect to these changes as well. The twin events of the 2014 World Cup finals and the 2016 Summer Olympics, by their very nature, are fueling substantial improvements in infrastructure – both to handle the expected influx of foreign visitors for these events, and to establish Brazil as a showplace in the world's eyes. Beyond new roads, ports or technology funding initiatives, however, the second decade of the 21st century represents an opportunity for Brazil to invest in its competitive posture, with these public events serving as a chance to highlight its successes. Many hurdles remain to be overcome, ranging from government reform to fiscal policy, but today there is more hope for Brazil to continue to emerge as a globally competitive economy and a source of policy and industrial innovation.

6
Sustaining Social Innovation

Government, in the abstract, exists for the sake of the public good. In the wake of two center-left[1] presidential administrations and a growing economy, modern Brazil has taken some of the world's strongest and most publicly visible strides toward this ideal, in areas such as education and the eradication of poverty, crime and corruption.

However, many of these initiatives are taking place against the backdrop of serious social problems, which in turn serve as the biggest challenges to Brazil's emergence as a world power. Levels of poverty, inequality, corruption and crime remain at some of the highest levels among major economies, critical deficits continue to exist in infrastructure, and its citizens are among the most poorly educated for a growth economy.

This chapter explores the current state of Brazil's social issues as of 2013, with a focus on both their impact on Brazil's rise as a world power, and the current and future prospects for these issues over time. It will focus on Brazil's human infrastructure needs to paint a picture of a country that has made substantial gains in addressing its worst problems, while recognizing that much remains to be done.

The future trajectory of Brazil's social issues, in a very real sense, will define its prospects as a global power and its "brand" as a nation. Its current political administration appears to be focused on harnessing the country's current economic growth as leverage to drive deep and permanent changes on the social front: for example, following the protests of June 2013, President Dilma Rousseff fought to direct the country's lucrative oil and gas royalties into funding for education.[2] The fate of both Brazil's economy and its social order will in all likelihood remain intertwined for some time to come.

Celebrating Brazil's strong civil society

The wave of demonstrations which hit Brazil in 2013 was a clear sign of growing dissatisfaction with the country's slow progress in many critical areas, including education, public health and transportation. At a deeper level, these protests are also a very healthy sign of participation from a strong civil society. Today, Brazilians are socially engaged and feel capable of instigating change at a grass roots level and its social policies and social entrepreneurs serve as models for the world. This has dovetailed in recent years with a growing capacity for various sectors of Brazilian society to address many core social issues, in the wake of a growing economy. Some of the tangible signs of these kinds of changes include the increasing implementation of corporate social responsibility (CSR) by companies, growing PPPs for the social good, social and human-rights-focused NGOs and The World Social Forum; and these are described below.

Increasing CSR: Businesses in Brazil are increasingly feeling the obligation – and the economic opportunity – to give back to the communities they serve. For example, the cosmetics firm Natura sources natural products from the Amazon rainforest from indigenous communities, and its business model has improved the life of the women selling their products. Service firm Renascer supplements hospital care for children from low-income communities to reduce the incidence of repeat hospitalization.[3] Organizations like Ethos Institute (Instituto Ethos) or the Businesses for Climate Platform (Empresas Pelo Clima) have also helped to mobilize the Brazilian business community in support of social and environmental goals.

Growing PPPs for the social good: As discussed in the previous chapter, PPPs promote the development of social or public infrastructure by leveraging the private sector. We have already cited the Pontal Irrigation Project, which transferred over 33,000 hectares of land in the semi-arid regions of Pernambuco state to the private sector for a period of 25 years, and in turn guarantees their revenues from user fees. Other programs serve the public more directly: the Federal government's "Light for All" (Luz para Todos) program teams up electric concessionaires with public utility Eletrobrás to provide universal access to electricity to more than ten million rural people. The "My House, My Life" (Minha Casa, Minha Vida) social housing initiative pairs state-owned bank Caixa Econômica Federal with private investors to provide low-cost 100% home financing for low- to middle-income households who normally would not be able to own a home.[4] The program started in 2009 and has provided 1.32 million homes for 4.6 million Brazilians.

Social and human-rights focused NGOs: A wide range of NGOs have sprung up in Brazil to address social and human rights causes. These operate mostly at a grass roots level – only 20%, for example, have budgets greater than US$1 million – however, their influence is steadily growing (Letelier, 2012).

The World Social Forum: The World Social Forum (Fórum Social Mundial) is a global meeting held annually in Brazil and other world cities to address global economic and political problems from the standpoint of civil society and social movements, as a counterpoint to the annual meeting of the World Economic Forum (WEF) held in Davos, Switzerland. Its speakers frequently include intellectuals, activists and other thought leaders. In January 2003, President Lula made a point of attending both the World Social Forum in Porto Alegre and the WEF meeting in Davos.

At another level, Brazil's current government is helping the world take a fresh look at the idea of *participatory democracy*, a bottom-up form of governance that gives people more direct input versus a traditional representative democracy. The term has a checkered history: from social movements such as the Occupy movement of 2011, to corporate cultures based on consensus decision making, it is widely viewed as ultimately leading to paralysis by analysis. In 1989, when the Workers' Party won the elections of the city of Porto Alegre, a city of 1.5 million people, it replaced a bureaucratic system that was rife with shortages, with a unique participatory democracy process where citizen assemblies – open to all, and with heavy participation from poorer residents – recommend budget priorities for approval by the city's municipal budget council and mayor. This system has led to substantial improvements in infrastructure, such as access to roads and sewers, particularly in poor neighborhoods, and continued even after the Workers' Party lost municipal power in 2004.[5,6]

While Brazil continues to face serious social problems, there is a renewed sense that change is in the air. Perhaps one popular example of this is *Avenida Brasil*, a soap opera that has become so hotly popular that even President Dilma Rousseff has changed her schedule to be able to watch it. *Avenida Brasil* is one of the first Brazilian soap operas to focus on the country's new middle class (rather than the super-wealthy) and the poor, showing the realities of living in the Brazilian shantytowns ("*favelas*"). As such, it reflects the growth of Brazil's middle class, which

Brazil's social entrepreneurs

Social entrepreneurship, as defined by Professor Felipe Santos of INSEAD, refers to those entrepreneurs who are looking for profit and, at the same time, social good. Rodrigo Baggio is a former Intel executive. Today, he heads the Center for Digital Inclusion (CDI), a successful business whose function is to bridge the digital divide for people in Brazil. Each of his centers is a self-sustaining operation that teaches people basic computer skills and literacy. The concept has spread to over 750 schools in Brazil, as well as over 100 abroad. Students learn to use computers in the context of creating a "social advocacy project", while teachers learn to improve their computer skills for use in the classroom. This chain has become very successful, and Baggio himself was named by *Time* magazine as one of the 50 Latin American Leaders of the new Millennium.[7]

This is an example of the kind of *social entrepreneurship* that is beginning to grow in Brazil. It has goals for the social welfare of the country, wrapped in the pragmatism of profit-making opportunities that often grow in supporting the CSR efforts of larger companies, or providing needed services in support of social goals. These include "green" businesses, educational firms and a host of other business ventures designed to improve the lives of Brazilians.

has been fueled by recent social change and economic recovery. This serves as one of many metaphors for a new spirit of change that has been sweeping the country.

Brazilians sometimes describe themselves using the word *jeitinho*, which is loosely translated as "find a way" to solve things: it speaks to having the street smarts, family connections, creativity or sheer will to make things happen. One could compare it with the Chinese concept of *guanxi* (favors given and received by insiders), or the *viveza criolla* (cunning) of Brazil's Latin American neighbors. Historically, it often spoke to the ability to survive in the challenging world of a developing country. Today, one could view modern Brazil through the lens of a renewed sense of *jeitinho* – one that speaks to the will of people to think beyond its past social issues, and forge a new and more promising society for all.

Overcoming poverty and income inequality

Brazil has the unfortunate distinction of having one of the largest gaps in income in the world between rich and poor. Roughly 10% of Brazil's population controls over 50% of the country's wealth. The country is home to some of the richest people in the world, while, as of 2011, 21% of Brazilians live below the national poverty line, translating to 40 million people.[8] This is comparable to the poverty rates for other Latin American nations, and naturally represents a major social issue. Coupled with relatively low unemployment rates this also translates to a relatively high level of working poor.[9]

Income inequality in a country can be quantified by what is known as the Gini coefficient, a number between zero and one that describes wealth patterns as a frequency distribution: countries with a coefficient of zero would have absolute income equality, while 1.0 would represent maximum inequality. With a Gini coefficient of roughly 0.53, as of 2011, Brazil has made substantial improvement from its 2002 score of approximately 0.64. However, this still ranks Brazil as having one of the worst levels of income inequality in Latin America, and in the world.[10]

The poor get richer

Recent economic figures are now starting to validate the outcomes from Brazil's anti-poverty initiatives: financially, the poor are currently gaining ground faster than any other segment of society.

As of 2012, according to figures from *Forbes* magazine, the poorest 10% of Brazil's workforce saw their wages increase by nearly a third, versus an 8.3% rise in wages for Brazilians as a whole – and nearly flat increases in real wages in the United States.[11]

Government-sponsored anti-poverty programs, such as the conditional cash transfer (CCT) programs (*Bolsa Família*) described below have clearly made a dent in this problem, as has a growing economy fueled by booming commodity exports. While rates of poverty and economic inequality remain high, particularly in relation to other developed countries, the rate of change of the past decade serves as a promising sign of Brazil's emergence as an economic power.

As a vast country with low population density (21 inhabitants/square km.), wealth in Brazil often takes a different form than in other more urban societies. Land equates to power, and many wealthy Brazilians own large amounts of land, several homes and a full complement of domestic help to maintain these properties. As in many countries, wealth tends to be concentrated in major states such as São Paulo, Rio de Janeiro and Minas Gerais, and economic conditions are better in the more prosperous and urban south of the country versus the more rural north. Conversely, poverty in Brazil often takes the form of either densely crowded urban shantytowns known as *favelas*, which are described elsewhere in this chapter, or pockets of rural poverty. While only 19% of Brazil's population lives in rural areas, more than half of them live in poverty, which is often a product of structural inequalities in the distribution of land.[12]

Throughout much of Brazil's history, its approach to poverty has been to attempt to marginalize them from society, through social segregation, as well as neglect and lack of infrastructure. Today, there has begun to be a fundamental change in tone toward the poor, which is aimed at giving them a voice and expanding their role in society. Beyond human respect, this stance is seen as creating economic benefits for Brazil, through programs ranging from the pacification of *favelas* to agrarian reform for family farms.

One of the more effective social interventions for poverty in recent years has been the success of conditional cash transfer programs, which leverage financial support for poor families against desirable social outcomes. One example is of Brazil's successful *Bolsa Família* program, created by President Lula in 2003 as a successor to existing cash transfer programs. As part of the government's larger Zero Hunger or *Fome Zero* program,[13] payments are predicated on compliance with school attendance and vaccination for children. For the 14 million families making US$70 or less per month, *Bolsa Família* provides approximately US$44 per month to nearly all of those households, with a budget of approximately US$11 billion in 2012 and a total expenditure of US$50 billion since its inception ten years ago.[14]

One of the subtle, but socially important, aspects of this program is that payments are generally made to the female head of household, giving mothers more of a voice. One of the key arguments against the program at first was the fear that direct cash compensation to male heads of households might get diverted to things such as drinking and gambling. Given the number of single mothers in poverty, this approach was designed to help ensure that money goes to support families, and it appears to be working.

As shown in Figure 6.1, poverty levels dropped by roughly 40% between 2003 and 2009, while levels of extreme poverty were cut in half – and relatively speaking, with extreme poverty defined as US$1.25/day, the eradication of extreme poverty is now in sight. It has also been a cost-effective intervention: These cash payments not only represent a substantial rise in income for their beneficiaries, but their social outcomes and economic benefits are also large, relative to the program costs. According to Minister of Social Development, Tereza Campello, speaking on the program's tenth anniversary, "We have managed to show that for every BRL1 that we invest in the *Bolsa Família*, BRL1.44 is returned to society. So who wins? The winners are the beneficiaries and their children. But the community also comes out a winner."[15] While there was some debate at first over whether to provide cash to poor families in this way, there is a broad consensus today that this program works well. Some argue that certain improvements should be brought to the way they are implemented, but very few voices (if any) call for their complete withdrawal (see Chapter 8).

Another recent success story is the growing integration of Brazil's *favelas* into society at large. Historically a product of migration from

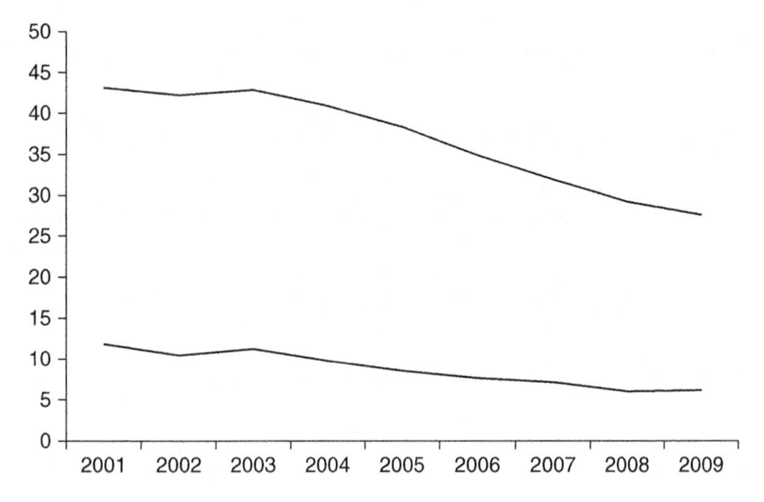

Figure 6.1 Trends in poverty ($4/day, upper line) and extreme poverty ($1.25/day, lower line) in Brazil, 2001–2009.

Source: Authors based on World Bank Poverty and Inequality Database (Accessed on 21 August 2013).

rural areas by people in search of opportunities in urban areas, these *favelas* grew in major cities such as Rio de Janeiro and São Paulo, often as crudely built housing lacking utilities or basic services. Police often avoided patrolling these areas, and as the drug trade grew as an economic reality for these communities, many became controlled by drug gangs, and remain so to this day.

Efforts to eradicate the *favelas*, including a large-scale effort in the 1970s under Brazil's military dictatorship, have generally met with failure, doomed by factors ranging from a lack of public funding for housing alternatives to a steady growth in urban migration. Today, the focus is more on integrating *favela* residents with society at large. For example, Rio de Janeiro's Favela Pacification Program (FPP) focuses on embedding a community police presence within *favelas*, wresting control from drug lords and paving the way for needed services to be provided. At a deeper level, local policing also builds community relationships that reduce the motivations for police brutality toward residents. To date, this program has exceeded expectations, and many of Rio's larger *favelas* have become pacified.

Ironically, *favela* tourism, which draws thousands of visitors to see some of these slums first-hand and interact with people in the community, is emerging as a source of community funding as well.[16] These programs, which are created in partnership with community leaders,

Favelas: The high-rent district?

Being poor in Brazil does not necessarily mean that your rent is cheap. Brazil's *favelas*, home to close to 6% of Brazil's population as of 2011, have recently undergone a significant increase in rental prices in conjunction with the expansion of Brazil's economy.

According to the *Financial Times*, rent for a small ramshackle apartment in the middle of Rio de Janeiro's Santa Marta *favela* now ranges from BRL400–500 (US$207–259), with prices even higher near the base of this hillside neighborhood, where there is better access to services and utilities. Factors ranging from a growing middle class, to strong appreciation in real estate prices – for example, growing over 20% in the year prior to April 2012 – have contributed to this rise. For slum dwellers who often took up residence in these neighborhoods by necessity, these increases form an added economic stress to an already impoverished lifestyle.[17]

are also part of larger social context to build social bridges with *favela* neighborhoods. For example, it is not unusual for young *favela* residents to attend college nowadays and return to their neighborhoods at night. Safety in general has continued to increase for residents as a whole.

Regional differences in poverty within the country remain an issue as well. However, Brazil continues to explore new options: for example, recent moves discussed elsewhere in this chapter to fund education and healthcare from future oil revenues may help redress inequalities between regions, and within regions. While much work remains to be done, the country is now on a promising trajectory with regards to poverty.

Brazil's education model and skills challenge

In education, like in poverty, Brazil has made huge advances, but the challenges are still plentiful. The quality of Brazil's educational system and, in particular, a lack of skilled and trained professionals, stands as one of the single biggest impediments to its growth. Moreover, better education for Brazil's children is seen as the key transformative influence for many of its other social problems, such as crime, poverty and lack of economic opportunity.

Unfortunately, the quality of basic education in Brazil remains extremely poor. Although Brazil's results are better than 10 years ago, of the 65 countries that participated in the 2012 OECD test for International Student Assessment (PISA[18]), Brazil ranks among the bottom dozen countries in mathematics, reading and science. On one hand, compliance levels with compulsory public education is high and improving: enrolment in compulsory education for those aged seven to 14 is now in excess of 95%, and has grown substantially to over 80% among those aged 15–17. On the other hand, over a third of 16-year-olds have never finished primary school, and nearly half of 19-year-olds fail to complete high school.

The situation is even more dire when it comes to skills mastery: 70% of Brazilian secondary school students lack basic competencies in mathematics, half of Brazilian 15-year-olds rank at the lowest functional level of the global standards of PISA, and nearly three-quarters of its adults cannot understand a simple text sentence.[19] Educational infrastructure is poor in many areas, and teachers suffer from lack of training and low pay: salaries averaged about 60% of what other educated people earn as of 2012, and some states even struggle to pay teachers the minimum salary of BRL1,451, or about US$820.[20]

While Brazil boasts an overall literacy rate of 90%, as of 2011, the lack of basic skills among its citizens serve as a critical deficit, particularly in a world that increasingly requires college-level capabilities for many jobs.

Many of these problems have their roots in public funding for education, which in turn is becoming a renewed focus for the Brazilian government. According to World Bank figures, Brazil spends barely a third as much on education as high-income countries such as the United States and South Korea: it is spending roughly 5% of GDP, versus around 15% for these other nations.[21] Brazil's 2012 National Educational Plan legislation sets an ambitious goal of doubling this spending level to 10% of GDP by 2022, together with improvements in other areas, such as teacher training and pay, improved efforts to reduce illiteracy, and increased enrolment in day care.[22]

Other proposals range from funding early childhood education to addressing regional economic inequalities. Even more aggressive interventions have been proposed more recently, fueled in part by public protest, such as a recent move by President Dilma Rousseff to try and have all net oil and gas revenues directed toward education. In response, Brazil's Congress agreed in summer 2013 to allocate 75% of revenues from oil extraction for education, and 25% for healthcare.[23]

Primary and secondary education

Modern Brazil is a country with nation-wide compulsory education for its children. Public education is divided into nine years of so-called "fundamental education", which is both free and mandatory for children aged 6 to 14, followed by three years of secondary education that is free but not mandated. Required courses at this level include Portuguese language and literature, mathematics, sciences, history, geography, philosophy, sociology and a foreign language.

Access to this free public education has gained substantial ground: for example, as of 2009, twice as many Brazilians aged 25–34 had completed secondary education (53%) versus those aged 55–64 (25%). However, the quality of this education often bears the burden of decades of neglect, and school infrastructures often lack basic necessities. Particularly as one moves away from the major cities into remote or rural regions of Brazil, the quality of public education is often a much greater problem than its availability.

Part of Brazil's gains lie in the success of the conditional cash transfer programs described in the previous section, where financial support

The elephant in the room: Brazil's technology education gap

As a historically agrarian nation that achieved independence in the 19th century, Brazil has traditionally lagged behind its counterparts in educating technology professionals – a gap that still exists today, and may threaten its growth in an increasingly technological global economy.

Before Brazil's first state-owned university, the Universidade de São Paulo, opened in São Paulo in 1934, postsecondary education was largely reserved for the elite and concentrated in areas such as medicine and law.[24] Today, Brazil boasts over 2,500 postsecondary institutions, yet few Brazilian universities have top global rankings; only six rank among the world's top 500 in the Academic Ranking of World Universities, and critical shortages exist in areas such as science, technology and engineering.[25]

The practical implications of this may impact the growth of areas such as technology and manufacturing: for example, Brazilian law professor Ronaldo Lemos noted that when Chinese electronic manufacturer Foxconn announced a manufacturing facility in Brazil, they projected hiring over 20,000 engineers, a number Lemos points out is simply unachievable given the current local workforce.[26] An even broader looming issue is the increasing level of technology required by today's workforce in nearly all professional areas of employment.

Current government efforts to address this issue include programs to fund Brazilian science and engineering students to study abroad (Science Without Borders or *Ciência sem fronteiras,* described in more detail below), as well as existing programs improving university access in Brazil to more people and encouraging technical study, such as the ProUni and Pronatec programs described below. Meanwhile, experts such as Lemos note the importance of opening Brazil's universities further to the outside world: for example, less than 3% of university students in Brazil are from abroad, and hiring foreign professors often requires a lengthy and complex approval process for their academic credentials. From here, educational policy promises to be an important factor in Brazil's future technology workforce.

to poor families is predicated on compliance with compulsory school attendance for their children. At another level, the introduction of higher standards and accountability has helped, such as former President Lula's introduction of the Basic Education Development Index (IDEB), a metric for measuring school performance and triggering intervention for poorly performing areas.[27] Finally, a renewed focus on funding for education holds promise to address the country's endemic educational quality issues for the longer term, particularly in the critical area of early childhood education.

University education

Brazil's Ministry of Education currently recognizes over 2,500 institutions of higher learning as of 2013. This number compares favorably with other developed nations; however, enrolment rates and institutional quality represent an ongoing issue for Brazil. As of 2011, less than 15% of people aged 18 to 24 were enrolled in postsecondary education, compared with over 40% in the United States – and roughly the same percentage as that of 30 years ago.[28] In poorer regions of Brazil, this rate can drop below 10%.

A deeper concern within these numbers is the lack of people choosing to study the critical skills that the country needs, such as science, technology and engineering. According to Brazil's National Institute of Studies and Educational Research (INEP, http://www.inep.gov.br), the agency responsible for college admissions testing, only 11% of students choose majors in engineering, manufacturing or construction, while science, mathematics and computer science enrolment rates are even smaller at 6.3%. This compares with figures in nations such as the United States, however, given Brazil's relatively small enrolment numbers, this represents a substantial skills gap for the future.

This is not to say that Brazil's government has not tried to address the problem of college attendance; in fact, an aggressive government partnership with private universities makes it possible for many academically qualified individuals to attend college at little or no cost. The University for All (*ProUni – Programa Universidade para Todos*) offers free college tuition for prospective students who graduate from secondary school and/or maintain a secondary school scholarship, and come from families who make no more than one and a half times the minimum wage, currently a total of approximately BRL1,000 (about US$420) per month. Partial scholarships are also available for applicants whose families make up to three times the minimum wage.

The quality of postsecondary education varies widely. Brazil's very best public universities, such as the University of São Paulo, are extremely competitive to get into: the ratio of applicants to admits at such top schools can exceed 30 to 40 students per accepted one. However, private schools tend not to be highly ranked or regarded; even in the example mentioned above, where the government sponsors all of the tuition costs for low-income attendees at private schools, there is often still a cultural perception that these schools are somehow "lesser" compared with the better public institutions.[29]

Science without borders: Giving Brazilians a global technology education

Brazil's Science without Borders (*Ciência sem fronteiras)* program is a unique public-private partnership that seeks to foster research, technological development and innovation, for the fewer than 15% of Brazilians who are enrolled in college – only 11% of whom study science and engineering. This program offers exchange scholarships for undergraduate and graduate students who are interested in studying and/or doing research in the world's most prestigious universities in the field of technology. Additionally, the program aims to attract international researchers who would like to settle in Brazil, or establish partnerships with Brazilian researchers in strategic areas for the country.

Established in 2011, this program has a goal of offering 101,000 scholarships by 2015 to promote exchange programs, so undergraduate and graduate students can study abroad and establish contact with competitive educational systems in technology and science.[30,31] Roughly a quarter of these will be financed by the private sector, with the rest financed by the Federal government. The private companies participate in the program by financing part of the scholarships, by receiving post doctorate students and special visiting researchers to work with them, and also by sending their employees to undertake internships and courses abroad.[32] To date, over 37,000 scholarships have been awarded, of which over 30,000 have gone to send Brazilian undergraduate students to study abroad.

Much more work lies ahead to not only encourage more young Brazilians to enter college, but to study within areas that are critical to the country's future. One such initiative in this direction is the National Programme of Access to Technical Schools (*Pronatec*), launched in 2011 by President Dilma Rousseff, which provides support for technical education at both the university and vocational school level, as well as a National Broadband Plan to improve school-level internet access. There are also calls to make Brazil's graduate schools more open to foreign students and become more globally competitive in producing graduates, particularly in critical areas such as science and technology.

Urban crime and violence

Between 2014 and 2016, the world's media spotlight will be on Brazil as it hosts the World Cup football championship and the Summer Olympics. Unfortunately, some of this spotlight is likely to fall on the country's endemic crime problems. Brazil has long been notorious for its rampant levels of criminal activity.

With an overall annual homicide rate of 21 murders per 100,000 people in 2011, Brazil ranks as one of the more dangerous major countries, according to the United Nations Office on Drugs and Crime (UNODC). While well below some smaller countries, such as Venezuela's 45.1 per 100,000 or Honduras' 91.6 per 100,000, it still far exceeds the 2011 rate of roughly one person per 100,000 in countries such as Germany and the United Kingdom, and 4.8 per 100,000 in the United States. An important trend, however, is the reduction in homicides over time in Brazil. In major cities such as Rio de Janeiro and São Paulo, murder rates have dropped substantially, by factors of roughly two and three, respectively, between 1997 and 2007, as shown in Figure 6.2. Factors in this decline include improved gun control laws, an increase in preventive policing and demographic factors such as a general aging of the population.[33]

Beyond homicides, street crime in general remains a serious social problem in Brazil. These crimes include robbery, assault, rape and theft. While most of the victims of these crimes are poor urban residents, much like the perpetrators, crime still affects all levels of society. It is still a given in major Brazilian cities that you should not display signs of wealth, leave valuables unattended or walk alone at night, including in major tourist areas. Exposure to such crimes often starts at a young age, with one 2008 study in Porto Alegre showing that over a quarter of eighth-grade youths had been mugged (Zdun, 2008).

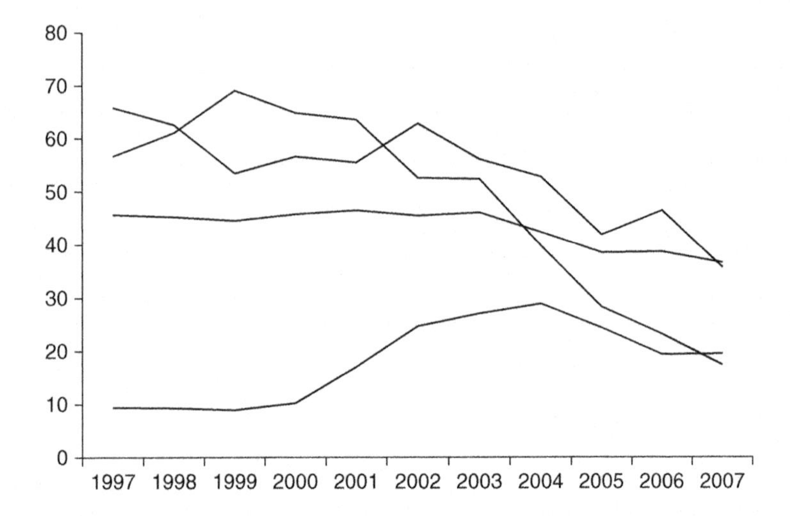

Figure 6.2 Murders per 100,000 people from 1997–2007 for Rio de Janeiro (upper line), Brazil (second line), São Paulo (third line) and Florianópolis (last line), and for all state capitals.

Source: Authors based on Waiselfisz, JJ, Mapa da Violência 2010: Anatomia dos Homicídios no Brasil, Instituto Sangari, 2011, http://mapadaviolencia.org.br/pdf2010/MapaViolencia2010.pdf (Accessed on 22 August 2013).

Another by-product of Brazil's high crime rate is police brutality and corruption, which is often fueled by frustration at the relentless crime levels, and a sense of vigilantism that is in turn supported by many segments of the public. In São Paulo, for example, while the actual murder rate has dropped by nearly two-thirds, rates of claimed justifiable homicide by police officers remain high, in the order of 400 to 700 per year.[34]

The epicenter of crime in Brazil is its urban areas, and it is often fueled by the dual pressures of extreme poverty and the violence associated with the drug trade. This means that, as discussed in the previous section on poverty, one of the key solutions to Brazil's crime problems lies in creating better overall economic opportunities, as well as specific ground-level initiatives, such as community policing. As these efforts continue to bear fruit, best practices are continuing to emerge. But crime prevention and social policies are strongly intertwined, and lasting results in this area may take time to materialize.

Corruption

Corruption is a fact of life in Brazil, as it is in much of Latin America – however, many Brazilians are now getting tired of it and are making their voices heard. One of the key demands of the massive 2013 protests in Brazil, along with protesting poor public services and the high cost of living, was an end to the corruption that plagues the country.[35] These protests did lead to changes, ranging from stronger corruption penalties to the arrest of a Brazilian lawmaker; however, fundamental social change in the culture that drives corruption will take longer.

Corruption is a common problem, according to the 2012 Corruption Perceptions Index published by Transparency International. Brazil, in fact, ranks slightly ahead of the other BRICS nations – however, its score of 43 (on a scale where 0 is the worst and 100 is the best) places it in the same category as other countries in Eastern Europe, the Middle East and elsewhere in Latin America.[36] Recent scandals have, unfortunately, uncovered some lawmakers who have been treating themselves to lavish dinners and events at the taxpayer's expense. According to private sources, public works projects often require mysterious "fees" to be paid to stakeholders before they can move forward, and over 7% of citizens in Rio report having had to pay bribes to the local police.[37]

As a practical matter, Brazil's corruption issues are rooted in longstanding social norms that plague some countries in the Americas. Academics and Brazil experts Timothy Power and Matthew Taylor frame these norms as a combination of weak institutions plus a sense of impunity that becomes ingrained over time.[38] At the same time, they both serve as an unlegislated tax on daily life and hurt Brazil's image abroad as a place to do business. Very recently, more public steps have been taken to address this issue by the Brazilian government, including new laws punishing domestic or international bribery, and the 2012 conviction of several aides to former President Lula, in what was the largest corruption trial in Brazilian history. A promising development is that this issue has recently become a subject of widespread social protest, and that politicians feel compelled to listen and act in response.

Will these socially innovative initiatives be enough?

For many years, a common joke among Brazilians stated that it was "the country of the future and it always will be". The truth in jest behind this statement continues to rest with Brazil's social issues. Crime, poverty and education issues are not only real daily problems for much of Brazil's population, but form global perceptions of its place in the world economic order.

The broader economic lesson of the 21st century is that social policy, when coupled with sustained economic growth, can make dramatic and fundamental changes in a country's standard of living. The lifetime of many adults has seen China transform from a country that once faced mass starvation and inept bureaucracy to one of the world's leading economic powerhouses – largely on the strength of policy interventions, ranging from agricultural reform to free-market incentives. Today, China is the world's second-largest economy, as well as its leading creditor nation, and is currently poised to overtake the United States in GDP by the year 2020.

Brazil today stands at the crossroads of a similar fundamental change in its economy, and its ascendancy as a major world power – and, in the process, as a beacon for the Latin America of the future. Its recent political administrations have shown that change is possible, by making substantial improvements in areas such as poverty levels, crime rates and access to higher education.

At the same time, Brazil's leaders realize that these recent gains are not enough, and what is needed is a more fundamental social and cultural transformation. For perhaps the first time in its modern history, such change appears possible. The key to such change is investment in education, in new approaches to policing, and in real solutions for tens of millions of low-income Brazilians.

While recognizing the current economic success of modern Brazil, from a standpoint of facts and figures, its true transformation will spring from the perceptions of its own people. China's growth, for example, has been fueled in part by the growth of a strong middle class, which includes now over 100 million people. Many young Chinese today no longer recognize the China of their parents, and take for granted that they live in a country that produces high-quality goods and provides economic opportunity. In much the same way, Brazilians must come to see the country they love as a model for the rest of the world, and this will require social as well as economic change. Brazilian social innovation programs are being replicated all over the world and are an example to follow. It is time to celebrate them.

The time is ripe for a new Brazil, where beyond economics lies a Brazil Dream – which we discussed in the book's introduction, and will explore in more detail in its conclusion – that captures Brazilians' aspiration of a just and ecological society that supports a wealth of social aims as well as financial ones.

7
In Search of a Role on the Global Stage

One of the greatest symbols of Brazil's new global prominence came from the revelation that the South American nation was one of the most targeted countries of the United States' electronic spying program that caused scandal across the world in 2013. Brazilian President Dilma Rousseff, whose own email communications reportedly had been monitored, canceled a state visit she was due to make to Washington at the end of the year. Unafraid to stand her ground, President Rousseff has been one of the most vocal leaders in expressing outrage at the United States.

As was the case for Europe and other Washington allies, United States spying on Brazil was not motivated by immediate security threats. The purpose was to keep an eye on one of the world's most strategic rising powers, whose moves and decisions could affect developments in areas such as trade, energy and global governance. Brazil is an active player in the G20 and a founding member of the BRICS group of emerging powers. It is making its presence felt at the United Nations, the IMF and the World Bank. Its latest victory came in May 2013, with the appointment of Roberto Carvalho de Azevêdo as Director General of the World Trade Organization (WTO), two years after another Brazilian national, José Graziano da Silva, landed the top job at the UN Food and Agriculture Organization.

The long road toward becoming a great power

"Brazil is poised to become one of the 21st century's great powers," President Lula told the Agence France-Presse toward the end of his second presidential term. Very few countries in the world, if any, can claim to have experienced such a spectacular rise in global prominence in such a short period of time. Two decades ago, the country was still battling with Argentina for regional leadership and largely remained at the periphery of world affairs. Brazil's economic boom throughout the 2000s explains much of the world's renewed interest in South America's largest nation. Yet, the country's global political "upgrading" came first and foremost as the result of an extremely pro-active diplomatic agenda led by its successive presidents, starting with Fernando Henrique Cardoso, and building on the longstanding experience of its highly regarded Ministry of Foreign Affairs, known as Itamaraty, after the palace in which it is housed (Cason and Power, 2009).

While Brazil's growing international clout is indisputable, its diplomacy has also experienced a number of important setbacks in recent years. The country's efforts to obtain a permanent seat at the United Nations Security Council fell short of receiving the crucial endorsement of the United States and China. Brazilian diplomats have even struggled to receive backing from their Latin American neighbors, with Argentina and Mexico expressing resistance to the idea. The United States' move to endorse India's bid in 2012 and to ignore Brazil's was a major blow for Brasília. But Brazil's most disappointing experience was arguably its failed attempt to act as a mediator in 2010 (together with Turkey) to settle the dispute between Teheran and the international community over Iran's nuclear program. The episode cast doubt over Brasília's effective diplomatic capabilities. In other words, Brazil is not yet the "great power" it aspires to become, and its capacity to influence global outcomes remains limited.

An emerging middle power

For now, Brazil can be safely classified as a "middle power", a term whose definition is the subject of debate among scholars. Eduard Jordaan defines middle powers as "states that are neither great nor small in terms of international power, capacity and influence, and demonstrate a propensity to promote cohesion and stability in the world system" (Jordaan, 2003). More precisely, Brazil falls into the category of what Jordaan calls "emerging middle powers".[1] This refers to "semi-peripheral, materially inegalitarian and recently democratised states that demonstrate much regional influence and self-association". According to Jordaan, emerging middle powers typically opt for reformist and not radical global change, exhibit a strong regional orientation, but also seek to distance themselves from the weaker states in their region.

While not yet a "great power", Brazil is clearly a player of increasing global relevance. A vibrant democracy, which seeks to project positive values to the outside world, it has long been opposed to the use of force in international relations and has consistently promoted dialogue and cooperation as a way to solve global issues and local conflicts. As a public defender of multilateralism, it has made clear that the global governance system should be reformed in order to better reflect the shift of economic weight toward emerging nations. In the current reconfiguration of power at the global level, Brazil and other emerging countries are seen as possible purveyors of solutions and leadership.

Brazil's soft-balancing strategy

Middle powers have historically put multilateralism at the top of their diplomatic agenda, and Brazil is a prime example in this respect (Lopes, Casarões and Gama, 2013). To accelerate the shift toward a multi-polar world, middle powers tend to "adopt 'soft-balancing' measures that do not directly challenge US military preponderance but use international institutions, economic statecraft, and diplomatic arrangements to delay, frustrate, and undermine US policies" (Pape, 2005).

In this spirit, Brazil has deployed a multi-pronged strategy, through which it has been able to increase its influence and acquire greater autonomy on the global stage. As we describe in this chapter, it has (i) formed coalitions with other emerging nations to advance its interests in multilateral forums; (ii) joined top-level diplomatic groupings at the core of the global governance system; (iii) led regional integration initiatives; (iv) used inter-regional bodies to extend its global reach; and (v) positioned itself as a champion of south-south cooperation.

Figure 7.1 summarizes Brazil's current presence in multilateral institutions, high-level diplomatic groupings,[2] regional bodies and interregional groupings, all of which are further described in this chapter. As we can see, the recent past was marked by an increasing focus on engagement in coalitions with other emerging and developing countries, whose rapid development would have unthinkable only ten years ago.

Brazil's multilateral breakthrough

Brazil's diplomatic rise first became evident within the sphere of multilateral institutions, and in particular in the World Trade Organization (WTO). As one of the world's agricultural superpowers, the country has stood as one of the most vocal supporters of the Doha Development Agenda, the latest round of multilateral trade negotiations launched by the WTO in Doha (Qatar) in November 2001. To advance Brazil's offensive interests in agricultural trade liberalization,[3] Celso Amorim,

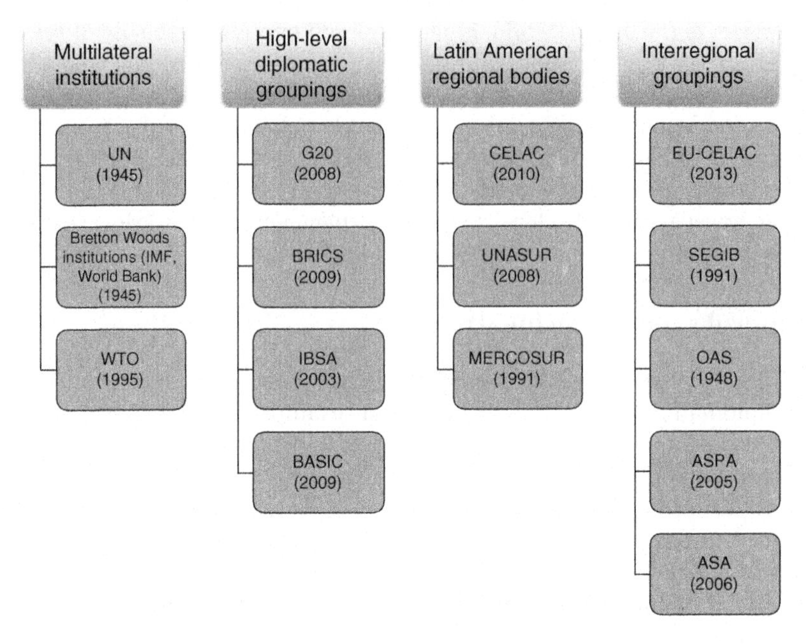

Figure 7.1 Main multilateral institutions, diplomatic groupings and Latin American regional bodies in which Brazil participates.

Note: Institutions which include only emerging and developing countries are indicated in bold. The date of creation or establishment is indicated in parenthesis.

in his former role as Minister of External Relations under President Lula, engaged in a bold negotiation strategy, which has transformed the way global trade talks are conducted within the WTO (Da Motta Veiga, 2004). In 2003, Brazil created and took the leadership (with India) of a coalition of 23 developing countries known as the G20[4] to jointly negotiate an ambitious deal on agriculture as an alternative to the framework proposed by the United States and the European Union. The creation of this new "Global South" coalition fundamentally changed the balance of power between developed and developing countries in the WTO. Notably, it prompted the spectacular breakdown of the fifth WTO Ministerial Conference in Cancún (Mexico) in September 2003.

While the G20 experience was not successful in obtaining significant concessions from the advanced economies, it propelled Brazil into the ranks of the top players in the WTO. Together with India, Brazil is the only emerging country to have been included in every new group of core negotiating states (such as the "Group of 4", the "Five Interested Parties" and the "Group of 6"), that were established to supplant the "old quad" (Canada, the European Union, Japan and the United States) that used to dominate negotiations behind the scenes. Brazil is also one of the most intensive users of the WTO dispute settlement system. Over the last decade, it has won landmark disputes against the United States and the European Union over their heavily subsidized and trade-distorting cotton and sugar regimes.

The strategy of siding with other emerging countries has been successfully replicated in another major multilateral forum, the UN climate change negotiations. The landmark 2009 UN Climate Change Conference in Copenhagen was marked by the emergence of a new bloc of emerging powers (Brazil, South Africa, India and China), referred to as the BASIC countries, which committed to act jointly and to resist any proposals that would be detrimental to their interests and those of the developing world. Their influence in Copenhagen was such that the United States was forced to negotiate the final Copenhagen Accord directly with them. While the four do not agree on all aspects of the negotiations, they continue to meet separately and to speak with one voice in climate change talks. Through its active participation in the group, Brazil has firmly established itself as a force to be reckoned with in shaping future global climate change initiatives (Qi, 2011).

IBSA: The club of rising democracies

The idea of creating coalitions of emerging states to influence multilateral negotiations has its roots in a wider, more institutionalized process initiated in 2003 by Brazil and two other rising powers, going by the name of IBSA, or the "India, Brazil and South Africa Dialogue Forum". Formally established by the Brasília Declaration of June 2003, IBSA (http://www.ibsa-trilateral.org/) describes itself as "a coordinating mechanism amongst three emerging countries, three multiethnic and multicultural democracies, which are determined to contribute to the construction of a new international architecture, to bring their voices together on global issues and to deepen their ties in various areas".

In its ten years of existence, IBSA has held five leaders' summits and led technical exchanges in the areas of agriculture, energy, science, technology and trade, while attempting to coordinate policy positions on global issues. In successive declarations, IBSA has emphasized its objective to push for a comprehensive reform of the United Nations – in particular the Security Council – in order to give a greater voice to developing countries on global political and security matters. As such, Brazil's participation in the tripartite coalition represents a key stepping stone in its strategy to obtain a permanent seat on the UN Security Council.

Faced with growing competition from other similar diplomatic initiatives, the IBSA experience has struggled to receive proper attention, both within and outside the group. The cancelation of IBSA's tenth anniversary summit – initially planned to take place in New Delhi in June 2013, but postponed due to "scheduling issues" – does not bode well for the future of the coalition, although its unique role in facilitating people-to-people ties between three of the world's biggest "rising democracies" makes it worth keeping.[5]

BRICS: Pushing for a multi-polar world

Using IBSA as a springboard, Brazil's quantum leap in terms of global status and influence came from its founding role in another, better-known diplomatic group: the BRICS group of rising powers. Initially called BRIC (an acronym standing for Brazil, Russia, India and China), and later renamed BRICS, with South Africa's inclusion in 2011, the role of this increasingly formal coalition is to encourage political and economic cooperation among its member countries and to speak with a collective voice in global and multilateral settings. While the BRIC concept initially came from the investment community (Jim O'Neill at Goldman Sachs), the foreign ministers of Brazil and Russia, Celso Amorim and Sergey Lavrov, played an instrumental role in making the group a political reality and establishing it as a permanent diplomatic platform. The leaders of the four countries have met in Russia (2009), Brazil (2010), China (2011), India (2012) and South Africa (2013), and are due to meet again Brazil in 2014. The coalition has become one of the most commented-on innovations on the global political scene.

The logic of Brazil's participation in the BRICS coalition is broadly similar to that of its involvement in IBSA (Soulé-Kohndou, 2011). Although China and Russia have not explicitly supported Brazil's demand for a permanent seat on the Security Council, Brasília hopes to gain worldwide credibility by deepening its political links with these two established powers. As many commentators have noted, divergences among the five countries' national interests will make it difficult for the BRICS to articulate a common vision on global issues (Valladão, 2012). However, they are starting to demonstrate an increasing level of cooperation. At their fifth summit in March 2013 in Durban, the five leaders announced the establishment of a BRICS-led development bank (see box below) and decided to create a US$ 100 billion "Contingent Reserve Arrangement" to address possible liquidity shortages faced by emerging economies. At their previous summit in New Delhi, BRICS leaders agreed to provide credit to each other in local currencies (instead of using United States dollars) for trade, project financing, and infrastructure projects. Through these timid steps, the BRICS countries are slowly becoming more assertive and beginning to challenge the hegemony of Western powers in political and economic fields.

A BRICS Development Bank

The possibility of creating a "New Development Bank" was first discussed in the fourth BRICS summit in New Delhi in 2012. BRICS leaders formally adopted the idea the following year at their fifth summit in Durban. According to the eThekwini Declaration, the New Development Bank will aim at "mobilising resources for infrastructure and sustainable development projects in BRICS and other emerging economies and developing countries".

Designed as an alternative to major global lenders such as the IMF and the World Bank, this bank – which Brazil will play a major role in capitalizing – will focus on infrastructure, an area where South Africa's finance minister estimated that over 2 trillion Rand (US$200 billion dollars) of funding will be needed over the next 20 years. Formal negotiations are underway to establish this bank as of late 2013, with analysts estimating an initial capitalization of approximately US$50 billion.[6]

A vocal partner in the G20

In 2008, at the peak of the Global Financial Crisis, the elevation of the G20 as the "premier forum" for international economic cooperation gave Brazil – and other rising powers – a unique opportunity to weigh in on global policy debates and take a direct part in the international decision-making process. A few days before the group's second summit in London in April 2009, President Lula set the tone by commenting to the press that the crisis "was caused and encouraged by the irrational behavior of white people with blue eyes".[7] As expected, Brazil used the G20 as a platform to advance the interests of emerging and developing nations. In 2009, it fought to secure greater access to credit for poor countries whose financing capabilities were greatly affected by the global "credit crunch". In 2010, it played an influential role in the G20's decision to accelerate governance and quota reforms of the IMF and the World Bank in favor of dynamic emerging markets and developing countries. The IMF reform, whose implementation has been dragging, will make Brazil one of its top ten shareholders.

By the end of 2010, Guido Mantega, Brazil's finance minister, gained worldwide attention for denouncing a looming "currency war" fed by loose monetary policies in the United States and China's alleged currency manipulation, as discussed in more detail in Chapter 3. In the ongoing debate over the best way to tackle the euro-zone's debt crisis, Mantega has been an outspoken critic of Europe's austerity measures and their effects on the wider global economy. Another Brazilian battleground in the G20 was the defense of capital controls (such as taxes and restrictions on foreign investments) as an acceptable policy measure to manage the inflows and outflows of "hot money" in emerging markets. In 2009, Brazil began to introduce capital controls to prevent the Brazilian real from appreciating too much, prior to a policy reversal in June 2013 to stop a sharp depreciation of the currency.

Brazil and its "backyard": Striking the right balance

As the largest Latin American country, both in terms of population and economic size, Brazil has played an instrumental role in the creation and advancement of the region's main integration processes. These include the Southern Common Market (MERCOSUR), an economic and political integration project between Argentina, Brazil, Paraguay and Uruguay founded in 1991 by the Treaty of Asunción;[8] the Union of South American Nations (UNASUR), a political and economic union of 12 South American countries whose constitutive treaty was signed in 2008 in Brasília, and the Community of Latin American and Caribbean States (CELAC), a wider regional bloc of 33 states created in Mexico in 2010. All of these regional ventures enjoy strong Brazilian support. President Dilma Rousseff has made clear on several occasions that South American (and to a lesser extent Latin American) integration would constitute a top priority of her foreign policy. The focus of Brazil's regional attention has been the promotion of UNASUR, which excludes Mexico, its main political rival in Latin America. As a sign of its commitment to further political integration, Brazil has prompted UNASUR to establish a defense council to strengthen regional cooperation on security matters.

Brazil's regional leadership is far from absolute, however, and its influence is increasingly being nibbled away by the emergence of subregional initiatives with strong ideological undertones. On its left, the Venezuela-led Bolivarian Alliance for the Peoples of Our America (ALBA) brings together eight Latin American and Caribbean nations around an anti-imperialist and anti-capitalist integration platform.[9] On its right, the Pacific Alliance gathers four countries from the Pacific Coast (Chile, Colombia, Mexico and Peru) that have embraced market-friendly integration. Formally launched in June 2012, the Pacific Alliance, which represent about 36% of Latin America's GDP, has already overtaken Mercosur as the most promising regional trade bloc, although Antonio Patriota, Brazil's foreign affairs minister between 2011 and 2013, described it as merely "a marketing success" with little potential for physical integration.[10] Another symbol of the rise of Pacific Latin American countries – from which Brazil is excluded – is the growing political energy spent by Chile, Mexico and Peru to successfully advance negotiations under the Trans-Pacific Partnership, a proposed trade agreement between major Asian and American economies from the Pacific Rim, including the United States and Japan but so far excluding China.

Brasília's regional strategy requires a careful balancing act. On the one hand, it must be careful not to overplay its role as regional leader so as not to upset other its neighbors from the "barrio", such as Argentina, Chile, Colombia and Venezuela, which are increasingly ill at ease with Brazil's political, economic – and increasingly military – domination of the region. On the other hand, Brazil's global ambitions and its participation in extra-regional diplomatic groupings (e.g., IBSA, BRICS, G20) may generate resentment among its neighbors if its enhanced status does not translate into clear benefits for the region – or if it decides to reduce its regional engagement to pursue global ambitions. In addition to this quandary, Brazil, as the regional heavyweight, is increasingly expected to intervene when democracy is at stake in its neighboring countries. Brasília received strong criticism for its relative silence during the social unrest that resulted in several fatalities in Venezuela in February 2014.

Creating inter-regional links

An interesting feature of Brazil's regional policy has been the extensive use of region-to-region diplomatic initiatives as part of its global role. The country has been an active participant at the annual Ibero-American Summit of Heads of State and Governments since its first meeting in 1991. Actively promoted by Spain, which hosts its Madrid-based secretariat (Secretaría General Iberoamericana or SEGIB), this cross-regional arrangement brings together 22 Spanish and Portuguese speaking countries from Europe and Latin America (with Equatorial Guinea and the Philippines as associate members) and acts as a "Latin Commonwealth". Parallel to these meetings, Brazil hosted the first European Union-Latin America and the Caribbean Summit in Rio de Janeiro in 1999. With the creation of CELAC, this process was elevated to a formal group-to-group dialogue and the first EU-CELAC summit was held in Santiago (Chile) in 2013. While both regions are keen to celebrate their mutual cultural understanding and show a willingness to work together, a certain fatigue can be detected in these different gatherings that have produced little tangible outcomes.

Within the Western Hemisphere, Brazil is also a founding member of the Organization of American States (OAS), based in Washington, which groups all 35 nations of the Americas.[11] The world's oldest regional organization was founded in 1948 with the aim of promoting democracy, human rights, security and development. The general assembly has convened every year since 1971 and is the main decision-making body. While Brazil generally maintains positive relations with the United States, the two countries took opposite stances in the context of OAS on recent cases involving Cuba and Honduras. The creation of CELAC was largely interpreted as way for Latin American nations to gain autonomy from the United States, which finances most of OAS's budget and has traditionally utilized the organization to advance its own economic, political and security objectives in Latin America and the Caribbean (Meyer, 2013).

Three other region-to-region initiatives are worth highlighting, especially since Brazil played an instrumental role in their founding. The first one is the South American-Arab Countries Summit (ASPA), which gathers 22 heads of state and governments from the two regions and which met in Brasília (2005), Doha (2009) and Lima (2012). The same model was replicated with Africa, and in 2006 Nigeria hosted the first Africa-South America Summit (ASA). A second summit was hosted by Venezuela in 2009 and a third one in Equatorial Guinea in 2013. An interesting feature of both interregional arrangements is that Latin participation is limited to the South American sub-continent and is formally channeled through UNASUR, thereby giving Brasília a strong say over their agendas and deliberations.

Brazil's south-south agenda

By fostering greater links with two of the world's most dynamic emerging regions through the ASPA and ASA processes, Brazil is faithful to another fundamental tenet of its diplomacy: the promotion of south-south dialogue and cooperation. Since the early 2000s, the country has sought to project greater influence in the developing world. In particular, it has forged closer relations with African countries, starting with the former Portuguese colonies Angola, Mozambique and Cape Verde. During his two terms as president, Lula visited 29 African nations and more than doubled the number of Brazilian embassies on the African continent.

While Brazil holds significant investments in several African countries, and nearly all of the big Brazilian companies operating in the continent are involved in the resources sector, its presence in the region is not purely driven by economic interests (Stolte, 2012). The Brazilian government has notably emerged as a major aid donor. More than half of the Brazilian Cooperation Agency's technical cooperation resources are directed toward the continent. Giving practical effect to its discourse on Southern solidarity, Brazil has offered African countries its expertise on a wide range of development issues, including agriculture, health and anti-poverty programs. In Mozambique, the Brazilian government funded a pharmaceutical plant to produce anti-retroviral drugs against HIV/AIDS. In 2012, it established a broad strategic partnership with Angola and is now helping the country to train its army and develop its defense industry. In Kenya, the Brazilian National Development Bank (BNDES) granted US$230 million of loans for the mechanization of agriculture and the construction of roads to decongest the capital city of Nairobi.

A second focal point of Brazil's south-south diplomacy is the Middle East (Baeza, 2011, Brun, 2011). The prospects of increasing trade and investment links with Arab nations certainly constitute a key motivation for its rapprochement with the region. Beyond economic considerations, Brazil sees the Middle East as a strategic testing ground for its global political ambitions.[12] In December 2010, Brazil, which has traditionally maintained good relations with Israel, initiated a wave of recognition of the Palestinian state by Latin American countries as a way to re-balance its relationships with both parts. While the move provided a clear example of Brazil's regional and even global leadership – Palestine was recognized as a state by the UN General Assembly in November 2012 – it also infuriated Israel and the United States.

This was not the first time that Brazil made a bold move regarding the Middle East. In May 2010, in an effort to find a diplomatic solution to the longstanding standoff between Iran and Western powers over its nuclear program, Brazil and Turkey brokered a separate deal with Iran. The diplomatic maneuver, which was initially encouraged by Washington, was eventually dismissed by the United States and the European Union, despite broad support from other UN member states.

As many observers have noted, Dilma Rousseff has taken a more muted approach to foreign policy than her predecessor Lula since she assumed presidential office in 2011. Rather than pushing for greater

Brazilian presence across-the-board, she has focused on countries and regions where Brazil has immediate interests. While the first impression was that of a recentralization toward the United States, Europe and Latin America, Dilma Rousseff's travel agenda for 2013 has shown a renewed attention to Africa. In the first three months of the year, she visited Equatorial Guinea, Nigeria, South Africa and Ethiopia. Brazil's relations with the Arab world may prove more difficult to sustain over time, due to the context of instability that has marked the region since the uprisings in 2011. The eviction of former Egyptian president Mohamed Morsi in July 2013, two months after he visited Dilma Rousseff in Brasília at the Planalto presidential palace to launch a new era of Brazilian-Egyptian relations, illustrates the complexity of long-term strategic planning in this field. While more discreet and less overtly political than during the Lula years, Brazil's web of bilateral south-south relationships is likely to grow and intensify, thereby consolidating the country's status as leading power of the Global South.

Decrypting Brazil's message to the world

Brazil's soft-balancing strategy has proved immensely successful at raising the country's profile and increasing its bargaining power on the international stage. As stressed by Andrew Hurrell, "A prominent theme of the Lula years has been the search for recognition, for securing Brazil's 'sovereign presence', via an assertive and activist foreign policy, not by means of direct confrontation in the style of Chávez, but rather through engagement and negotiation within the changing circuits of global decision-making" (Hurrell, 2010b).

Brazil has pushed for, and subsequently benefited from, the emergence of formal and informal diplomatic groupings, either within the framework of multilateral institutions or in the wider context of the global governance system. By openly challenging the status quo, but without radically questioning the global order, the country has managed to maintain positive relationships with the United States and Europe, while at the same time winning the respect of its peers across the developing world.

One key difficulty, however, is determining what Brazil and its leaders want to do with its newfound global prestige and influence. While the South American giant has a greater voice than ever before, its message to the world remains unclear. The observation is valid for other rising powers as well. For Alfredo Valladão, this is explained by the simple fact that "BRICS countries want 'voice' not 'change.' They are not fighting for another 'order' but only to acquire the political tools to better defend their own national interests inside the present framework, which by the way they are not ready to be responsible for" (Valladão, 2012).

This proposition is particularly troubling in the case of Brazil. On the one hand, it is characterized by an ambitious and progressive diplomacy, which it readily uses to defend the interests of the Global South and to push for a pro-development reform of global governance institutions. On the other hand, Brazil retains the image of an inward-looking nation, which is generally reluctant to interfere in the internal affairs of other countries or to allow others to interfere in its own.

To some extent, the two positions are not incompatible. Developing countries have traditionally emphasized the importance of protecting their national sovereignty to prevent a resurrection of colonial patterns in their interactions with their old ruling powers or the United States. Yet, emerging global powers cannot ignore the inherent contradiction which comes with asking for greater influence in world affairs while constantly resorting to the principles of sovereignty and non-interference to justify inaction or to defend their own interests when global issues are at stake.

In the case of Brazil, this contradiction has become evident in both the economic and political arenas, where policy strategies oscillate between self-centered motives, sometimes at the expense of its progressive objectives, and a desire to take the lead on global issues. This brings to light the inherent tension between the globalist Brazil, which fully embraces its global role and contributes to the creation of common public goods and solutions, and the more self-contained Brazil that tends to shy away from making any moves that do not directly serve its domestic interests.

The following section looks at two areas in which the country will be increasingly expected to clarify its position and make a more decisive contribution to the shaping of global solutions. One is world trade, and in particular reforming the framework of policies and rules which govern trade and investment flows. The other is the protection of human rights, and in particular addressing the complex dilemmas that the international community has to face when deciding whether to intervene – or not intervene – to stop atrocities taking place in other parts of the world.

Protectionism or open trade?

The appointment of Roberto Azevêdo as the new head of the WTO is symptomatic of Brazil's duality in trade matters. Azevêdo's victory over the candidate proposed by Mexico had a special significance, marking

Brazil's ascendancy over its main Latin American contender for regional and global influence. The rivalry between Brazil and Mexico is not only economic; it is also a rivalry between two political orientations. While the Mexican government supports open markets and close relations with the United States, Brasília favors a more pro-development approach and seeks to accelerate the move toward a multi-polar world.

For many observers the choice of a Brazilian diplomat came as a surprise given the country's reputation as a champion of trade protectionism. According to Global Trade Alert, the country has implemented 56 trade-restrictive measures since November 2008, many of which have directly hurt exports from other developing nations. Only eight other countries have resorted to protectionist measures more often. The world's seventh economy ranks 67th (out of 75) in the 2013 edition of the Open Market Index by the International Chamber of Commerce, making it the most protectionist country among G20 and BRICS members.

However, as stated above, Brazil is a historical supporter of the Doha Development Agenda. In January 2011, Brazil's trade minister joined his counterparts from India and South Africa to call for the conclusion of multilateral trade talks as early as possible. During the G20 summit in Los Cabos in June 2012, President Rousseff proposed to re-open the Doha Round by 2014, but the idea gained little traction among other G20 leaders. Together with Gita Wirjawan, the former Indonesian Trade Minister, Azevêdo played an instrumental role in sealing the WTO's first global trade deal in its 18 years of existence during its ninth Ministerial Conference in Bali in December 2013. The agreement, known as the "Bali Package", covers several sub-sets of the Doha Development Agenda.

Contrary to what one might think, the North-South divide was not the main force behind Azevêdo's appointment as head of the WTO. He clearly enjoyed the backing of BRICS nations, Portuguese-speaking countries and a wide range of developing nations. But according to Matias Spektor, an Associate Professor at the Getulio Vargas Foundation, Azevêdo was also the preferred candidate of the European Commission and of many European countries. In Washington, his appointment was well received, in spite of the official support given by the United States administration to the Mexican candidate, which was mainly motivated by domestic politics.[13] Beyond the personal qualities of the Brazilian diplomat, the broad support (or at least lack of formal opposition) enjoyed by Azevêdo is partly explained by the tacit wish of the United States and the European Union to have Brazil confront its contradictions regarding trade policy matters. In that sense, the election of Azevêdo may be a Pyrrhic victory for Brazil. As Director General of the WTO, he will no longer represent the interests of the Brazilian government but will clearly be expected to help build bridges between the positions of Brazil and those of its trading partners.

Mercosur's internal disputes provide another illustration of Brazil's ambiguous position on trade matters. Two decades after its inception, many observers feel that Mercosur was barely successful in creating a common market among its members through the progressive establishment of a free-trade zone, a customs union, and greater coordination of their macroeconomic policies. Trade between members of Mercosur has increased, but still represents a low fraction of their total trade. The numerous exceptions to the association's trade rules, and their frequent violations, have led some practitioners to describe Mercosur as an "incomplete" customs union – or sometimes, even worse, as "irrelevant". In spite of its natural position of leadership, Brazil was unable to solve many of these internal disputes and even took protectionist measures itself, prompting the *Financial Times* to ask: "If Brazil cannot boost regional trade, how can it boost trade globally?"[14] In a world where trading blocs compete for preferences through bilateral, regional and inter-regional trade deals, Mercosur (including Brazil) remains isolated. Outside of Latin America, the only comprehensive free trade agreements Mercosur has signed with third parties are with Egypt, Israel and Palestine.

While Brazil is prompt to erect trade barriers to protect its industrial sector, it turns into unabashed advocate of free trade when it comes to agriculture. For years, it has advocated for an end to the trade and price-distorting subsidies of advanced economies, a battle which Brazil was easily able to drape in Southern rhetoric. Yet, the position of Brasília is not always as pro-development as it may seem. The country, which accounts for 19% of the world's arable land, is one of the dominant exporters of food commodities for international markets. As such, it is *de facto* one of the main regulators of the global food supply. However, Brazil's response to the challenge of global food insecurity, which directly concerns 1 billion people around the world and threatens to affect another billion, has been largely inaudible. In the G20, it sided with the United States and China to water down France's proposed communiqué on agriculture, which included proposals to reduce the use of biofuels and export controls.[15] Together with the United States, it fiercely opposed attempts to introduce price control mechanisms in agricultural markets. While Brazil has made impressive strides in reducing food insecurity at home, it is not clear whether its agricultural commercial interests are always compatible with the interests of net food-importing countries around the world.

Protecting human rights or sovereignty?

Likewise, Brazil's position toward humanitarian intervention has been difficult to gauge in recent years.

Brazilian diplomats regard the respect of sovereignty, non-interventionism and the peaceful resolution of conflicts as their sacrosanct guiding principles, a longstanding position which partly explains Brazil's abstention from voting the March 2011 UN resolution that approved the establishment of a no-fly zone over Libya as well as "all necessary measures" (excluding foreign occupation) to protect Libyan civilians under attack by Muammar el-Qaddafi. The subsequent perception that the North Atlantic Treaty Organization (NATO) went beyond its mandate through the excessive use of force, subsequently reinforced Brazil's conviction that humanitarian intervention is in reality a cover for Western powers to enforce imperialist policies of regime change. This mistrust is one of the major reasons behind Brasília's opposition to any kind of military intervention to resolve the Syrian crisis. In 2011, Brasília even voted against the imposition of UN sanctions against the Syrian regime at the UN Security Council. In line with its BRICS counterparts, Brazil has since then called for a peaceful transition through a broad national dialogue between Syrian President Bashar al-Assad, the opposition and all sectors of Syrian society.

However, Brazil is not the unconditional defender of non-intervention and national sovereignty, which some observers like to describe.[16] The country has long assumed a leadership role in the United Nations Stabilization Mission in Haiti (MINUSTAH), a peacekeeping mission directly involved with the establishment of a transitional government after Haiti's coup d'état of 2004. The Brazilian army has led the mission's military component and the force is under Brazilian command. Brasília was willing to infringe the principle of non-interference as it saw this involvement as an opportunity to establish its regional leadership as a military power, a position criticized as a new "Brazilian imperialism" by some civil society organizations. Since 2011, Brazil has also led the Maritime Task Force of the United Nations Interim Force (UNIFIL) in Lebanon.

For many observers, the somewhat inconsistent positioning of Brasília over matters concerning human rights and sovereignty should prompt it to rethink its longstanding deference to the principle of non-intervention, and become a more energetic advocate of democracy and human rights. Conectas, a Brazilian human rights organization, which actively monitors Brazil's foreign policy, has regularly denounced the passivity of Brasília regarding the massive violations of human rights in Syria since 2011. The idea here is not that Brazil should transform itself into a belligerent power, or blindly follow the United States and European nations into military intervention campaigns against unfriendly governments. The call is for Brasília to "present concrete alternatives and set an example through its own actions".[17] As Conectas' Camila Asano argues, Brazil "is critical of the selective and somewhat undemocratic functioning of the international and regional bodies, but it has rarely followed up with a more purposeful or constructive posture".

To demonstrate that its reluctance toward foreign intervention is more the result of a genuine concern over the negative consequences of the use of force rather than a covert means of defending its own sovereignty against possible future interferences, Brazil's diplomacy has pioneered an innovative idea that could have strong repercussions going forward. During her opening speech to the UN General Assembly in September 2011, President Rousseff argued that military deployments for humanitarian purposes should be held responsible for the unwanted damage they provoke, and that better mechanisms were needed to keep such damage to a minimum – a concept she referred to as "responsibility while protecting" (RwP). Presented as a complement to the "responsibility to protect" (R2P) doctrine adopted by the United Nations in 2005, RwP highlights the need for those undertaking humanitarian intervention to consider alternative measures first, to take extra care when using military intervention to protect civilians, and to report continually to the United Nations Security Council.

The Brazilian concept of RwP represents a very welcome contribution at a time when military interventionism is increasingly being criticized as an unsatisfactory solution, which brings more harm than good if left unchecked. However, it is still a work in progress. The idea has been judged by Western powers as too restrictive, potentially blocking any possibility of intervention in the future. Moreover, the concept is yet to receive the backing of other emerging powers. Indeed, the Syrian crisis has exacerbated the divergence between them. In the face of opposition from Russia and China, Brazil was unable to include any reference to RwP in BRICS declarations. As several observers have noted, Brazil seems today less keen to pursue the development of RwP, or at least not pursue it as vigorously as before. For Oliver Stuenkel, from the Getulio

Vargas Foundation, the "enigmatic retreat" of Brazil (as diplomats in New York privately describes it) may frustrate its future attempts to act as an agenda-setter because of a general uncertainty about Brazil's willingness to follow-up and withstand the initial criticism that its original contribution has elicited.[18]

Defining Brazil's future global agenda

Brazil's new role in world affairs offers an intriguing paradox. The country is both praised for its role as a champion of multilateralism and as a leading voice of the Global South as well as criticized for being overly protectionist and a staunch defender of its domestic interests as a sovereign state. While the same can be said of many of today's rising powers, the contrast is particularly stark in the case of Brazil.

As it gains influence in world affairs, thanks to its diplomatic activism or simply as a result of its ever-growing economic weight, Brazil inevitably raises new expectations. As the saying goes, "with power comes responsibility". To sustain its move to global power status, the country and its leaders will be increasingly expected to contribute to the design of the common good. In this context, the challenge for Brazil will be to identify and formulate "third way" alternatives that move away from the Western-dominated intellectual framework while going beyond the narrow defense of sovereignty and national interest that characterizes most of today's emerging powers.

Looking forward, Brazil's search for a role on the global stage should not only be about winning seats, seeking status, and defying established powers just for the sake of earning their respect. Rather, Brazilian leaders should focus on making an impact and presenting alternative means to secure peace and spread prosperity that differ from those championed by the West, which have evidently reached their limits.

The areas in which it could make a decisive contribution are plenty. Will Brazil find a way to broker a deal between advanced and developing economies to reform global trading rules and finally bring the WTO Doha round to a successful conclusion? Will it use its new status as an agricultural power to help resolve the problem of global food security? Will it find a role to play as part of the international community to address today's most pressing political and security issues, whether at a regional or global level? Will it further elaborate and promote its innovative "Responsibility while Protecting" concept to help the international community better approach acute crises and prevent massive human rights violations around the world?

In all these fields, Brazil's biggest resource is its own wealth of experience as a developing economy – which has gone through good times and bad times – a multicultural society and a vibrant democracy. One area in which Brazil has begun to take the lead is the right of privacy on the internet and electronic communications. Following the spying scandal of 2013, Brazil and Germany jointly presented a draft resolution to the UN General Assembly calling internationally recognized rights to privacy and urging an end to global electronic espionage. Brazilian leaders announced the hosting of an international summit on internet governance in 2014, with the participation of government, industry, civil society and academia. The meeting could prove a key test for Brazil's future capabilities to become a global agenda-setter and rule-maker.

8
Looking for Answers

The previous chapters of this book have shown some of the huge progress that Brazil has achieved on the political, economic and social fronts. Recently, however, the notion of a "winning Brazil" has become a hard sell to many of its citizens. In June 2013, for the first time in decades, hundreds of thousands of Brazilians took to the streets to express their frustration with the growing mismatch between rising living costs, high taxes and decaying public services. Worried that the country might be stuck in a middle-income trap, Brazil's weekly publication *Exame* touched a nerve by asking on its cover in August 2013: "Will we ever be rich?" As authors, we were frankly taken by surprise by this unprecedented wave of protests and pessimism, along with many outside observers.

To get a better grasp of the big challenges facing Brazil in the years to come, we felt it was important for us to get the opinions of experts, decision-makers and ordinary practitioners from business, academia, government and civil society, on the country's recent accomplishments and its future prospects. In an era of instant information, it made sense to put Brazil's cyclical difficulties into perspective. Numbers never tell the entire story, and we wanted to incorporate the views of opinion leaders to get a greater understanding of how Brazil views itself, where Brazil wants to go, and which economic model will take Brazil to the developed world.

Methodology

With the support of the Inter-American Development Bank,[1] we conducted a series of interviews between July and October 2013, through which we invited mainly Brazilians and some foreign stakeholders from different genders, ages and background to share their opinions about Brazil's strengths and challenges.

Thirty-four interviews were conducted through a questionnaire sent by email from mid-July to mid-September 2013.[2] The remaining 11 interviews were conducted by the authors, in order to obtain a more intuitive reaction from respondents.

The questionnaire included four questions around Brazil's achievements, Brazil's economic model and foreign policy:

1. In your view, what are the main accomplishments of Brazil over the last decade?
2. What should Brazil seek to achieve/improve over the next decade, in general and in your own field?
3. Where should Brazil focus its investments and foreign policy in the world: South America, Latin America, BRICS, Asia, Africa, Europe or the United States? Mention three and rank them according to their priority.
4. What should be Brazil's economic model: more open or closed trade, more state in the economy or more free market, more private-public partnerships or not, more social policies or not?

This questionnaire was sent to close to 100 individuals. The overall response rate (including written responses to the questionnaire and interviews conducted in person) was high, with a total of 45 answers received.

We have classified our respondents according to seven broad categories: (i) business: senior executives and middle managers from Brazilian corporations and banks; (ii) government: Brazilian civil servants working at the municipal, state or federal level, or individuals working for inter-governmental organizations; (iii) academia: faculty and researchers from leading universities in Brazil and abroad; (iv) Brazilian and foreign civil society: individuals working in think-tanks, business organizations, and other non-governmental and not-for-profit organizations (NGOs); (v) Brazilian media; (vi) Brazilian low-income workers; and (vii) Brazilian students. Several of our interviewees fall between various categories. For example, some business or civil society respondents had previous public sector experience at high levels of government. In such cases, the categorization was made according to the position held at the time of the interview.

About half of our respondents (25) originate from the business sector, ranging from middle managers (four of them were young professionals who had just joined Cornell University's Master of Business Administration (MBA) program) to founding board members. Seven are academics, most of whom had lived in Brazil but now lived in Europe or in the United States. Six are members of civil society and work either in think-tanks or NGOs, including business organizations. Only four are government officials. It is worth noting that 2014 is election year in Brazil, which may explain the rather low number of responses from public sector representatives.

Our respondents include 34 men and 11 women. It should be noted that most of the interviewees selected belong to Brazil's political and economic elite, or the country's upper middle class. To obtain a more balanced view, we made a special effort to reach out to people at the bottom of the pyramid through interviews with two Brazilian low-income workers. We also interviewed two undergraduate students enrolled at Cornell University through the Brazilian government's *Ciência sem fronteiras* program, which provides scholarships to Brazilian students, predominantly in the fields of science, technology, engineering and mathematics.

All of our interviewees are Brazilian nationals, but 11 of them who, as mentioned above, have lived in Brazil for periods ranging from a few months to a couple of years. It was important for the authors to get the views from "inside" Brazil and that's why all persons interviewed either lived in Brazil or were very familiar with the country.

The result is not a quantitative survey, but a set of qualitative answers that we have analyzed and classified according to the topics that, sometimes, were spontaneously cited by interviewees in their answers. The sample of people interviewed is not large and representative enough to give a scientific value to the findings. In particular, the over-representation of respondents from the business sector has inevitably influenced the general tone of the answers we received. We believe, however, that in their entirety the results provide interesting leads that will need to be verified in further research.

Below, we summarize the answers, identifying major agreements as well as areas which still generate debate. In order to keep the confidentiality of some of the interviewees, we have highlighted some quotes and identified the person with the category where they belong.[3]

A basis for consensus: Brazil's accomplishments

Several points of agreement emerge among the interviewees, both with respect to Brazil's achievements and needed improvements. Beyond the political divide between those who support the current administration and those who take a more critical stance, there is a great deal of consensus in several areas like the reduction of poverty, the rise of the middle class, the success of Brazil in sustaining macroeconomic stability and, to a lesser extent, the consolidation of democracy and Brazil's rise on the global stage. Looking to the future, interviewees generally agreed that Brazil should seek to balance economic growth with social inclusion. In order to achieve that, the overall feeling was that Brazil needs to improve the private sector productivity by improving its education system, reducing the "Brazil cost" and upgrading its infrastructure.

Key achievements of the past decade: poverty reduction, macroeconomic stability, democracy and global status

Two-thirds of the respondents to our written questionnaire cited the **reduction of poverty** and its corollaries – the rise of the middle class and the fall in inequalities – as one of the country's biggest accomplishments in the past ten years. Several figures were quoted to prove this trend. One interview noted that the Human Development Index of Brazilian municipalities went from 0.493 in 1991 to 0.727 in 2010, that formal employment grew from 42% in 2001 to 55% in 2011 and that education was universalized for children aged 7 to 14 years. Some interviewees highlighted the positive economic effects resulting from the arrival of these new consumers. For one corporate leader, a key accomplishment was having "30 (in fact, there are 35) million people who lived in poverty entering the consumer market and becoming part of the country's middle class". One respondent from civil society emphasized the human dimension of what can be described as Brazil's "social debt". She noted however that the new middle class was "still vulnerable" and "include[s] people who live in poor housing, with no sanitation, and often dangerous areas, such as the hills where the slums are built", before concluding that "[the reduction of poverty] is a big achievement considering that the situation before was even more critical".

About a third of the respondents highlighted the key role of targeted social policies – such as *Bolsa Família* and *Minha Casa, Minha Vida* – for combating poverty in Brazil, a country with one the highest rates of inequality in the world. As one member of civil society pointed out, "no matter how high our GDP is, the 10% poorest Brazilians gets only 1.2% of the country total income and this is simply not right. Having this in mind, Brazil needs social policies: many of them and in different areas." One public official noted that "the success of some social programs, [such] as the internationally praised *Bolsa Família*, as well as the increase in the number of children and adolescents with access to basic education has ensured an important advance in the struggle against absolute poverty and hunger. In fact, *Bolsa Família* and the access to basic education are interconnected events, as school attendance is a conditionality of the cash transfer system."

The **macroeconomic stability** was the second most cited accomplishment, with over half of the interviewees making an explicit reference to the progress achieved in this area. Many of them referred to the sustained GDP growth, the control of inflation, the rise of private consumption and a historically low unemployment rate "with several regions having reached full employment". One respondent from a Brazilian business organization placed emphasis on external indicators: "We managed to build a strong level of foreign exchange reserves, our vulnerability was reduced, [leading] international financial markets to lend us money at lower interest rates. Our foreign trade has grown remarkably, new commercial partnerships were forged, and we were able to gain international respectability as a result of our new economic position." One civil society respondent added that the "Brazilian industry has acquired a high level of efficiency, diversification and technological innovation". One young interviewee also stressed that "Brazil has a very solid and well-structured banking system". The fact that the country proved to be resilient during the peak years of the world recession was considered as an extraordinary economic and social performance. This appraisal was particularly strong among the older generation, who are still haunted by the experience of hyperinflation in the 1980s and therefore prioritize macroeconomic stability. There was also a relatively strong consensus about the need for open trade and free market policies but, as we will discuss below, some of the views were more nuanced in this area, with some respondents telling us that the state should keep a role in regulating the economy.

Another major achievement, cited by a third of respondents, was **the consolidation of democracy**. Several interviewees underlined how remarkably "smooth" was "the transition between the right-wing government of [President] Fernando Henrique Cardoso and the left-wing government of [President] Lula". After 21 years of dictatorship (until 1985), it was the first time that the country experienced a political change of this kind. As noted by one interviewee, Brazil has not witnessed any evidence of fraud in recent elections, which means that "the most important tool for real democracy (elections) is in place and working well". One expert pointed out the ability of President Lula and President Dilma to govern in a "fair way", by being inclusive in the way they relate to other political actors. One consultant for an inter-governmental body argued that "having the Workers' Party leading the Federal Government for so long is, in a fact, a democratic accomplishment in itself". The June 2013 demonstrations were also considered by seven interviewees as a major step in the strengthening of the Brazilian democracy. For one business leader, "protesting is part of the role of a democratic civil society and hopefully it will help to shape Brazil's agenda for the future". One young professional stressed that "the government [was pushed by the protests] to actively listen to the public's opinion and this is a great accomplishment for Brazil".

Although we expected more, surprisingly, only a handful of our interviewees chose to mention the **rise of Brazil on the international stage** as one of the striking accomplishments of the last decade. Only one interviewee – a former government official – referred to the major role played by Brazil in the G20, the IMF and the United Nations, and highlighted the recent appointment of a Brazilian diplomat, Roberto Azevêdo, as the new head of the World Trade Organization.

Brazil's most pressing challenges for the future: improve education, infrastructure and reduce *Brazil cost*

There were also several areas of agreement regarding what Brazil should be doing in terms of looking to the future.

One corporate leader offered a blueprint for the country's national project, which resonated well with many of the responses we received: "Brazil must **balance economic growth and social development**, leveraging its internal market, natural resources and industrial footprint (which has lost significance over the last two decades, but is still relevant) to increase wealth generation and distribution".

Two-third of our interviewees insisted on the fact that **education** is the most important challenge facing Brazil in the years to come, and one of the key factors **to increase the productivity in the private sector**. All demanded a tangible improvement of the quality and efficiency of the educational system, with better use of resources, a focus on primary and secondary education, better trained teachers, and improved infrastructure of schools in general. The need to improve the university system was also emphasized. *Ciência sem fronteiras* (which we described further in Chapter 6) is recognized by several interviewees as a positive initiative. Two respondents stressed the need for the state to work in partnership with companies and academic institutions to prepare the workforce of the future. In light of the important shortages of skilled labor faced by Brazilian firms, one senior business executive argued that the new generation of Brazilian professionals would benefit from more university exchanges in other countries as well as more language courses, starting from primary school. As one member of civil society emphasized, the issue of education also has far-reaching implications for the future of the country: "I believe education is the basis of a society that questions standards, fights for [its] rights, and chooses [its] leaders well".

Another key challenge, cited by 21 of our interviewees, related to the urgent need for Brazil to **upgrade its infrastructure**, through the improvement of ports, airports, roads, railways, public transportation and sewage. To frame the discussion, one respondent from civil society noted that in order to secure 5% annual growth, Brazil needs close to BRL300 billion (about US$128bn) of investment annually. 16 respondents considered that public private partnerships (PPPs) could be an effective way to meet these needs, although some also noted that the implementation of such partnerships may raise practical problems, as we further explore in the next part of this chapter.

As a third priority area, 16 respondents stressed that the country has to make enormous efforts to improve the business environment and **reduce the "Brazil cost"** (see Chapter 4), which one interviewee described as a "huge barrier" for the private sector "to produce and supply goods at competitive prices". Beyond education and infrastructure gaps, which also explain part of the "Brazil cost", several respondents noted that Brazil needs to reduce corruption (cited 13 times) and to launch a comprehensive reform of the state (cited 10 times). Further reforms in the areas of taxation (cited 14 times), the electoral system (cited 7 times), labor laws (cited 6 times), the pension system (cited 3 times) were mentioned as key priorities. Some respondents also emphasized the need to promote the rule of law by ensuring the predictability of policies and regulations (cited 3 times) and to improve the management of public institutions and government, as well as to enhance their transparency and accountability (cited 3 times).

Finally, two other challenges mentioned by respondents included improving the country's health system (cited 10 times) and securing public safety (cited 6 times).

Key points for debate: the role of state in the economy and Brazil's international focus

While there was a relatively strong consensus about the country's recent accomplishments and most pressing challenges, our survey also revealed a variety of viewpoints on specific questions which are central to Brazil's democratic debate. First, a key discussion relates to the role of the state in the economy, and whether Brazil should fully embrace free-market policies or seek to preserve a proactive role for the government in the economy. A second area which steered debate revolves around PPPs: while they are widely considered as an attractive solution for meeting the country's infrastructure needs, several voices also warn against existing pitfalls in their practical implementation. Two other heated topics were whether Brazil's diplomatic and outward investment efforts should focus on developed countries or the "Global South", and whether President Fernando Henrique Cardoso (1995–2002) or President Lula (2003–2010) should take the most credit for Brazil's recent economic and social achievements. Finally, a controversial issue related to the country's social policies (further described in Chapter 6). While many celebrate their achievements, some believe they still carry many flaws and should be either substantially improved or phased out entirely.

The following section examines each of these five areas and highlights some of the main arguments raised by respondents in their answers.

What should be the role of the state in the economy?

How to strike the right balance between state intervention and free markets is a question that every country has to face, and which we further explored in Chapter 2 and other parts of this book. Our respondents shared a variety of views on what exactly should be the role of the Brazilian state in the country's economy.

One economist made a plea for caution:

> Brazil is not ready for economic openness in the short run. The vast majority of Brazilian companies lack the business management acumen necessary to compete with multinational companies. Brazil must therefore seek for a balance between protection of the national industry and enough external competition to stimulate progress. Alternatively, private-public partnerships, as well as the current policy of supporting the creation of big companies, (...) might be an alternative for those few markets in which Brazil is in better position to compete.

Many interviewees disagreed with this vision. 20 respondents believed that Brazil needs to embrace open trade, with 16 of them adding that Brazil's economic potential can only be unleashed through a diminution of the state and free-market reforms. As one respondent from civil society framed it: "The model of the state subsidizing the growth of companies instead of letting them rely on market forces needs to be seriously reviewed." This opinion was particularly prevalent among the young managers we surveyed. One of them argued that tariffs on imported manufactured goods should be slowly reduced in order to force domestic companies to become more competitive and innovative. Another frequent criticism related to Brazil's high levels of taxation (mentioned 14 times), which were similar to those of OECD countries although the quality of public services continued to lag behind.

In the same vein, one senior business executive stated: "[Brazil should have] a market driven economy, where the state focuses [on] guaranteeing the rule of law for its citizens and corporations, improving its efficiency, and establishing the necessary conditions for sustainable investment and economic development." This position was shared by another interviewee from a prominent business organization who "support[s] the concept of a state with a free market, acting with transparency and in partnership with the private sector" while stressing the importance of controlling public spending and lowering taxes.

By contrast, 11 respondents believed that Brazil should strike the right balance between free-markets and state intervention, but still with greater emphasis on the former. They often insisted on the crucial role of the state and public institutions in creating the right environment for boosting economy activity through investment in education, infrastructure and health. The role of government for sustaining demand was also mentioned. For a senior governmental official, "the role of the private sector should be expanded, with the government focusing more on the creation of stimuli". Another public official highlighted the need for "a strong but not huge state", noting also that "Brazil has made significant progress in fostering strong institutions, but corruption is still an issue and regulations should be more predictable". According to this respondent, two key goals of the state were "to ensure competition through a reliable and strong anti-trust agency, such as CADE [Brazil's Administrative Council for Economic Defense]" and "simplifying procedures for patents and strengthening INPI [Brazil's National Industrial Property Institute], the agency responsible for intellectual property".

On a separate note, stressing the importance of public policies for strengthening the country's private sector, another interviewee called for "clearer and more open and proactive immigration policy to attract talents, specially qualified workers in key sectors where we face shortage".

Are PPPs the solution for the country's infrastructure needs?

As stated in Chapter 5, Brazil will need to devote tremendous efforts to increase public investment in education, health, urban transportation and infrastructure at large in order to overcome the bottlenecks that continue to prevent its further rise as a world economic power. In many cases, these investments will also require capital from private sources, and PPPs are often presented as a way to combine the skills and resources of both the public and private sectors.

As mentioned above, 16 of our interviewees, government and business included, saw PPPs as a way to overcome meet the country's gaps in infrastructure. Nevertheless, some of them raised important concerns about the way these have been implemented in Brazil. As a Brazilian professor noted, "PPPs are an interesting model but their execution has been very slow in Brazil. Several bids are still under discussion and development."

One respondent from civil society considered that "the use of PPPs to develop infrastructure is a solution that should be explored, but it requires the government to ensure transparency and, in addition to economic viability, all the rights of those involved in the contract".

Another concern related to the risks of corruption associated with PPPs, particularly during the public auctions and subsequent awarding processes. One respondent from a leading business organization strongly insisted on the importance of "transparency", "clear and well defined rules" and "good public governance" to implement such partnerships.

Beyond the nature of each arrangement, it is also the scope of PPPs, which is at stake. For a former governmental official, now in the business sector,

> a new step should be taken by applying successful models [of public-private partnerships] – as in the case of airports – to [more areas, such as] daycares, prisons, health, defense, integrated transport infrastructure, environment, or other sectors with structural deficiencies, in which the lack of resources and agility prevents the public sector to bear alone the enormous changes that need to be launched and implemented.

One corporate leader was of the view that "the investment can and should be private, but the overall conditions to enable them must be put in place by the state, including clear and stable rules and adequate return on capital. While he believed that "public-private partnership can be the way to go", he also emphasized that Brazil's development process should first and foremost build upon "private investment and capital markets".

Does this mean that Brazil should engage in a new wave of privatizations? From the answers we received, it does not seem so. Only 4 respondents said that privatizations should be favored over PPPs. One interviewee argued that "the state has a role to play in the economy as a regulator, but not as a service provider". The underlying idea was that "services provided by private companies are of higher quality than the public ones".

Furthermore, one member from civil society noted that the inequality gap in Brazil was precisely due to "unequal access to health and education". In that sense, she feared that privatized, market-based delivery systems for basic social services and urban infrastructure could exacerbate income inequality by providing fewer and worse services to the poor.

Brazil's global projection: Should it head north or south?

In Chapter 7, we described the rise of Brazil on the global stage and the ability of Brasília to establish enduring relations with countries and leaders from all regions of the world. When asked to tell us which countries or regions should be the focus of Brazil's future diplomatic and economic investment efforts, the experts we surveyed came up with a particularly diverse set of answers.

A total of 23 respondents said the United States should be part of Brazil's top three priorities, which represents the highest rate of the survey. However, it is interesting to note that only seven respondents placed it as the top priority. For one senior corporate executive, "the most natural business and geopolitical partner for Brazil is the United States. Unfortunately for both countries, this partnership has never realized its full potential. It should be the first priority." This opinion was shared by other interviewees, who also see a linkage between Brazil's strategy of pushing for South American integration and its relative disinterest for the United States and Europe. As one business leader noted, "its Latin American geography makes it natural and necessary for Brazil to focus in the region, but not in detriment of the relations with the United States or Europe. Some viewed these as mutually exclusive, but that should not be the case".

Not far behind, Asia received a total of 19 mentions, including eight times as number one priority for Brazil. In addition, ten respondents opted for the BRICS countries in general, and three of them mentioned

China in particular. Japan was cited twice. Nevertheless, one respondent noted that "language and cultural differences seem to be a barrier for [these] relationships to grow faster".

Overall, Latin America and South America were mentioned slightly less frequently than the United States and Asia, with a total of 13 and 10 mentions respectively. However, those who did cite Brazil's neighborhood often placed it as their top priority.

Mercosur was either ignored or criticized. About a fifth of interviewees tended to see Brazil's participation in the economic bloc as an obstacle to an effective international insertion. One young professional judged Brazil's link to Mercosur as "very harmful", because it "prevents the country [from seeking] other agreements, as countries like Chile, Peru, Colombia and Mexico [successfully did]". This view echoed the opinion of another respondent: "Above all Brazil should leave Mercosur, which is an ideological barrier for the country's trade development." According to another interviewee from civil society, "the current economic bloc (Mercosur) is no longer serving the interests of the country."

One former government official was more cautious by stating that Brazil needs to "evaluate Mercosur's conditions, in order to facilitate some free trade agreements with other partners". This was also the position shared by a former government official, who believed Brazil should pursue bilateral trade agreements outside the framework of Mercosur.

South America as a whole seemed to be preferred to only Mercosur. For a professor specializing in strategy and innovation, "Brazil is the most industrialized country of South America, which is also an important market for its manufacturing industry. Therefore, the country should use its soft power and investment [capabilities] to seek greater economic integration in the region." Another respondent from a Brazilian think-tank supported this view: "we should certainly focus on South America, and do so by promoting productive complementarities, a basic condition to convince the economic agents of the neighboring countries that it is important to strengthen the negotiation process of commercial preferences".

By contrast, one former government official considered that South America should be Brazil's priority, but also believed that the main focus should be on Mercosur:

> Brazilian foreign policy is heavily influenced by its participation in Mercosur, whose consolidation has been one of the main Brazilian goals for the last 20 years. The bloc represents a significant

> destination for Brazilian exports and investment, with the integration of production chains such as in the automotive industry.

Interestingly, 15 of the experts we surveyed said Africa should be part of Brazil's top three priorities. One former government official noted that "during the Lula administration, Brazil significantly improved its image on the African continent". According to one public official,

> it is important to invest in Africa [for economic motives, but] also for geopolitical reasons, so as to enhance Brazilian importance in a continent that shares with our country a colonial past and is struggling to find partners not linked to the colonizers or not identified with the United States. It is interesting to act as a counterweight to China in its aggressive search for influence and energy resources in Africa.

Finally, 11 respondents cited Europe among Brazil's top three focus areas, sometimes in combination with the United States, but almost never as a number one priority.

Who should take the credit for Brazil's recent achievements: President Fernando Henrique Cardoso or President Lula?

In Chapter 2, we analyzed the key foundations of what has been called the "Brasília Consensus". As we argued, two important pillars of the "Brasília Consensus" – macroeconomic stabilization and social programs – trace back to the policies of President Fernando Henrique Cardoso (1995–2002) but were further consolidated by President Lula (2003–2010) and President Dilma Rousseff since her accession to power in 2011.

However, a small but vocal minority of the stakeholders we interviewed made a point of emphasizing the role of Cardoso's administration in the successful social and economic changes of Brazil. One young respondent formulated it in a very straightforward manner: "As a brief introduction statement, I am a harsh critic of the Partido dos Trabalhadores (PT) [Workers' Party]; I strongly believe that the main developments of Brazil in the past decade have been a result of actions and policies implemented before the PT government."

Not all the commentaries were as trenchant, but a handful of interviewees considered it unfair that the important reforms undertaken during the 1990s were sometimes underplayed by the current administration and media reports.

Regarding macroeconomic stabilization, one senior business executive highlighted the fact "that some of the basis for these improvements were established not one, but two decades ago, when inflation was finally tamed, an ample and successful privatization program was implemented, and fiscal discipline was adopted by the Federal government". Another respondent from civil society insisted on the "wave of microeconomic reforms [that were implemented] between 1994 and 2002", such as greater access to consumer credit and new bankruptcy regulations. In addition, a business school professor stressed that "income transfer mechanisms were initiated during the 1990s, but were consolidated and expanded in the last decade". As one interviewee summarized it, "the basis for the 'social and economic inclusion' was paved by the previous government".

A handful of respondent tempered and even denied the performance of President Lula's government: "A common mistake some analysts frequently do is to associate [recent] improvements with the ruling party (PT). Brazil could grow in the past decade by a combination of external factors, not by any merit of the government." A professor concurred with this statement by arguing that "growth was a consequence of the boom of commodities at the global level. The Brazilian state was a beneficiary not an agent of change."

Social policies: Where do we go from here?

In Chapter 2 and Chapter 6, we showed that social policies played a key role in the drastic reduction of poverty and inequalities that Brazil was able to accomplish over the last decade. As we mentioned in the first part of this chapter, about a third of our respondents explicitly recognized the benefits of these social policies. However, seven of them also stressed that these policies come with major distortions that will need to be addressed by Brazilian policy-makers. Also, while five respondents called for an extension of these social policies, six of them thought exactly the opposite and argued that it was now time to phase them out.

A key aspect of this debate relates to the modalities of these social policies (how recipients of social benefits are actually selected) and their outcomes over time (is there an exit strategy for recipients?) The underlying question could be summarized in the following way: should the government focus on improving the programs already in place in order to address their deficiencies, as several respondents suggest, or expand them by extending their reach to more people?

One respondent from academia observed that "social policies are important and should be maintained, but the government must be more cautious in granting benefits (there are many cases of people of average income who are in the program)". Some went further and raised the point that the targeting process encouraged "patronage and corruption".

Four interviewees emphasized that the question of the "exit strategy" remained unsolved and currently represented the most important challenge of targeted social programs. One respondent from a business organization considered that "[there needs to be] conditions to enter and also to get out of government social programs." Another respondent added: "I agree that social policies have had an important role on increasing family income and moving a great percentage of the population to middle class. However, I think that they will become an issue on the long term, since the population will become highly dependent on it."

One young respondent raised the point that social programs discouraged people from seeking better jobs and did not promote education. However, on the positive side, it seems that some real efforts have been made to prevent such a risk. As one of the low-income workers we interviewed noted, "The government has offered many courses for free, and through these courses many people already have found employment."

Several interviewees also noted that cash transfers were not enough for solving the issue of poverty. As a respondent from the public sector put it: "there is no possibility of reducing inequality and promoting inclusive development without a strong commitment from the state to face the root causes of inequality". One senior public official insisted that "the trend for the next decade should be the consolidation of the achievements in the social field and its progressive improvement, especially in the fields of public services in the areas of health and education". Another former public official said the same thing: "once people are rescued from misery, the focus [of social policies] should be education and employment, and gradually adapt them to the new demands of the population, such as public transport".

Time to reflect: Where should Brazil go?

Our survey is a first attempt to understand how Brazil's recent achievements and future prospects are perceived by some of the *movers and shakers* of the Brazilian economy. As we have already noted, most of our respondents belong to the country's upper and upper middle class, which has the advantage of offering a unique insight into the thinking of current and future opinion leaders in Brazil's policy debates.

As could be expected in an electoral year, the majority of interviewees coming from the business sector clearly favored a move toward more market-friendly solutions to address the country's economic challenges. One respondent even claimed that "we need a tropical Margaret Thatcher in Brazil". Naturally, respondents from the public sector were more inclined to express pride in the progress achieved over the past ten years, while recognizing the important challenges that continue to lie ahead.

The one issue that triggered the widest range of conflicting responses was the geographical focus that the country should give to its future diplomatic and outward investment efforts. While many believed that Brazil should revive its traditional partnerships with Europe and the United States, others argued that the country should gradually move its attention toward those regions which offer new opportunities, such as Africa, BRICS countries and Latin America itself. Such variety of viewpoints may be the signal that the Brazilian leadership has not yet succeeded in designing a convincing and coherent roadmap for the country's global integration.

Turning back to the question of Brazil's economic model, the analysis of survey responses leads us to believe that efforts will be required from both sides in order to achieve the Brazil Dream. On one hand, the government will need to pay heed to the private sector's calls for further reforms to improve the business environment. On the other hand, the business community should recognize more readily that the government has been and must continue to be a crucial partner, and an enabler, to revive economic growth and pave the way for Brazil's future successes.

Conclusion: Building the Brazil Dream

This book revolves around one question: is Brazil ready to take its place among the world's leading powers?

In the Introduction, we framed Brazil in the context of a country that has undergone cycles of promise and disappointment. It was – and always will be – the country that built its capital of Brasília from scratch in less than four years, and was once declared an economic miracle in the 1970s. And yet, in the lifetimes of most adults in Brazil today, the country has been wracked by hyperinflation and economic instability. The golden decade of the 2000s, during which the country experienced continuous economic growth and a dramatic fall in poverty rates, has now given way to a new period of uncertainty. Are today's economic and social difficulties the sign of a profound reversal of Brazil's fortunes, or the last major obstacle in the long road toward global-leader status?

We believe it is the latter. The foundations of Brazil's economic and political strength are more solid than ever before. As discussed in the opening chapters of this book, Brazil's biggest force lies in its soft power. Through its diplomatic capabilities, and the success of its social-economic model, Brazil has accumulated a great amount of goodwill, if not outright admiration, across the world. But today, for the first time, Brazil's soft power is complemented by the hard power of its economy. At a key point in history, with growing worldwide needs for food, energy and resources, Brazil's abundance now gives it a seat at the global table of power and influence. The world has always liked Brazil – but today, and from now on, the world needs it.

Brazil's emergence as a global power can be understood via Joseph Nye's framework of soft and hard power. However, this book has also emphasized that these aspects have to be augmented by a third

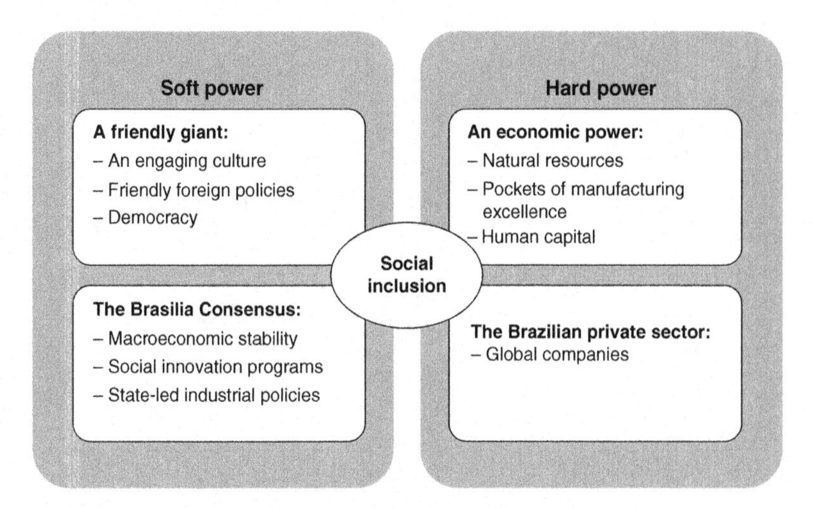

Figure C.1 The emergence of a global power: Soft power, hard power and social inclusion.

dimension: the need for social inclusion. We believe that emerging global powers need inclusive policies to involve all its citizens (see Figure C1). Figure C2 summarizes the strengths and weaknesses of Brazil on the three dimensions of soft power, hard power and social inclusion, which we have addressed in this book.

The survey we conducted for this book, among participants ranging from business leaders to members of civil society, corroborates the view of a country that can be proud of its recent accomplishments. The stabilization of the economy, the emergence of a new middle class, the consolidation of democracy, and Brazil's higher standing in the world, are among the biggest victories of modern Brazil – and a real cause for celebration.

The answers we received also gave a clear view of the vast challenges ahead, from improving public services and simplifying the tax system, to strengthening public accountability and upgrading its infrastructure. Unsurprisingly, for a democracy as vibrant as Brazil, the survey also revealed a wide spectrum of views about how the country should frame its policies in these crucial areas. While some call for a greater reliance on market forces, others emphasize the importance of creating synergies between the state and the private sector. Some consider that Brazil should look to reinforce its historical links with the United States and Europe, others believe that the country should increasingly bet on the Global South, starting with its Latin American neighbors.

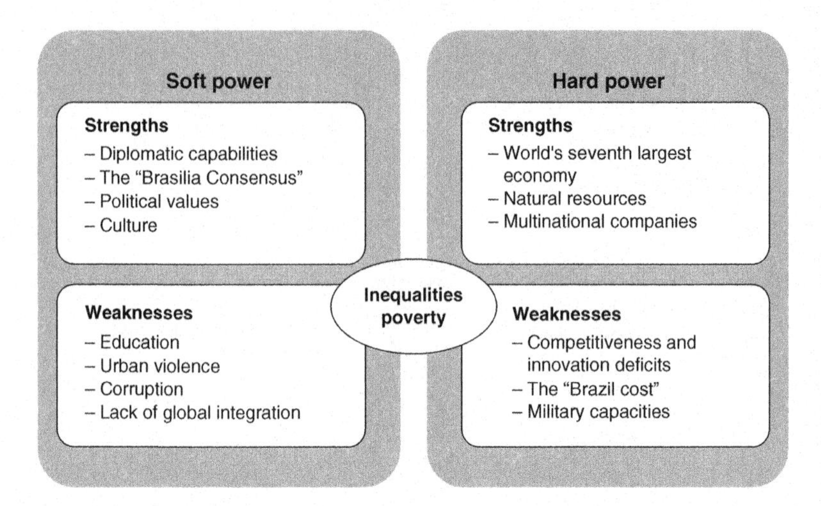

Figure C.2 Brazil's hard power/soft power/social inclusion matrix: Strengths and weaknesses.

Building the Brazil Dream

Throughout this book we have framed the components of a "Brazil Dream" that form the blueprint for its future as a world power: an end to social determinism, a growing middle class, a social safety net and, above all, a robust, independent and diversified economy.

Although there is still work to be done, today, 21st-century Brazil has come far toward institutionalizing the first three of these components. Poverty is no longer a birthright for many of its citizens. Broadly accepted policy interventions such as the *Bolsa Família* program, now entering its second decade, have come close to eradicating extreme poverty. Some *favelas* are becoming pacified, primary education has become close to universal, and growing personal wealth has created a vibrant consumer society. The trajectory of Brazil's legendary economic inequalities is improving, and a deep economic divide is no longer accepted as the status quo.

On the broader issue of the economy, Brazil's defining moment is in front of us. The combination of substantial gains in agricultural productivity, the discovery of massive oil reserves, and its leadership in mining and minerals are all quickly moving Brazil from good neighbor to power broker. These areas also give Brazil new financial resources to deal with the weaker aspects of its economy. The country is now starting to take steps to address a serious infrastructure deficit and the result of decades of underinvestment in public services, which in large part drove the social unrest of mid-2013. Its educational system, public and private, needs work to be on a par with global standards, and in turn create the kind of skilled professionals who will be required to build a competitive manufacturing and technology base. And the "Brazil cost" of doing business, fueled by bureaucracy and inefficiency, still needs to be drastically reduced. While the world today wears Brazilian Havaianas and travels in Brazilian airplanes, its growth as an industrial power is a work in progress that will in time have a major impact on its prosperity.

Turning to world affairs, Brazil has already made immense strides in lifting its global standing and gaining respect both from established powers and its peers from the emerging world. The next step of the Brazil Dream will be for the country to successfully transform itself from a rule-follower into a rule-maker. This will require a deep and continuous effort to develop and defend alternative approaches, which builds on Brazil's experience as a developing country and its attachment to peaceful cooperation and the promotion of multilateralism. The areas in which Brazil could make a decisive contribution, from global trade and food security to internet privacy and the resolution of conflicts, are plentiful. Expectations are now growing and the South American giant faces one of its biggest tests.

Engaging the people

Implementing the Brazil Dream will require the energy and engagement of its population and ironically, one of the best examples of this lies in the massive social protests of mid-2013. First of all, these protests represented the pluralism of a healthy democracy. Second, in a very real sense, they were arguing to improve key issues standing in the way of the Brazil Dream, such as strained services, high taxes and an educational system that needed to modernize, in the face of high public spending for the upcoming 2014 World Cup and 2016 Summer Olympics. The protestors were not arguing against repression or pressing for regime change – they wanted lower bus fares, better infrastructure and less corruption.

Above all, these protesters were heard at the highest levels of government, culminating in legislative victories ranging from public transport pricing to the landmark 2013 bill ceding future oil and gas revenues toward education and healthcare. Viewed in its entirety, this body of legislation – which also included bills criminalizing corruption and embezzlement, ending secret votes in Congress for forfeiture of office, and implementing new inflation control measures – helped further codify many of the social values that drive the BrazilDream.

According to a piece in *Euromoney* magazine, these protests were actually seen by many in the business community as a good thing: "[If] these protests wake up the dozing giant, the *manifestações* could be the biggest boost to Brazil bulls for years."[1] At a deeper level, they are an example for how Brazil's social and economic values are now being driven by the engagement of its people. For a country that was ruled by a military dictatorship for 20 years until 1985, its responsiveness to the voice of the public – a process that began with the peaceful transfer of power between opposition parties in January 2003 – are signs of a stable and progressive democracy that drives its current global standing.

In search of a new model: Working together the public and the private sector

A common denominator among world powers is economic competitiveness. This means that the Brazil Dream is built on relationships, with not just its people, but also its business community. One of the lessons of recent history is that the most successful emerging growth economies have been fueled by effective partnerships between the public and private sector.

The emergence of Asian economies over the past few decades also serves as an example on how Brazil and other BRICS countries can grow through the right level of government involvement. For example, Japan's Ministry of Economy, Trade and Industry (METI) played a key planning role in the "Japan, Inc." boom of the 1980s and beyond, Singapore's high level of investment in science and technology has built a highly successful city-state in the 21st century, and China's moves from a communist, centrally planned economy to a market-based government partnership have created an economic powerhouse.

Brazil is developing its own unique sense of economic model, in part through the seeds of its business-oriented Cardoso administration in the late 1990s, and today the trademark of a Workers' Party government that has learned to govern from the center and work collaboratively with the private sector. It leverages institutional resources such as its development bank (BNDES), its state agricultural research organization (EMBRAPA) or the innovation body (FINEP) as instruments of policy, fostering critical areas ranging from Brazil's huge growth as a food producer to needed enhancements for technology, energy, infrastructure and innovation.

A view for the future

In our view, it is time for Brazil to lead. Its rich and expanding natural resources have given it a unique opportunity to move past cyclical economies and economic inequality, and its culture and worldview are giving it an increasingly important place in global affairs.

The world's eyes will be on Brazil in 2014 and 2016 for two major sporting events. More importantly, its eyes will be on Brazil in the years to come as a key supplier of food, energy, natural resources and, increasingly, global leadership. We share the view of many inside and outside Brazil's government and private sector that this very visible point in its history is a turning point for its role on the world stage.

We are in a world where no single model fits all. While it still has many issues to overcome in the near future, the Brazil of today is quickly turning the corner as an economic and political giant, and becoming an economic and societal inspiration for the future of Latin America and the broader emerging world in the process. It is time to celebrate the achievements and to move ahead. We are watching a new world order unfold before us, and Brazil is poised to play a major part in it.

Notes

Introduction

1. Brazil's military dictatorship ran from 1964 to 1985.
2. The American Dream was first mentioned by James Truslow Adams in 1931 (Adams, 2001) and revisited by a number of authors, among them Cullen (2004).
3. Jeremy Rifkin (2004) describes the differences between European and American values and contrasts Europe's soft power with American hard power. In spite of the current crisis, the European Union represents for some countries still a different model, which they may want to follow.
4. The *Chinese Dream* was the title of a book published by Helen H. Wang (2010). The author defines the Chinese dream around sustainable development, national renewal, individual dreams and economic and political reform and connects it with the American Dream. More recently, Milton Friedman also spoke in a widely quoted 2012 article in the *New York Times* (http://www.nytimes.com/2012/10/03/opinion/friedman-china-needs-its-own-dream.html) about the need for China to have its own dream. In May 2013, Xi Jinping, President of the People's Republic of China, mentioned the need to have a "Chinese Dream".

1 A Friendly Giant

1. http://news.bbc.co.uk/2/hi/americas/8580560.stm (Accessed on 16 September 2013).
2. http://www.ft.com/intl/cms/s/2/37685a5c-7bbd-11e2-95b9-00144feabdc0.html#axzz2e3HkImDB (Accessed on 16 September 2013).
3. http://www.largeur.com/?p=3976 (Accessed on 16 September 2013).
4. In 2001, Jim O'Neill, then Head of Global Economic Research at the investment bank Goldman Sachs, coined the term BRIC, an acronym standing for Brazil, Russia, India, and China – the four largest and rapidly growing developing countries that have come to symbolize the shift in global economic power.
5. http://www.theguardian.com/inside-brazil/young-and-vibrant (Accessed on 16 September 2013).
6. http://www.csmonitor.com/World/Americas/Latin-America-Monitor/2012/0406/Brazil-neglecting-culture-in-quest-for-power (Accessed on 16 September 2013).
7. http://www.braziliality.org/ (Accessed on 16 September 2013).
8. http://www.futurebrand.com/images/uploads/studies/cbi/CBI_2012-Final.pdf (Accessed on 16 September 2013).
9. http://www.futurebrand.com/foresight/cbi/country-brand-index-latin-america (Accessed on 16 September 2013).

10. http://www.project-syndicate.org/commentary/a-more-robust-defense-policy-for-brazil-by-celso-amorim (Accessed on 16 September 2013).
11. http://www.midiaindependente.org/pt/red/2010/03/467090.shtml (Accessed on 16 September 2013).
12. Business as usual levels are based on projections of future emissions if no action is taken.
13. http://www.wfp.org/stories/brazils-president-lula-honoured-wfp-champion-against-hunger (Accessed on 16 September 2013).
14. http://www.globaltimes.cn/NEWS/tabid/99/ID/683010/Brazil-is-world-leader-in-the-battle-against-hunger-WFP.aspx (Accessed on 16 September 2013).
15. mercury.ethz.ch/serviceengine/Files/ISN/137671/ ... 3fbb ... /no21.pdf (Accessed on 20 October 2013).
16. http://www.realinstitutoelcano.org/wps/portal/rielcano_eng/Print?WCM_GLOBAL_CONTEXT=/wps/wcm/connect/elcano/Elcano_in/Zonas_in/ARI62-2010 (Accessed on 16 September 2013).
17. http://www.ey.com/Publication/vwLUAssets/Rapid-growth_markets_soft_power_index:_Spring_2012/$FILE/softpowerindex.pdf (Accessed on 16 September 2013).
18. http://monocle.com/film/affairs/soft-power-survey-2012/ (Accessed on 16 September 2013).
19. http://www.ft.com/intl/cms/s/0/0bd55672-f482-11e2-a62e-00144feabdc0.html#axzz2dlyDDJL5
20. http://www.nybooks.com/blogs/nyrblog/2010/aug/17/talking-about-brazil/ (Accessed on 16 September 2013).
21. http://mtv.uol.com.br/memo/brasil-tem-mais-de-16-milhoes-de-pessoas-viv endo-em-condicoes-de-extrema-pobreza (Accessed on 16 September 2013).
22. http://www.economist.com/node/21543494 (Accessed on 16 September 2013).
23. http://www.huffingtonpost.com/2013/03/17/race-in-brazil-offers-lesson-to-us_n_2895325.html (Accessed on 16 September 2013).
24. http://www.economist.com/blogs/americasview/2013/04/affirmative-action-brazil (Accessed on 16 September 2013).
25. http://www.csmonitor.com/World/Americas/2013/0820/Chasing-the-Brazilian-dream-migrants-strain-the-country-s-immigration-laws (Accessed on 16 September 2013).
26. "Rising Brazil Tackles Immigration Question", *CNN*, 31 January 2012, http://edition.cnn.com/2012/01/28/world/americas/brazil-immigration/index.html (Accessed on 16 September 2013).
27. "Influx of Haitians Into the Amazon Prompts Immigration Debate in Brazil", *New York Times*, 7 February 2012, http://www.nytimes.com/2012/02/08/world/americas/brazil-limits-haitian-immigration.html (Accessed on 16 September 2013).
28. http://www.reuters.com/article/2012/08/24/brazil-immigration-idUSL2E8JNAK920120824 (Accessed on 16 September 2013).
29. http://www.theguardian.com/world/2013/aug/28/brazil-doctors-jeer-cubans (Accessed on 16 September 2013).
30. http://www.theguardian.com/commentisfree/2013/jul/08/brazil-football-violence-symptom-collapsed-justice-system (Accessed on 16 September 2013).

31. http://www.bbc.co.uk/blogs/worldtonight/2010/03/brazil_hard_cop_or_soft_cop.html (Accessed on 16 September 2013).
32. http://www.reuters.com/article/2012/04/13/us-brazil-borders-idUSBRE83C0KB20120413 (Accessed on 16 September 2013).
33. http://www.ft.com/intl/cms/s/0/f07fcaf0-e0fd-11da-90ad-0000779e2340.html#axzz2eR2DQm00 (Accessed on 16 September 2013).
34. http://www.project-syndicate.org/commentary/a-more-robust-defense-policy-for-brazil-by-celso-amorim (Accessed on 16 September 2013).

2 The Brasília Consensus: Still a Valid Model?

1. http://mag.newsweek.com/2013/09/27/the-comeback-queen-brazil-president-dilma-rousseff-reverses-her-declining-popularity.html, 29 September 2013 (Accessed on 1 October 2013).
2. See also: Casanova, L., 2010. *Del "consenso de Washington" al "consenso brasileño": El nuevo poder empresarial brasileño* http://www.globallatinas.org/docs/aeconomia2010final.pdf América Economía, Santiago de Chile, April 2010.
3. As the United States and parts of Europe struggle to rise from the crisis, emerging markets are looking more closely at China's state-controlled economic model, which has produced economic growth, reduced poverty and helped make the country the second biggest economy in the world.
4. Using the exchange rates of September 2013. The same study considers those living under BRL291 per capita as "low class", which means that they are in a precarious situation and can fall back into poverty.
5. http://hdrstats.undp.org/images/explanations/BRA.pdf (Accessed on 30 September 2013).
6. Conditional cash transfer programs rely on a "social contract" with the beneficiaries. In exchange for direct cash transfers, poor individuals or households commit to taking certain actions, such as sending children to schools or sending them to health centers.
7. Pinhoni, Marina, "Brazil is the 12th Country in Spending to Fight Poverty," Exame.com, 23 September 2013, http://exame.abril.com.br/english/brazil-now/brazil-is-the-12th-country-in-spending-to-fight-poverty.shtml (Accessed on 5 October 2013).
8. It should be noted that many Brazilian workers still receive monthly stipends that are well below the minimum wage.
9. http://data.worldbank.org/indicator/TG.VAL.TOTL.GD.ZS (Accessed on 30 September 2013).
10. http://www.brazilchamber.no/?p=1035 (Accessed on 30 September 2013).
11. These types of policies seem to have gained support from the majority of Brazilians who kept voting in favor of the Workers' Party.
12. http://www.economist.com/debate/days/view/802 (Accessed on 30 September 2013).
13. http://www.mckinsey.com/insights/public_sector/state_capitalism_and_the_crisis (Accessed on 30 September 2013).
14. http://www.economist.com/node/21542924 (Accessed on 30 September 2013).

15. http://blogs.reuters.com/ian-bremmer/2012/07/03/are-state-led-economies-better/ (Accessed on 30 September 2013).
16. The China Development Bank, with about US$1 trillion of assets, remains the largest of its kind.
17. http://www.economist.com/node/16748990 (Accessed on 30 September 2013).
18. http://www.jbs.com.br/ri/ (Accessed on 30 September 2013).
19. http://fibria.infoinvest.com.br/static/enu/estrutura-acionaria.asp?idioma =enu (Accessed on 30 September 2013).
20. http://ri.embraer.com.br/show.aspx?idCanal=ltPlKaoPDWiQ1uj7aoUw6Q (Accessed on 30 September 2013).
21. http://www.vale.com/EN/investors/company/shareholding-structure/Pages/default.aspx (Accessed on 28 April 2013). BNDES's participation in Vale is in fact higher if taking into account its direct participation in Valepar, Vale's controlling entity.
22. http://www.economonitor.com/blog/2010/10/brazil-creative-accounting-and-fiscal-risk/ (Accessed on 30 September 2013).
23. http://economia.estadao.com.br/noticias/economia-geral,bndes-decide-abandonar-a-politica-de-criacao-de-campeas-nacionais,151356,0.htm (Accessed on 28 April 2013).
24. http://www.slideshare.net/carmencampollo/how-latin-america-pension-unds-invest-their-assets-april-2013 (Accessed on 30 September 2013).
25. http://ri.embraer.com.br/show.aspx?idCanal=ltPlKaoPDWiQ1uj7aoUw6Q== (Accessed on 30 September 2013).
26. http://www.brasilfoods.com/ri/siteri/web/conteudo_en.asp?idioma=1&conta =44&tipo=32223 (Accessed on 30 September 2013).
27. http://ri.invepar.com.br/invepar/web/conteudo_en.asp?idioma=1&conta =44&tipo=45015 (Accessed on 30 September 2013).
28. See also: Casanova, L., 2010. *Del "consenso de Washington" al "consenso brasileño": El nuevo poder empresarial brasileño* http://www.globallatinas.org/docs/aeconomia2010final.pdf América Economía, Santiago de Chile, April 2010.
29. *ibd.morningstar.com/ERR/500/VALE.pdf* (Accessed on 30 September 2013).
30. http://br.advfn.com/noticias/ADVNEWS/2013/artigo/58479291 (Accessed on 30 September 2013).
31. US–Brazil Business Council, *A Greater Brazil? Industrial Policy, Competitiveness, and Growth* (report). http://www.brazilcouncil.org/sites/default/files/17875_BrazilReport_Final.pdf (Accessed on 10 October 2013).
32. http://en.mercopress.com/2013/06/24/three-out-of-four-brazilians-fed-up-with-poor-public-services-support-street-protests (Accessed on 30 September 2013).
33. This dispersed leadership made it difficult at first to establish negotiations between the government and the protesters.

3 Brazil's Economic Power

1. The third big rating agency and the only non-American one, Fitch, the UK rating agency, upgraded Brazil's sovereign grade to investment grade in April 2011.

2. Brazil was the world's sixth biggest economy (bigger than UK's) during 2011. The variation in the nominal GDP is due, in part, to the changes in the value of the Brazil currency with respect to the United States dollar.
3. Nye, JS, "Has Economic Power Replaced Military Might?" Project Syndicate, 6 June 2011, http://www.project-syndicate.org/commentary/has-economic-power-replaced-military-might (Accessed on 26 August 2013).
4. According to *The Economist* special report on Brazil's future: "Has Brazil blown it?" (28 September 2013), taxes in Brazil account for 36% of GDP and this represents (with Argentina) the highest in the emerging market world. Public spending, according to the same source is at 38.5% of GDP. http://www.economist.com/news/leaders/21586833-stagnant-economy-bloated-state-and-mass-protests-mean-dilma-rousseff-must-change-course-has (Accessed on 28 September 2013).
5. Leahy, Joe, "Brazilian President Dilma Rousseff Defends Record on Economy," *Financial Times*, 16 June 2013, http://www.ft.com/intl/cms/s/0/aff5a652-d6a1-11e2-9214-00144feab7de.html?siteedition=intl#axzz2WUAZ8wwD (Accessed on 26 August 2013).
6. http://www.er-co.com/ (Accessed on 23 August 2013).
7. Green City Times, "Curitiba," http://www.greencitytimes.com/sustainable-cities/curtiba.html (Accessed on August 2013).
8. Soon after its IPO, Petrobras lost its position as the fourth largest company in the world by market capitalization. Petrobras moved from a value of US$60 billion in 2007 to US$314 billion at its peak in 2010, to its current value of US$103 billion as of September 2013. According to financial analysts, the volatility is due to the economic context of Brazil, currency swings and the recent doubts about Petrobras's capabilities to extract the oil from the "pre-salt" fields.
9. Citibank report, "The Brazilian Energy Sector," September 2012.
10. As of 2013, the seven biggest national oil companies are: Gazprom (Russia), National Iranian Oil Company (Iran), China National Petroleum Corporation (China), Petrobras (Brazil), PDVSA (Venezuela), Petronas (Malaysia) and Saudi Aramco (Saudi Arabia).
11. WPP. 2012. Brandz top 50 Most Valuable Latin American Brands. http://www.millwardbrown.com/brandz/2012/LATAM/Documents/2012_BrandZ_LATAM_Top50_Report.pdf (Accessed on 30 August 2013).
12. The World Factbook. https://www.cia.gov/library/publications/the-world-factbook/ (Accessed on 15 August 2013).
13. The earthquake and subsequent tsunami in Japan on 11 March 2011 that caused the terrible accident in the nuclear plant of Fukushima Daiichi brought the attention back to the benefits of alternative energy sources such as solar energy, wind and biofuels.
14. Brazil's sugarcane production in 2011 was 734,000 tons, more than double that of the second biggest producer, India, at 342,000 tons.
15. Mercosur (Mercosul in Portuguese, Southern Common Market) members include Argentina, Brazil, Paraguay, Uruguay and Venezuela with seven more associated countries and two observers.
16. According to some estimates, the production of Brazilian sugar cane based ethanol starts to be profitable when the price of a barrel of oil goes beyond US$30.

17. USGS Mineral Commodity Summaries. http://www.usgs.gov/ (Accessed on 25 August 2013).
18. Vale, "Vale Obtains Operation License for Salobo," 14 November 2012, http://www.vale.com/en/aboutvale/news/pages/vale-obtains-operation-license-for-salobo.aspx (Accessed on 25 August 2013).
19. Butler, Rhett A., "Calculating Deforestation Figures for the Amazon," Mongabay.com, 2010, http://rainforests.mongabay.com/amazon/deforestation_calculations.html (Accessed on 5 October 2013).
20. "Brazil will Forge its Own Path for Developing the Amazon." Conservation news and environmental science news, 26 January 2009.
21. The Economist, "Brazil's Agricultural Miracle: How to Feed the World," 26 August 2010, http://www.economist.com/node/16889019 (Accessed on 12 October 2013).
22. Pellissier, Hank, "Brazil: Future Farm of the Planet?" Institute for Ethics & Emerging Technologies, 22 September 2010, http://ieet.org/index.php/IEET/more/pellissier20100922 (Accessed on 12 October 2013).
23. Ortiz, F., "Billions of Brazilian Health Dollars Going Up in Smoke," InterPress Service, 7 June 2012, http://www.ipsnews.net/2012/06/billions-of-brazilian-health-dollars-going-up-in-smoke/ (Accessed on 1 August 2013).
24. WHO, "Brazil and Tobacco Use: A Tough Nut to Crack," *Bulletin of the World Health Organization,* 87(11), November 2009, http://www.who.int/bulletin/volumes/87/11/09-031109/en/; Tobacco Control Laws, "Country Details for Brazil," January 2013, http://www.tobaccocontrollaws.org/legislation/country/brazil/summary (Accessed on 1 August 2013); UnfairTobacco.org, "Country Profile: Brazil," December 2012, http://www.unfairtobacco.org/en/atlas/brasilien/ (Accessed on 20 July 2012).
25. Amorim, Celso, "Hardening Brazil's Soft Power," Project Syndicate, 16 July 2013, http://www.project-syndicate.org/commentary/a-more-robust-defense-policy-for-brazil-by-celso-amorim (Accessed on 2 August 2013).
26. Mari, A, "IT Sector Creates Majority of Jobs in Brazil," ZDNet.com, 13 July 2013, http://www.zdnet.com/it-sector-creates-majority-of-jobs-in-brazil-7000017662/ (Accessed on 2 August 2013).
27. Geromel, R., "Brazil's Top 10 Most Innovative Companies," Forbes, 21 February 2012, http://www.forbes.com/sites/ricardogeromel/2012/02/21/brazils-top-10-most-innovative-companies/2/
28. The help of Barbara Marchiori de Assis, Research Assistant and student at CIPA in Cornell University, in this section is gratefully acknowledged.
29. World Population Review, Population of Brazil 2013, http://worldpopulationreview.com/population-of-brazil/
30. 2009 figures, The World Factbook (United States) Central Intelligence Agency.
31. Trading Economics, http://www.tradingeconomics.com/brazil/unemployment-rate (Accessed on 27 February 2014).
32. Brazilian Institute of Geography and Statistics (IBGE).
33. Development Economics, Brazil at a Glance, 17 March 2013.
34. In June 2013, Standard & Poor's gave a negative outlook to the Brazilian debt and announced that it may cut its credit status and loose its investment grade at the beginning of 2014. During the summer of 2013, investors left emerging markets and moved back to the United States following

declarations by the Federal Reserve saying that the quantitative easing was coming to an end and, as a consequence, yields were going to become more attractive in the United States.

4 Brazilian Companies Going Global

1. http://unctad.org/en/docs/webiteiia200416_en.pdf (Accessed on 10 April 2013).
2. These are Petrobras, Banco do Brasil, Banco Bradesco, Vale, JBS, Itaúsa-Investimentos Itaú, Ultrapar Holdings, Brazilian Distribution (CBD) (Brazil), Pemex, América Móvil, CFE (Mexico), PDVSA (Venezuela) and Ecopetrol (Colombia).
3. *Source:* www.latinbusinesschronicle.com (Accessed on 12 June 2013).
4. The help of Barbara Marchiori de Assis, Research Assistant and student at CIPA in Cornell University, in this section is gratefully acknowledged.
5. The Transnationality Ranking of Brazilian Companies assesses the level of internationalization of Brazilian firms based on three indicators: percentage of revenues of foreign subsidiaries with respect to total revenues, percentage of foreign assets with respect to total assets and percentage of foreign employees with respect to the total number of employees. To establish its ranking, FDC focuses on corporations with "physical presence abroad", using the following criteria: commercial offices, distribution centers, production and assembly unit, services, research and development with constant personnel abroad and banking agencies.
6. http://www.vcc.columbia.edu/files/vale/documents/EMGP-Brazil-Report-2010-Final.pdf (Accessed on 10 April 2013).
7. SOBEET and Columbia Vale Center (2012), *Outward Foreign Direct Investment from Brazil and its Policy Context, 2012,* http://www.vcc.columbia.edu/files/vale/documents/Profile-_Brazil_OForeign Direct Investment_10_May_2012_-_FINAL.pdf (Accessed on 25 April 2013).
8. SOBEET and Columbia Vale Center (2012), *Outward Foreign Direct Investment from Brazil and its Policy Context, 2012,* http://www.vcc.columbia.edu/files/vale/documents/Profile-_Brazil_OForeign Direct Investment_10_May_2012_-_FINAL.pdf (Accessed on 25 April 2013).
9. http://assets.vale.com/docs/Documents/en/investors/Company/Fact-sheet/factsheeti.pdf (Accessed on 28 April 2013).
10. Petrobras has lost a lot of market value since then, as discussed in Chapter 3.
11. https://icsid.worldbank.org/ICSID/FrontServlet?requestType=ICSID PublicationsRH&actionVal=ViewBilateral&reqFrom=Main# (Accessed on 28 April 2013).

5 Strengthening Brazil's Competitiveness

1. Wilson, Mike, "Embrapa: The Engine Behind Brazil's Miracle," Farm Futures, 3 May 2011, http://farmfutures.com/blogs-embrapa-the-engine-behind-brazils-miracle-2264 (Accessed on 15 September 2013).
2. Ukon, M. et al., "Brazil: Confronting the Productivity Challenge," Boston Consulting Group, 20 January 2013, https://www.bcgperspectives.com/

content/articles/growth_value_creation_strategy_brazil_confronting_the_productivity_challenge/

3. *The Economist*, "Has Brazil Blown It?" 28 September 2013, http://www.economist.com/news/leaders/21586833-stagnant-economy-bloated-state-and-mass-protests-mean-dilma-rousseff-must-change-course-has
4. *Custo Brasil* refers to the higher operational cost of doing business in Brazil due to the deficits in hard (roads, airports, etc.) and social (lack of skilled workers, corruption, etc.) infrastructure, with respect to other countries.
5. MercoPress (Uruguay), "Brazil Highways' Maintenance to the Private Sector on Ten Year Contracts," MercoPress (Accessed on 5 September 2013).
6. Rathbone, John Paul, "Coming of Age," *Financial Times* special report: The New Brazil, 29 June 2010, http://www.ft.com/intl/cms/s/0/73e73bbc-7d12-11df-8845-00144feabdc0.html (Accessed on 20 August 2013).
7. Pearson, Samantha, "Rousseff Reform Aims to Consign Clogged Ports to History," FT Special Report: Brazil Infrastructure, *Financial Times*, 10 September 2013 (Accessed on 15 September 2013).
8. Wright, Robert, "Leaders Seek to End Nation's Love Affair with the Automobile," FT Special Report: Brazil Infrastructure, *Financial Times*, 10 September 2013 (Accessed on 15 September 2013).
9. Pearson, Samantha, "Airport Upgrades Suffer a Slow Takeoff," FT Special Report: Brazil Infrastructure, *Financial Times*, 10 September 2013 (Accessed on 15 September 2013).
10. Bombardier Inc., "BOMBARDIER INNOVIA Monorail – São Paulo, Brazil," http://www.bombardier.com/en/transportation/projects/project.innovia-sao-paulo-brazil.html
11. Goldsmith, Daniel, "Walt Disney World Monorail Crash Kills Conductor, No Passengers were Hurt," *New York Daily News*, 5 July 2009, http://www.nydailynews.com/news/world/walt-disney-world-monorail-crash-kills-conductor-passengers-hurt-article-1.426373
12. Carrico, Thalita, "Waterways are a Decongestant for Transport," FT Special Report: Brazil Infrastructure, *Financial Times*, 10 September 2013 (Accessed on 15 September 2013).
13. PPP Brazil (website), available at: http://www.pppbrasil.com.br/portal/ (Accessed on 30 April 2013).
14. State of Pernambuco, Brazil, "Projeto de irrigação Pontal," available at: http://www.pontal.org/projeto.html (Accessed on 30 April 2013).
15. Governo do Estado de Minas Gerais. "Projetos de PPPs Concluídos." Available at: http://www.ppp.mg.gov.br/projetos-ppp/projetos-celebrados (Accessed on 15 September 2013).
16. Governo do Estado de São Paulo. "Parceria Público-Privada: um excelente negócio para você, uma ótima ação para São Paulo." Available at: http://www.investe.sp.gov.br/usr/share/documents/Folder_PPPs_port.pdf (Accessed on 30 April 2013).
17. *New York Times*, "Do Olympic Host Cities Ever Win?" 2 October 2009. http://roomfordebate.blogs.nytimes.com/2009/10/02/do-olympic-host-cities-ever-win/ (Accessed on 2 September 2013).
18. Ainsworth-Wells, Martine, "London 2012 Olympics: What is London's Tourism Legacy?" *The Telegraph*, 15 November 2012, http://www.telegraph.

co.uk/travel/ultratravel/9680322/London-2012-Olympics-what-is-Londons-tourism-legacy.html (Accessed on 2 September 2013).
19. Ainsworth-Wells, Martine, "2016 Olympic Games: Rio de Janeiro's Reputation is at Risk," *The Telegraph*, 28 January 2013, http://www.telegraph.co.uk/travel/ultratravel/9831577/2016-Olympic-Games-Rio-de-Janeiros-reputation-is-at-risk.html (Accessed on 10 September 2013).

6 Sustaining Social Innovation

1. The Workers' Party has been in power since former President Luiz Inacio da Silva (Lula) came to power in 2002 and the former President Fernando Henrique Cardoso pioneered many of these policies.
2. Pearson, Samantha, "Dilma Wants Oil Royalties in Education," *Financial Times (United Kingdom)*, 20 November 2012, http://blogs.ft.com/beyond-brics/2012/11/20/dilma-wants-oil-royalties-in-education/
3. Casanova and Dumas (2010), "Corporate social responsibility and Latin American multinationals: Is poverty a business issue."
4. Barbara Marchiori de Assis, "Public-Private Partnerships in Brazil" and "Social Public-Private Partnerships in Brazil," unpublished working papers, Cornell University, 2013. The contribution of Barbara in this chapter is gratefully acknowledged.
5. Kingsley, Patrick, "Participatory Democracy in Porto Alegre," *The Guardian (United Kingdom)*, 10 September 2012, http://www.theguardian.com/world/2012/sep/10/participatory-democracy-in-porto-alegre
6. Pateman, Carole, "Participatory Democracy Revisited (APSA Presidential Address)," *Perspectives on Politics*, 10(1), March 2012, http://www.cf.ac.uk/europ/resources/presidential%20address.pdf (Accessed on 29 August 2013).
7. Center for Digital Innovation, www.cdi.org.br (Accessed on 27 August 2013).
8. Development Economics, *Brazil at a Glance*, 2012.
9. Trading Economics, Brazil Unemployment Rate, http://www.tradingeconomics.com/brazil/unemployment-rate, 2013 (Accessed on 28 August 2013).
10. ECLAC, *Social Panorama of Latin America*, 2012.
11. Rapoza, Kenneth, "In Brazil: The Poor Get Richer Faster," *Forbes Magazine*, 25 September 2012, http://www.forbes.com/sites/kenrapoza/2012/09/25/in-brazil-the-poor-get-richer-faster/ (Accessed on 21 August 2013).
12. United National IFAD (International Fund for Agricultural Development), "Rural Poverty in Brazil," http://www.ruralpovertyportal.org/country/home/tags/brazil (Accessed on 28 August 2013).
13. www.fomezero.gov.br (Accessed on 21 August 2013).
14. Barbara Marchiori de Assis, "Conditional Cash Transfer Programs: 'Bolsa Família' and 'Oportunidades,' " unpublished working paper, Cornell University; Brazil. Data Ministério do Desenvolvimento Social e Combate à Fome. "Relatório de Informações Sociais." http://www.mds.gov.br/bolsafamilia (Accessed on 16 April 2013).
15. Instituto Lula, "Each one Real Invested in the Bolsa Família Returns R$1.44 to the Economy, says Minister," http://www.institutolula.org/eng/?p=501#.Uk7FdYaTiSo (Accessed on 4 October 2013).
16. Baena (2011).

17. Pearson, Samantha, "Real Estate Becomes Target for Investors," *Financial Times (UK)*, 17 May 2012 (Accessed on 21 August 2013).
18. "PISA is an international study launched by the OECD in 1997. It aims to evaluate educational systems worldwide every three years by assessing 15-year-olds' competencies in the key subjects: reading, mathematics and science. To date over 70 countries and economies have participated in PISA." http://www.oecd.org/pisa/ (Accessed on 23 August 2013).
19. A Transformação da Qualidade da Educação Básica Pública no Brasil (Converting the Quality of Basic Education Public in Brazil).
20. Kuehne, Tina, "In Brazil, Teachers Struggle for Fair Pay," *United Press International*, 5 April 2012, http://www.upi.com/Top_News/World-News/2012/04/05/In-Brazil-teachers-struggle-for-fair-pay/UPIU-7201331691154/ (Accessed on 23 August 2013).
21. Economist Intelligence Unit, Scoring Brazil: Innovation and Competitiveness in an International Context, 2012.
22. Reis, Guilherme, "What Brazil Needs to Do to Achieve Excellence in Schools?" *Brazilian Post*, 23 July 2012, http://brazilianpost.co.uk/23/07/2012/public-education-in-debate/ (Accessed on 25 August 2013).
23. Real News Network, "In Response to Protests, Brazil's Congress Votes to Invest 100% of Oil Revenue into Education and Healthcare (transcript)," http://therealnews.com/t2/index.php?Itemid=74&id=31&jumival=10386&option=com_content&task=view (Accessed on 25 August 2013).
24. Organization for Economic Cooperation and Development (OECD), Brazil 2010.
25. Academic Ranking of World Universities, 2011, http://www.shanghairanking.com/World-University-Rankings-2013/Brazil.html (Accessed on 24 August 2013).
26. Lemos, Ronaldo, "Universities in Brazil are too Closed to the World, and that's Bad for Innovation," Freedom to Tinker blog (Princeton University), 15 June 2011, https://freedom-to-tinker.com/blog/rlemos/universities-brazil-are-too-closed-world-and-thats-bad-innovation/ (Accessed on 20 August 2013).
27. Funeka Yazini April, "SA should take Educational Leaf from Brazil," Polity.org.za, 28 August 2013, http://www.polity.org.za/article/sa-should-take-educational-leaf-from-brazil-2013-08-28 (Accessed on 20 August 2013).
28. Adapted from INEP, "Resumo Técnico do Censo da Educação Superior 2011." http://www.inep.gov.br/ (Accessed on 28 August 2013) and Barbara Marchiori de Assis; National Center for Educational Statistics, http://nces.ed.gov/fastfacts/display.asp?id=98 (Accessed on 26 August 2013).
29. Barbara Marchiori de Assis, "University for All" Program (ProUni – Programa Universidade para Todos), unpublished working paper, Cornell University.
30. Available at: http://www.cienciasemfronteiras.gov.br/web/csf/o-programa (Accessed on 22 September 2013). The fields of interest are mostly: Engineering; Physical Sciences; Clinical and Health Sciences; Computing and Information Technology; Aerospace Technology; Pharmaceuticals; Sustainable Agricultural Production; Oil, Gas and Coal; Renewable Energy; Minerals Technology; Biotechnology and New Materials; Technologies for Prevention and Mitigation of Natural Disasters; Bioprospecting

and Biodiversitiy; Marine Sciences; Creative Industry; New Technologies Construction Engineering; Practical Technologists. Available at: http://www.cienciasemfronteiras.gov.br/web/csf/areas-contempladas (Accessed on 22 September 2013).

31. It should be noted that "Science without Borders" has also accepted students from other fields, such as social science, due to resolutions by the district courts on equity grounds. For instance, the district court of the State of Ceará determined on 18 December 2012 the inclusion of 20 fields, most of them from humanities, in the "Science without Borders" selection process. However, the federal court of appeals overruled this decision in January 2013, stating that the expansion of the scholarships to other areas would not only damage the financing of the program, but also distort the program's goals. Available at: http://exame.abril.com.br/brasil/noticias/trf-tira-novamente-humanas-do-ciencias-sem-fronteiras (Accessed on 23 September 2013).
32. Among the private companies that participate in the "Science Without Borders" program, there are: (1) BG Group; (2) Boeing; (3) Eletrobras; (4) Funttel; (5) Hyundai; (6) Natura; (7) Petrobras; (8) Posco; (9) Vale. Available at: http://www.cienciasemfronteiras.gov.br/web/csf/empresas (Accessed on 22 September 2013).
33. *The Economist*, "Brazil: Not as Violent as You Thought," 21 August 2008, http://www.economist.com/node/11975437 (Accessed on 22 August 2013).
34. Lyons, John, "As Crime Rattles Brazil, Killings by Police Turn Routine," *The Economist*, 12 July 2013, http://online.wsj.com/article/SB100014241278873238365045785536434351194 34.html (Accessed on 24 August 2013).
35. Boadle, Anthony, "After Post-Protest Flurry, Brazil's Politicians Resist Reform," *Reuters*, http://www.reuters.com/article/2013/07/22/us-brazil-politics-corruption-idUSBRE96L0MS20130722 (Accessed on 29 August 2013).
36. Transparency International, "2012 Corruption Protection Index," http://www.transparency.org/cpi2012/results (Accessed on 29 August 2013).
37. Cawley, Marguerite, "Rio Police Most Corrupt in Brazil: Govt Survey," *InSight Crime*, 9 April 2013, http://www.insightcrime.org/news-briefs/rio-police-most-corrupt-in-brazil-govt-survey (Accessed on 29 August 2013).
38. Power, Timothy and Matthew Taylor, "Political Accountability in Brazil," *Focal (Canada)*, 31 April 2011, http://www.focal.ca/en/publications/focalpoint/431-april-2011-power-and-taylor (Accessed on 3 October 2013).

7 In Search of a Role on the Global Stage

1. Argentina, Malaysia, South Africa and Turkey are other examples of emerging middle powers according to Jordaan. States excluded from the middle-power category are non-Western nuclear powers (e.g., China, India and Pakistan) and alleged "sponsors of terrorism" (e.g., Iran).
2. The high-level diplomatic groupings described in Figure 7.1 may have a high degree of institutionalization but, unlike multilateral institutions or

regional bodies, they do not derive their authority from an international treaty between their participating states.

3. Brazil continues to lobby for an end to agricultural subsidies in Europe, the United States and Japan, and to open up the sector to open trade. Agriculture is a key sector for developing countries who want to be able to export their products to Europe, the United States and Japan.
4. The G20 group of developing countries currently includes 23 members countries (Argentina, Bolivia, Brazil, Chile, China, Cuba, Ecuador, Egypt, Guatemala, India, Indonesia, Mexico, Nigeria, Pakistan, Paraguay, Peru, Philippines, South Africa, Tanzania, Thailand, Uruguay, Venezuela and Zimbabwe). The group only exists in the context of the WTO and is distinct from the similarly named governance forum, the Group of 20 (G20), which was launched to address the global economic and financial crisis of 2007–2009.
5. http://www.postwesternworld.com/2013/07/04/is-ibsa-dead/ (Accessed on 16 September 2013).
6. Powell, Anita, "BRICS Leaders Optimistic About New Development Bank," Voice of America, 27 March 2013, http://www.voanews.com/content/brics-summit-leaders-optimistic-about-new-development-bank/1629583.html (Accessed on 11 October 2013).
7. http://news.bbc.co.uk/2/hi/7967546.stm (Accessed on 16 September 2013).
8. Venezuela joined the Mercosur in 2012, while Paraguay was suspended the same year.
9. The member states of ALBA are Antigua and Barbuda, Bolivia, Cuba, Dominica, Ecuador, Nicaragua, St Vincent and the Grenadines, and Venezuela
10. http://en.mercopress.com/2013/06/22/pacific-alliance-in-a-marketing-success-and-no-concern-for-mercosur-says-brazil (Accessed on 16 September 2013).
11. The government of Cuba was excluded from participation in the OAS in 1962. The OAS General Assembly revoked Cuba's suspension in 2009 but the country has not rejoined the organization.
12. http://www2.anba.com.br/noticia_diplomacia.kmf?cod=9661945&indice=320 (Accessed on 16 September 2013).
13. http://www1.folha.uol.com.br/colunas/matiasspektor/2013/05/1278742-os-porques-de-azevedo.shtml (Accessed on 16 September 2013).
14. http://www.ft.com/intl/cms/s/0/c7a8b5b2-b7ef-11e2-bd62-00144feabdc0.htm (Accessed on 16 September 2013).
15. http://www.ft.com/intl/cms/s/0/aca4d56a-9da8-11e0-b30c-00144feabdc0.html#axzz2d2iVMBDu (Accessed on 16 September 2013).
16. Brun, E. (2013). "Le Brésil n'est pas souverainiste!", Le Monde, 18 February 2013, retrieved from http://www.lemonde.fr/idees/article/2013/02/18/le-bresil-n-est-pas-souverainiste_1834526_3232.html (Accessed on 16 September 2013).
17. http://www.opendemocracy.net/openglobalrights/camila-asano/can-brazil-promote-change-without-changing-itself (Accessed on 16 September 2013).
18. http://www.postwesternworld.com/2013/08/01/brazils-enigmatic-retreat-the-case-of-the-responsibility-while-protecting-rwp/ (Accessed on 16 September 2013).

8 Looking for Answers

1. The financial support of the Inter-American Development Bank for conducting the survey is gratefully acknowledged.
2. The questionnaires were sent via email to the stakeholders by Barbara Marchiori de Assis, Research Assistant, Cornell University, on behalf of Lourdes Casanova, who was copied into the emails. For those who had not answered, a reminder was sent after two weeks. Barbara's help and comments on this chapter are gratefully acknowledged. The oral interviews were all conducted by Lourdes Casanova.
3. Interviewees were free to answer the questionnaire in English or Portuguese and many chose Portuguese. The corresponding quotes are based on free translation.

Conclusion: Building the Brazil Dream

1. *Euromoney* magazine, http://www.euromoney.com/Article/3229910/Brazil-The-positives-of-protests.html (Accessed on 16 October 2013).

Bibliography

Adams, James Truslow (2001). (first published January 1932). *The Epic of America*. New York City: Simon Publications.

Agtmael, A. V. (2007). *The Emerging Markets Century: How a New Breed of World-Class Companies is Overtaking the World*. New York, NY: Free Press.

Ambos, T. C., & Ambos, B. (2009). The impact of distance on knowledge transfer effectiveness in multinational corporations. *Journal of International Management, 15*(1), 1–14.

Amighini, A., & Rabellotti, R. (2010). Outward FDI from developing country MNEs as a channel for technological catch-up. *Seoul Journal of Economics, 23*(2), 239–261.

Ang, S. H., & Michailova, S. (2008). Institutional explanations of cross-border alliance modes: The case of emerging economies firms. *Management International Review, 48*(5), 551–576.

Araujo Jr., J. T. (2013). *The BNDES as an Instrument of Long Run Economic Policy in Brazil*. Retrieved from http://www.ecostrat.net/files/bndes-as-an-instrument-of-long-run-economic-policy.pdf.

Armijo, L. (2013). The public bank trilemma: Brazil's new developmentalism and BNDES, Draft of 24 July 2013. Prepared for inclusion in P. Kingstone, & T. Power (Eds.). *Democratic Brazil Ascendant* (forthcoming).

Armijo, L. E., & Burges, S. W. (2010). Brazil, the entrepreneurial and democratic BRIC*. *Polity, 42*(1), 14–37.

Aulakh, P. S. (2007). Special issue on emerging multinationals from developing economies: Motivations, paths, and performance. *Journal of International Management, 13*, 235–402.

Baena, V. (2011). Favelas in the spotlight: Transforming the slums of Rio de Janeiro. *Harvard International Review. 33*(1), 34–37.

Baer, W. (2008). *The Brazilian Economy: Growth and Development*. 6th edition. Boulder, CO: Lynne Rienner.

Baeza, C. (2011). O reconhecimento do estado palestino: Origens e perspectivas. *Boletim Meridiano, 47, 12*(126), 34–42.

Barbosa-Filho, N. H. (2008). Inflation targeting in Brazil: 1999–2006. *International Review of Applied Economics, 22*(2), 187–200.

Barney, J. (1991). Firm resources and sustained competitive advantage. *Journal of Management, 17*, 99–120.

Barral, W., & Haas, A. (2007). Public-Private Partnerships (PPP) in Brazil. *The International Lawyer, 41*(3), 957–974.

Bartlett, C. H., & Ghoshal, S. (2000). Going global: Lesson from late movers. *Harvard Business Review, 78*, 75–82.

Berg, J. (2009). *Brazil, the Minimum Wage as a Response to the Crisis*. International Labour Office. Retrieved from http://www.ilo.org/wcmsp5/groups/public/—americas/—ro-lima/documents/article/wcms_limd3_11_en.pdf.

Blank, F. F., Baidya, T. K. N., & Dias, M. A. G. (2009). *Real Options in Public Private Partnership – Case of a Toll Road Concession.* Retrieved from http://www.realoptions.org/papers2009/37.pdf.

Bodman, S. W., Wolfensohn, J. D. (Chairs), & Sweig, J. (Project Director) (2011). *Global Brazil and U.S.-Brazil Relations.* Council on Foreign Relations. Independent Task Force Report nr. 66.

Borenstein, S. (1991). The dominant-firm advantage in multiproduct industries: Evidence from the U. S. airlines. *The Quarterly Journal of Economics, 106*(4), 1237–1266.

Boston Consulting Club – BCG (2011). *Companies on the More: Rising Stars from Rapidly Developing Economies are Reshaping Global Industries.* Retrieved from http://www.bcg.com/documents/file70055.pdf.

Bourne, R. (2008). *Lula of Brazil: The Story so Far.* Berkeley and Los Angeles, CA: University of California Press.

Brainard, L., & Martínez Díaz, L (Eds.) (2009). *Brazil as an Economic Superpower: Understanding Brazil's Changing Role in the Global Economy.* Washington, DC: Brookings University Press.

Brazilian Development Bank – BNDES (2013). *Institutional Presentation BNDES (English)* [PowerPoint slides]. Retrieved from http://www.slideshare.net/bndes/institutional-presentation-bndes-english-24592414.

Brun, E. (2011). Brazil into the mediterranean strategic outbreak on socio-historical background. *Conjuntura Austral, 1*(5), 26–44.

Campello, D. (2013). *What is the Left of the Brazilian Left?* Retrieved from http://papers.ssrn.com/sol3/papers.cfm?abstract_id=2243118. Under review.

Campos Mello, P. (2012). The Brasília consensus. *The Brazilian Economy,* Getulio Vargas Foundation, *4*(1).

Casanova, L. (2004). *Multinational Strategies in Latin America: Comparing East Asian, European and North American Multinationals.* INSEAD – Faculty &Research Working Paper Series. Retrieved from http://www.insead.edu/facultyresearch/research/doc.cfm?did=47937.

Casanova, L. (2009a). *From Multinationals to Global Latinas: The New Latin American Multinationals* (Compilation case studies). Washington, DC: Inter-American Development Bank.

Casanova, L. (2009b). *Global Latinas: Latin America's Emerging Multinationals.* New York, NY: Palgrave Macmillan.

Casanova, L. (2011). El ascenso de las multilatinas en la economia mundial. *Informacion Comercial Espanola Monthly Edition, 859,* 21–32.

Casanova, L., Castellani, F., Dayton-Johnson, J., Dutta, S., Fonstad, N., & Paunov, C. (2011). *InnovaLatino: Fostering Innovation in Latin America.* Madrid: INSEAD/OECD/Fundación Telefonica.

Casanova, L., & Dumas, A. (2010). Corporate social responsibility and Latin American multinationals: Is poverty a business issue? *Universia Business Review.* Retrieved from http://ubr.universia.net/pdfs_web/25010-07.pdf.

Casanova, L., & Kassum, J. (2013a). *From Soft to Hard Power: In Search of Brazil's Winning Blend.* INSEAD – Faculty & Research Working Paper. Retrieved from http://www.insead.edu/facultyresearch/research/doc.cfm?did=52407.

Casanova, L., & Kassum, J. (2013b). *Brazilian Emerging Multinationals: In Search of a Second Wind.* INSEAD – Faculty & Research Working Paper. Retrieved from http://www.insead.edu/facultyresearch/research/doc.cfm?did=52564.

Casanova, L., & Kassum, J. (2013c). *Brazil: In Search of a Role on the Global Stage*. INSEAD – Faculty & Research Working Paper. Retrieved from http://www.insead.edu/facultyresearch/research/doc.cfm?did=52793.

Casanova, L., & Kassum, J. (2013d). *Brazil: In Search of a Social Innovation Model*. INSEAD – Faculty & Research Working Paper.

Cason, J. W., & Power, T. J. (2009). Presidentialization, pluralization, and the rollback of itamaraty: Explaining change in Brazilian foreign policy making in the Cardoso-Lula era. *International Political Science Review, 30*(2), 117–140.

Caves, R. E. (1971). International corporations: The industrial economics of foreign investment. *Economica, 38*(149), 1–27.

Confederação Nacional da Indústria – CNI (2010). *A Indústria e o Brasil: Uma agenda para crescer mais e melhor.* Brasília: CNI.

Confederação Nacional da Indústria – CNI (2010). *Competitividade Brasil 2010: Comparaçao com Países Selecionados. Uma chamada para a ação.* Brasília: CNI.

Cuervo-Cazurra, A. (2012). Extending theory by analyzing developing country multinational companies: Solving the goldilocks debate. *Global Strategy Journal, 2*(3), 153–167.

Cuervo-Cazurra, A., Maloney, M. M., & Manrakhan, S. (2007). Causes of the difficulties in internationalization. *Journal of International Business Studies, 38*(5), 709–725.

Cuervo-Cazurra, A., & Ramos, M. (2005). Explaining the process of internationalization by building bridges among existing models. In S. Floyd, J. Roos, C. Jacobs, & F. Kellermanns (Eds.). *Innovating Strategy Processes* (pp. 111–122). Malden, MA: Blackwell Publishing.

Cullen, James (2004). *The American Dream: A Short Story of an Idea that Shaped a Nation*. Oxford: Oxford University Press.

Cyrino, A. B., & Tanure, B. (2009). Trajectories of Brazilian multinationals: Coping with obstacles, challenges and opportunities in the internationalization process. In J. Ramsey, & A. Almeida (Eds.). *The Rise of Brazilian Multinationals: Making the Leap from Regional Heavyweights to True Multinationals* (pp. 13–14). Rio de Janeiro, RJ: Elsevier-Campus.

Da Motta Veiga, P. (2004). *Brazil and the G-20 Group of Developing Countries*. World Trade Organization. Retrieved from http://www.wto.org/english/res_e/booksp_e/casestudies_e/case7_e.htm#bibliography.

Davidson, J. D. (2012). *Brazil is the New America: How Brazil Offers Upward Mobility in a Collapsing World*. New Jersey: John Willey & Sons Inc.

De Onis, J. (2008). Brazil's big moment-a South American giant wakes up. *Foreign Affairs, 87*, 110–122.

Economic Commission for Latin America and the Caribbean – ECLAC (2012). *Social Panorama of Latin America* [PDF Document]. Retrieved from http://www.eclac.org/publicaciones/xml/4/48454/SocialPanorama2012DocI.pdf.

Economic Commission for Latin America and the Caribbean – ECLAC (2013). *Foreign Direct Investment in Latin America and the Caribbean* [PDF document]. Retrieved from http://www.eclac.org/noticias/paginas/1/33941/2013-371_PPT_FDI-2013.pdf.

Fleury, A., & Fleury, M. T. (2011). *Brazilian Multinationals: Competences for Internationalization*. New York, NY: Cambridge University Press.

Flores-Macias, G. A. (2012). *After Neoliberalism? The Left and the Economic Reforms in Latin America*. New York, NY: Oxford University Press.

Fundação Getulio Vargas – FGV (2010). *The New Middle Class: The Bright Side of the Poor*. Coordination: Marcelo Neri. Retrieved from http://www.cps.fgv.br/ibrecps/ncm2010_eng/NMC_Research_FGV_CPS_Neri_FORMAT_ENG_FIM_apres_SITE.pdf.

Gordon, L. (2001). *Brazil's Second Chance: En Route Toard the First World*. Brookings Institute Press.

Gras, G. L. (2001). *The New New World: The Re-emerging Markets of South America*. New Jersey, NJ: Pearson Education.

Grosse, R., & Mesquita, L. F. (2007). *Can Latin American Firms Compete?* New York, NY: Oxford University Press.

Guillén, M. F., & García-Canal, E. (2009). The American model of the multinational firm and the "new" multinationals from emerging economies. *The Academy of Management Perspectives, 23*(2), 23–35.

Guillén, M., & García-Canal, E. (2010). *The New Multinationals: Spanish Firms in a Global Context*. New York, NY: Cambridge University Press.

Guillén, M., & García-Canal, E. (2013). *Emerging Markets Rule: Growth Strategies of the New Global Giants*. New York, NY: McGraw-Hill.

Hakim, P. (2010). *Rising Brazil: The Choices of a New Global Power*. Inter-American Dialogue. Retrieved from http://www.thedialogue.org/page.cfm?pageID=32&pubID=2273.

Hall, A. (2006). From Fome Zero to Bolsa Família: Social policies and poverty alleviation under Lula. *Journal of Latin American Studies, 38*(4), 689–709.

Hannan, M. T., & Carroll, G. (1992). *Dynamics of Organizational Populations: Density, Legitimation, and Competition*. New York, NY: Oxford University Press.

Hart, S. L. (2010). *Capitalism at the Crossroads: Next Generation Business Strategies for a Post-Crisis World*. New Jersey, NJ: Pearson Education.

Hitt, M. A., Bierman, L., Uhlenbruck, K., & Shimizu, K. (2006). The importance of resources in the internationalization of professional service firms: The good, the bad, and the ugly. *Academy of Management Journal, 49*(6), 1137–1157.

Hitt, M., Hosskisson, R. E., Ireland, R. D., & Harrison, J. (1991). Effects of acquisitions on R&D inputs and outputs. *Academy of Management Journal, 34*(3), 693–706.

Hitt, M., Hosskisson, R. E., & Kim, H. (1997). International diversification: Effects on innovation and firm performance in product-diversified firms. *Academy of Management Journal, 40*(4), 767–798.

Hurrell, A. (2010a). Brazil and the new global order. *Current History, 109*(724), 60–68.

Hurrell, A. (2010b). Brazil: What kind of rising state in what kind of institutional order? In A. S. Alexandroff, & A. F. Cooper (Eds.). *Rising States, Rising Institutions: Challenges for Global Governance* (pp. 128–150). Baltimore, MD: The Brookings Institutions.

Hymer, S. (1976). *The International Operations of National Firms: A Study of Direct Foreign Investment*. Cambridge, MA: MIT Press.

Inter-American Development Bank – IDB (2010). *Ten Years After the Take-off: Taking Stock of China-Latin America and the Caribbean Economic Relations*. Retrieved from http://idbdocs.iadb.org/wsdocs/getdocument.aspx?docnum=35410652.

International Monetary Fund – IMF (2012). *Brazil: Consumer Credit Growth and Household Financial Stress*. Technical Note. Financial Sector Assessment Program. Retrieved from http://www.imf.org/external/pubs/ft/scr/2013/cr13149.pdf.

International Monetary Fund – IMF (2013). *Brazil: Staff Report for the 2013 Article IV Consultation.* Technical Note. IMF Country Report No. 13/312.

Jaruzelski, B., & Dehoff, K. (2010). *The Global Innovation 1000: How the Top Innovators Keep Winning.* Retrieved from http://www.booz.com/media/file/sb61_10408-R.pdf.

Johanson, J., & Vahlne, J. E. (1977). The internationalization process of the firm: A model of knowledge development and increasing foreign market commitments. *Journal of International Business Studies, 8*, 23–32.

Jordaan, E. (2003). The concept of a middle power in international relations: Distinguishing between emerging and traditional middle powers. *Politikon, 30*(1), 165–181.

Khanna, T., & Palepu, K. (1999). Policy shocks, market intermediaries, and corporate strategy: The evolution of business groups in Chile and India. *Journal of Economics & Management Strategy, 8*(2), 271–310.

Khanna, T., & Palepu, K. (2010). *Winning in Emerging Markets: A Road Map for Strategy and Execution.* Boston, MA: Harvard Business Review Press.

Kingstone, P., & Power, T. J. (Eds.) (2008). *Democratic Brazil Revisited.* Pitt Latin American Series. Pittsburgh: University of Pittsburgh Press.

Kohli, H. Loser, C, Sood, A. et al. (2010). *Latin America 2040. Breaking Away from Complacency: An Agenda for Resurgence.* 2nd edition. CAF. SAGE Publications Inc.

Kuczynski, P. P., & Williamson, P. (2003). *After the Washington Consensus: Restarting Growth in Latin America.* Washington, DC: Institute for International Economics.

Letelier, L. (2012). Journey into Brazil's Social Sector. *Stanford Social Innovation Review.* Retrieved from http://www.ssireview.org/articles/entry/journey_into_brazils_social_sector.

Lindert, K. (2006). Brazil: Bolsa Familia Program–Scaling-up Cash Transfers for the Poor. In *Emerging Good Practice in Managing for Development Results – Source Book* (pp. 67–74). OECD/World Bank. Retrieved from http://www.mfdr.org/Sourcebook/1stEdition/MfDRSourcebook-Feb-16-2006.pdf.

Lopes, D. B., Casarões, G., & Gama, C. F. (2013). *Tragedy of Middle Power Politics: Traps and Contradictions in Brazil's Quest for Institutional Revisionism.* International Studies Association Annual Meeting. Retrieved from http://files.isanet.org/ConferenceArchive/333aa12f007e4707890062d2999ec733.pdf.

Low, J. L., & Brito Low, C. (2013). *They Don't Speak Spanish in Brazil. A Guide to Live, Management, and Taxes for Doing Business in Brazil.* Jhl3 Publications. Kindle Edition.

Madhok, A., & Keyhanim, M. (2012). Acquisitions as entrepreneurship: Asymmetries, opportunities, and the internationalization of multinationals from emerging economies. *Global Strategy Journal, 2*(1), 26–40.

Makino, S., Lau, C. M., & Yeh, R. S. (2002). Asset-exploitation versus asset-seeking: Implications for location choice of foreign direct investment from newly industrialized economies. *Journal of International Business Studies, 33*, 403–421.

Marcovitch, J. (2009). *Pioneirismo Empresarial no Brasil.* São Paulo, SP: Edusp.

Mathews, J. A. (2006). Dragon multinationals: New players in 21st century globalization. *Asia Pacific Journal of Management, 23*(1), 5–27.

Mauro, David (2012). *Brazil as a Global Power: Rising or Risen?* Retrieved from http://www.academia.edu/1582049/Brazil_as_a_Global_Power_Rising_or_Risen_Draft_.

Meyer, P. (2013). *Organization of American States: Background and Issues for Congress*. Washington, DC: Congressional Research Service.

Nayar, D. (2008). The internationalization of firms from India: Investment, mergers and acquisitions. *Oxford Development Studies, 36*(1), 111–131.

Negroponte, D. V. (2013). *The End of Nostalgia: Mexico Confronts the Challenges of Global Competition*. Washington, DC: The Brookings Institution.

New Generation Consulting – NGC (2013). *Making Sense of Brazilian Protests* [PDF Document]. Retrieved from http://www.new-gen-consulting.com/resources/Brazilian-Protests-NGC-Special-Report.pdf.

Nye Jr, J. S. (2004). The benefits of soft power. *Harvard Business School Working Knowledge, 2*.

Nye Jr, J. S. (2009). Get smart: Combining hard and soft power. *Foreign Affairs*, 160–163.

Nye, J. S., & Alterman, E. (1990). *Bound to Lead: The Changing Nature of American Power*. Cambridge, MA: Basic Books.

Oliveira Junior, M. M. (2010). *Multinacionais Brasileiras: Internacionalização, Inovação e Estratégia Global*. Porto Alegre, RS: Bookman.

O'Neill, J. (2011). *The Growth Map: Economic Opportunity in the BRICs and Beyond*. Penguin Group.

Onis, J. de (2008). Brazil's Big Moment. *Foreign Affairs 87*, nr. 6. November–December Council of Foreign Relations.

Organization for Economic Cooperation and Development – OECD (2010). Brazil: Encouraging Lessons from a Large Federal System. In *Strong Performers and Successful Reformers in Education: Lessons from PISA for the United States* (pp. 177–196). Paris: OECD.

Organization for Economic Cooperation and Development – OECD (2011). *OECD Economic Surveys: Brazil 2011*.

Organization for Economic Cooperation and Development – OECD (2013). *OECD Economic Surveys Brazil: Overview*. Retrieved from http://www.oecd.org/eco/outlook/48930900.pdf. Paris: Organization for Economic Cooperation and Development.

Pape, R. A. (2005). Soft balancing against the United States. *International Security, 30*(1), 7–45. MIT Press Journals.

Pellissier, H. (2010, September 22). *Brazil: Future Farm of the Planet?* Institute for Ethics & Emerging Technologies. Retrieved from http://ieet.org/index.php/IEET/more/pellissier20100922.

Penrose, E. (2009). *The Theory of the Growth of the Firm*. New York, NY: Oxford University Press.

Perryman, M. (2012). *Why the Olympics Aren't Good for Us and How They Can Be*. New York, NY: OR Books.

Peteraf, M. A., & Bergen, M. E. (2003). Scanning dynamic competitive landscapes: A market-based and resource-based framework. *Strategic Management Journal, 24*(10), 1027–1041.

Porter, M. E. (1990). The competitive advantage of nations. *Harvard Business Review*, March issue: 73–93.

Prusa, A. (2011). *The "Soft Power" Power? Brazil's Soft Power Strategy in World Politics During the Lula Presidency*, a Thesis submitted to the Faculty of the Elliott School of International Affairs of The George Washington University.

Qi, X. (2011). The rise of BASIC in UN climate change negotiations. *South African Journal of International Affairs, 18*(3), 295–318.

Ramamurti, R. (2012). What is really different about emerging market multinationals? *Global Strategy Journal, 2*(1), 41–47.

Ramsey J., & Almeida, A. (Eds.) (2009). *The Rise of Brazilian Multinationals: Making Leap from Regional Heavyweights to True Multinationals.* Rio de Janeiro, RJ: Elsevier-Campus.

Ravallion, M. (2009). A comparative perspective on poverty reduction in Brazil, China and India. *World Bank Policy Research Working Paper Series No 5080.*

Reid, M. (2007). *Forgotten Continent: The Battle for Latin America's Soul.* Suffolk, UK: St. Edmundsbury Press Ltd.

Reis, J. B. M. (2012). Cooperação internacional para o desenvolvimento. Brasil um país doador: panorama e interesses. *Relaciones Internacionales, 21*(42), 99–117.

Rezende, S. M. (2010). Brazil: Challenges and achievements. *Issues in Science and Technology.* Retrieved from http://www.issues.org/26.3/rezende.html.

Rifkin, J. (2004). *The European Dream: How Europe's Vision of the Future is Quietly Eclipsing the American Dream.* New York: Tarcher/Penguin.

Roett, R. (2010). *The New Brazil.* Washington, DC: Brookings Institution.

Rohter, L. (2011). *Brazil on the Rise. The Story of a Country Transformed.* New York: Palgrave Macmillan.

Salama, P. (2010). Brésil, bilan économique, succès et limites. *Problèmes d'Amérique Latine,* (4), 47–61.

Sampaio, D. F. C. (2011). Estratégias e efeitos da política da boa vizinhança no Brasil [PDF Document]. Retrieved from http://bdm.bce.unb.br/bitstream/10483/2408/1/2011_DanielaFerreiraCoelhoSampaio.pdf.

Santiso, J. (2013). *The Decade of the Multilatinas.* New York, NY: Cambridge University Press.

Sauvant, K. P. (2008). *The Rise of Transnational Corporations from Emerging Markets: Threats or Opportunity?* Northampton, MA: Edward Elgar Publishing.

Scheman, R. L. (2003). *Greater America: A New Partnership for the Americas in the Twenty-First Century.* New York, NY: New York University.

Schwab, K. (2010). *The Global Competitiveness Report 2010–2011.* Centre for Global Competitiveness and Performance. World Economic Forum. Retrieved from http://www3.weforum.org/docs/WEF_GlobalCompetitivenessReport_2010-11.pdf.

Secretaria de Assuntos Estratégicos da Presidência da República. 2012. *Vozes da Classe Média: É ouvindo a população que se constroem políticas públicas adequadas.* Brasilia. Governo Federal. 20 September 2012.

Sennes, R., & Camargo Mendes, R. (2009). Public Policies and Brazilian Multinationals. In J. Ramsey, & A. Almeida (Eds.). *The Rise of Brazilian Multinationals: Making the Leap from Regional Heavyweights to True Multinationals* (pp. 157–174). Rio de Janeiro, RJ: Elsevier-Campus.

Sinha, J. (2005). Global champions from emerging markets. *McKinsey Quarterly, 2*, 29–37.

Skidmore, T. E. (1999). *Brazil: Five Centuries of Change.* Oxford: Oxford University Press.

Soares, S. S. D. (2012). *Bolsa Família: A Summary of Its Impacts* (No 137). International Policy Center for Inclusive Growth. Retrieved from http://www.ipc-undp.org/pub/IPCOnePager137.pdf.

Soulé-Kohndou, F. (2011, May 24). IBSA, BRICS: l'intégration des pays émergents par les clubs? *Le Monde*. Retrieved from http://www.lemonde.fr/idees/article/2011/05/24/ibsa-brics-l-integration-des-pays-emergents-par-les-clubs_1526561_3232.html.

Sotero, P. (2012). Uma reflexão sobre a frustrada iniciative Brasil-Turquia para superar o impasse nuclear entre o Irã e a comunidade internacional. *Política Externa, 20*(3), 75–79.

Sotero, P., & Armijo, L. E. (2007). Brazil: To be or not to be a BRIC? *Asian Perspective, 31*(4), 43–70.

Srivastava, R. K., Fahey, L., & Christensen, K. (2001). The resource-based view and marketing: The role of market-based assets in gaining competitive advantage. *Journal of Management, 27*(6), 777–802.

Stillman, A. (2013, September 9). Rio's Olympic deadline forces transport upgrades. *Financial Times*. Retrieved from http://www.ft.com/cms/s/0/b6ad8048-efb8-11e2-a237-00144feabdc0.html#axzz2j1qc9PkX.

Stolte, C. (2012). Brazil in Africa: Just another BRICS country seeking resources? *Chatham House Briefing Paper*.

Suppo, H. R., & Lessa, M. L. (2007). O estudo da dimensão cultural nas relações internacionais: Contribuições teóricas e metodológicas. In M. L. Lessa & W. S. Gonçalvez (Eds.). *História das Relações Internacionais. Teorias e Processos* (pp. 223–250). Rio de Janeiro: EdUERJ.

Tallman, S. (1991). Strategic management models and resource-based strategies among MNEs in a host market. *Strategic Management Journal, 12*(S1), 69–82.

Tsai, H. T., & Eisingerich, A. B. (2010). Internationalization strategies of emerging markets firms. *California Management Review, 53*(1), 114–135.

United Nations Conference on Trade and Development (UNCTAD) (2006). *FDI from Developing and Transition Economies: Implications for Development*. Retrieved from http://unctad.org/en/Docs/wir2006_en.pdf.

United Nations Conference on Trade and Development (UNCTAD) (2012). *World Investment Report*. Geneva. United Nations Conference on Trade and Development.

Valladão, A. (2012). *BRICS: Path Openers or Reluctant Followers?* Madariaga College of Europe Foundation. Retrieved from http://www.madariaga.org/publications/other/728-brics-path-openers-or-reluctant-followers.

Vernon, R. (1966). International investment and international trade in the product cycle. *The Quarterly Journal of Economics, 80*(2), 190–207.

Wang, Helen H. (2010). *The Chinese Dream: The Rise of the World's Larges Middle Class and What it Means to You*. Brande, Denmark: Bestseller Press.

Williamson. P. (1990). *The Progress of Policy Reform in Latin America*. Washington, DC: Institute for International Economics.

Wernerfelt, B. (1984). A resource-based view of the firm. *Strategic Management Journal, 5*(2), 171–180.

World Bank (2013). *Doing Business 2013: Smarter Regulations for Small and Medium-Size Enterprises*. Retrieved from http://www.doingbusiness.org/~/media/GIAWB/Doing%20Business/Documents/Annual-Reports/English/DB13-full-report.pdf.

World Bank Institute (2012, January). *Best Practices in Public-Private Partnerships Financing in Latin America: The Role of Guarantees* [PDF Document]. Retrieved from http://einstitute.worldbank.org/ei/sites/default/files/Upload_Files/BestPracticesPPPFinancingLatinAmericaguarantees.pdf.

World Trade Organization – WTO (2013, May 17). *Trade Policy Review: Report by the Secretariat – Brazil*. Retrieved from http://www.wto.org/english/tratop_e/tpr_e/s283_e.pdf.

Yeoh, P. (2011). Location choice and the internationalization sequence: Insights from Indian pharmaceutical companies. *International Marketing Review, 28*(3), 291–312.

Yiu, D. W., Lau, C., & Bruton, G. D. (2007). International venturing by emerging economy firms: The effects of firm, home country networks, and corporate entrepreneurship. *Journal of International Business Studies, 38*(4), 519–540.

Zdun, S. (2008). Violence in street culture: Cross-cultural comparison of youth groups and criminal gangs. *New Directions For Youth Development, 2008*(119), 39–54.

Index

Note: Letter '*f*' '*t*' and 'n' followed by locators refers to figures, tables and notes respectively.

CPSIA information can be obtained at www.ICGtesting.com
Printed in the USA
LVOW04*1736230715

447369LV00002B/5/P

9 781137 352354